ULTIMATE

CORE = CHURCH ON THE RADICAL EDGE

15.89

WINKIE PRATNEY has helped and trained young people of all ages for forty years and speaks to over five hundred thousand annually in his work with many leading international youth organizations, including Youth With a Mission, Operation Mobilization, and Campus Life. He originally hails from New Zealand.

TREVOR YAXLEY and his wife, Jan, pursue their heart's passion of evangelizing, training, and equipping people to bring positive change to their home country of New Zealand. They are the parents of three children and have three granddaughters.

———◆———

Space does not allow us to cover topics as fully as we would like. For further study in these areas and others, visit *www.ultimatecore.net*. Designed to be the best single source for free youth ministry materials on the planet, it will enable youth and discipleship workers to access constantly updated contemporary and cross-cultural illustrations and in-depth studies for each major life principle of Scripture.

TREVOR YAXLEY :: WINKIE PRATNEY

ULTIMATE CORE

BETHANYHOUSE
MINNEAPOLIS, MINNESOTA

Library of Congress Cataloging-in-Publication Data

Pratney, Winkie, 1944–.
   The ultimate core : maximum life transformation for the third millennium / by Winkie Pratney and Trevor Yaxley.
      p. cm.
   ISBN 0-7642-2803-X (pbk.)
   1. Youth—Religious life.   2. Evangelistic work.   3. Witness bearing (Christianity)
I. Yaxley, Trevor. II. Title.
   BV4531.3.P73   2003
   248.8'3—dc21   2003002570

CORE

CONTENTS

CORE

DEEP CENTER: pertains to the interior
   heart, crux
INNER ESSENCE: heart and fundamental
   life of a living entity
MAIN: principal, primary, central thing
SAMPLE: example—a small typical represen-
   tation of the original substance
TEST: to try something out

   CORE TEMPERATURE is the life-
sustaining middle section of a living body. To
drop below this core means death. A core represents a FOUNDATION, a mainstay, a hub out
of which all other things connect and function.
Core refers to the risky, radioactive fissionable
heart of a FUNCTIONING NUCLEAR
REACTOR that (when governed and regulated)
brings enough light, heat, power, and energy to
empower and enlighten everything, from an individual home to an entire city.
   The CORE are the Christians Of Revival
Encounters, a Company Of Reconstructed Expectations Committed Out and Out to the Ruler of
Everything. The CORE Wants More.

The Sermon on the Mount

MATTHEW 5:1-16
[1]And seeing the multitudes, He went up on a mountain, and when He was seated His disciples came to Him. [2]Then He opened His mouth and taught them, saying:

[3]"Blessed are the poor in spirit,
For theirs is the kingdom of heaven.
[4]Blessed are those who mourn,
For they shall be comforted.
[5]Blessed are the meek,
For they shall inherit the earth.
[6]Blessed are those who hunger and thirst for righteousness,
For they shall be filled.
[7]Blessed are the merciful,
For they shall obtain mercy.
[8]Blessed are the pure in heart,
For they shall see God.
[9]Blessed are the peacemakers,
For they shall be called sons of God.
[10]Blessed are those who are persecuted for righteousness' sake,
For theirs is the kingdom of heaven.

[11]"Blessed are you when they revile and persecute you, and say all kinds of evil against you falsely for My sake. [12]Rejoice and be exceedingly glad, for great is your reward in heaven, for so they persecuted the prophets who were before you.

[13]"You are the salt of the earth; but if the salt loses its flavor, how shall it be seasoned? It is then good for nothing but to be thrown out and trampled underfoot by men.

[14]"You are the light of the world. A city that is set on a hill cannot be hidden. [15]Nor do they light a lamp and put it under a basket, but on a lampstand, and it gives light to all who are in the house. [16]Let your light so shine before men, that they may see your good works and glorify your Father in heaven.

And seeing the multitudes, He went up on a mountain, and when He was seated His disciples came to Him. NKJV

Now when he saw the crowds, he went up on a mountainside and sat down. His disciples came to him. NIV

WHEN JESUS SAW THE CROWDS, HE WENT UP ON THE MOUNTAIN; AND AFTER HE SAT DOWN, HIS DISCIPLES CAME TO HIM. NASB

When Jesus saw his ministry drawing huge crowds, he climbed a hillside. Those who were apprenticed to him, the committed, climbed with him. Arriving at a quiet place, he sat down. THE MESSAGE

SEEING THE CROWDS, HE WENT UP ON THE MOUNTAIN, AND WHEN HE SAT DOWN, HIS DISCIPLES CAME TO HIM. ESV

One day as the crowds were gathering, Jesus went up the mountainside with his disciples and sat down to teach them. NLT

1

CORE VISION

THE ONE AND ONLY CHRIST

And seeing the
multitudes, He went
up on a mountain, and
when He was seated His
disciples came to Him.

MATTHEW 5:1

Mountain heights draw and captivate in wonder something core within the human heart. The majestic splendor of the mountain ranges of God's world calls us to adventure, to lift our gaze from valleys and plains to the towering peaks. They capture our imagination with the promise of a grander view, a greater perspective, a clearer vision of what is before us.

For the church on the radical edge, God's CORE, this is where it begins: We need God's mountaintop perspective to challenge and realign our thinking according to His infinitely perfect view of His world.

A God's-Eye View of the World

God sees it all. Nothing is hidden from His eyes. He sat on heaven's throne long before He sat on the Galilean hillside to teach the crowds and give the world His core blessing. God, the Infinite, who sees things no one else can see, sits on the mountain looking over His creation. God is here, saying something special to His world if only we will hear and respond.

You live in a world now more globally connected than at any other time in human history. We are told it takes at most only seven linked people to connect any two different people in the world. Almost no one can live in isolation anymore. So many tribes of people, so many loyalties, so much history lies in the inheritance you have in the twenty-first century of God's dealings with His world.

Nebuchadnezzar, the greatest king in human history, had a dream. It scared him so badly he forgot what it was about when he woke up.

He called for all the psychic advisers of Babylon to help him remember and interpret it. No one could except Daniel, the young man who dreamed great dreams and believed in the one great God. Daniel, a man of faith who could see the future, told the king what he had seen in his dream—a towering man with a head of gold, arms and chest of silver, hips of bronze, legs of iron, and feet of rusty clay. But that image is not what had scared the king silly. It was a rock, a little rock that hit that giant statue on its fragile foundation and brought it tumbling to the ground. And that Rock grew until it filled the whole earth.

We live in the day of the Rock. The global family founded by and on Jesus now includes billions, the largest belief system on our planet. All around the earth, the Rock is filling the world.

"Many people shall come and say, 'Come, and let us go up to the mountain of the LORD, to the house of the God of Jacob; He will teach us His ways, and we shall walk in His paths.' For out of Zion shall go forth the law, and the word of the LORD from Jerusalem" (Isaiah 2:3).

Why would the God of Jacob attract such a global following? And why would people from all walks of life willingly learn from and follow Him?

Come As You Are

For millions, religion is part of their cultural, social, or even national identity; to belong, they believe. Converting to another religion is almost unthinkable, like trying to change who you are. Yet what you do and what you think always affect your life, your family, and your nation. Brokenness, sadness, suffering, and sin are rampant everywhere, and altering that seems completely beyond the scope of the top world religions. There is an ache, an emptiness, a God-sized gap no earthly religion can fulfill.

But written in the world around us and deep in every heart is a wonderful witness to what *can* fill that gap—and perfectly. The Bible's core message is different from that of any other religion. The God of the Bible is both infinite and personal, and there is no other god like Him. The Bible God really deserves to be loved and worshiped. Why put anyone else before Him? If people attempt to serve gods lesser than we are, we deny our *minds;* if we serve gods *unlike* us, we deny what it means to be human. We can say that "God is an infinite everything," but that leaves us searching for an answer to the origin of our own unique personalities. Yet if we say on the other hand that "God is personal and little," we will have to find something else worth worshiping. We can even say within that we *are* God, but our lives will show the lie.

No matter what fantasies and idolatries we embrace, the true God will always be there, loving us, sad for us. We can consistently live sanely, morally, meaningfully, and virtuously only if we worship God as both infinite and personal. *We become like the God we worship.*

Throughout history multiplied millions of people have tried to make a home like heaven in one of the great alternatives. Yet the very sadness and emptiness of people who give themselves to something that cannot satisfy has become painfully obvious. A god just like us and no better has no power to make us good. Nations that give themselves to false peace lie poor and devastated. And no living Eastern guru has enough enlightenment to prove what is on the other side of death.

God has not left us to wander alone in the dark, unable to know the truth. Check out the credentials. See who is worth your trust, and then listen to the Leader who not only tells you there is a real difference between heaven and hell and life and death but has experienced that very difference. Only one Man in history ever did that, and all history splits around His birth.

The One and Only Christ

"Now it shall come to pass in the latter days that the mountain of the LORD's house shall be established on the top of the mountains, and shall be exalted above the hills; and peoples shall flow to it. Many nations shall come and say, 'Come, and let us go up to the mountain of the LORD, to the house of the God of Jacob; He will teach us His ways, and we shall walk in His paths.' For out of Zion the law shall go forth, and the word of the LORD from Jerusalem" (Micah 4:1–2).

Why have so many found in Jesus Christ the one true God? Out of our world's many different religions and belief systems, what makes Jesus unique?

HIS BIRTH ✦ THE STRANGEST

No one was ever born the way Jesus was. He is the first and only baby with a human mother but without a human father. "The virgin shall conceive and bear a Son, and shall call His name Immanuel [God is with us]" (Isaiah 7:14).

In every individual we find all the genetic characteristics of that person's parents. From Mary, Jesus received true humanity, dating back to Adam; from God, Jesus' Father, Jesus received true deity, dating from eternity. How the limitless love and life of the Ruler of the Universe could have compressed down into one person is incomprehensible, but that fact is central to the Bible record: "And the Word became flesh and dwelt among us, and we beheld His glory, the glory as of the only begotten of the Father, full of grace and truth" (John 1:14).

HIS WISDOM ✦ THE SMARTEST

No one ever spoke like Jesus. The Bible is full of accounts of those who were amazed by how and what Jesus communicated: "The people were astonished at His teaching, for He taught them as one having authority, and not as the scribes" (Matthew 7:28b–29). "They were astonished at His teaching, for His word was with authority" (Luke 4:32). "No man ever spoke like this man" (John 7:46). Think of the Sermon on the Mount, the Lord's Prayer, the parables. Any of these simple, powerful words would do honor to a writer of the greatest genius. Did early Christians compose these and later attribute them to Christ? They could not have done it. Where did a peasant carpenter find such wisdom? Only God could be the source.

Listen to Jesus' own words:

"Heaven and earth will pass away, but My words will by no means pass away" (Luke 21:33). "He who hears My word and believes in Him who sent Me has everlasting life, and shall not come into judgment, but has passed from death into life" (John 5:24). "For whoever is ashamed of Me and My words, of him the Son of Man will be ashamed when He comes in His *own* glory, and *in His* Father's, and of the holy angels" (Luke 9:26, emphasis added).

His claims, His words, His warnings are huge and ring with authority and majesty. "I am the way, the truth, and the life. No one comes to

CORE VISION

13

the Father except through Me" (John 14:6). "I am the light of the world. He who follows Me shall not walk in darkness, but have the light of life" (John 8:12). No one had ever spoken like Jesus did, without a moment's hesitation or uncertainty and to all people, curious, hostile, or admiring. He spoke to critics, lawyers, professional debaters, religious specialists, and scoffers so masterfully and convincingly, their carefully planned tricks fell apart and they were filled with rage. Look at the story of the woman found committing adultery (John 8:1–11), the lawyer with his question about eternal life (Luke 10:25–37), the chief priests discussing authority (Matthew 21:23–46), and the Pharisees' taxation trap (Matthew 22:15–22). Are Jesus' answers those of a mere man?

Church historian Phillip Schaff wrote,

This Jesus of Nazareth without money and arms conquered more millions than Alexander, Caesar, Mohammed and Napoleon; without science and learning, He shed more light on things human and divine than all the philosophers and scholars combined; without the eloquence of schools, He spoke such words of life as were never spoken before or since, and produced effects which lie beyond the reach of orator or poet; without writing a single line, He set more pens in motion, and furnished themes for more sermons, orations, discussions, learned volumes, works of art and songs of praise than the whole army of great men of ancient and modern times.

In short, no one has ever equaled Jesus.

HIS PURITY ✦ THE HOLIEST

No one ever lived like Jesus. Imagine anyone else saying what He said and getting away with it. "You are from beneath. I am from above. If you do not believe that I am He, you will die in your sins" (John 8:23–24). "I came forth from the Father and am come into the world" (John 16:28). "He who has seen Me has seen the Father" (John 14:9). Jesus said things many would find outrageous, but the purity of His life gave His words weight. As Catherine Booth, cofounder of the Salvation Army, noted in *Popular Christianity,* "His character supported His assumptions. For over 1800 [2000] years the best of the human race have accepted these without being shocked by them." Only Someone who was truly holy *and* divine could say what Jesus said and still have credibility.

Jesus was born a Jew and lived a Jewish life under Jewish laws in a Jewish land. Yet to the end of His days, He never offered a sacrifice for sin. No other person living under Moses' law could claim that he did not need to offer sacrifice for sin. Jesus admonished His disciples, "[When you pray, say . . .] 'forgive us our debts, as we forgive our debtors'" (Matthew 6:12), but *He* never prayed for forgiveness because He had nothing to ask forgiveness for. Jesus taught that we all need *regeneration,* or rebirth in God, from the loyal disciples who followed Him to His mother, Mary. Every person in history has needed regeneration—except for Jesus. Only He was perfect.

Perfection. No other word could describe the humanity of Christ. Perfection is so rare that the saying "no one is perfect" seems obvious. But Jesus Christ was. "Nineteen centuries of more or less constant progress have lifted the levels of living among civilized people . . . yet after those long years the life of Christ is still recognized as the perfect moral pattern for all ages and all races" (Harry Rimmer, *The Magnificence of Jesus*).

Jesus' *friends*, the people who knew Him best, said He was without sin. "[Jesus] committed no sin," Peter said, "nor was deceit found in His mouth" (1 Peter 2:22). Even Jesus' *enemies* had to admit it. Pilate said, "I find no fault in Him at all" (John 18:38). The thief on the cross said, "This Man has done nothing wrong" (Luke 23:41). The centurion who crucified Him remarked, "Certainly this was a righteous Man!" (Luke 23:47). Jesus himself said, "I always do those things that please [My Father]" (John 8:29), and to His critics, "Which of you convicts Me of sin?" (John 8:46).

None of the great religious leaders of the world could claim to be perfect, and none of them would have dared. But Jesus did. He could forgive sins because He was God in the flesh, and He never sinned.

HIS POWER ✦ THE STRONGEST

Forty-nine miracles surround the life of Jesus from His birth to His Ascension, seven showing His power over demons (Mark 1:23–26) and many the healing of sickness or impairment (John 4:46-54).

Jesus performed miracles of deliverance (John 6:17-21) and judgment (Matthew 21:18-21). He supplied food and drink by means of miracles (Luke 5:1-11). Jesus even raised three people from the dead: a widow's son (Luke 7:11-16), Jairus's daughter (Mark 5:22-24, 35-43), and Lazarus, who had been dead four days! (John 11). Then Jesus *himself* rose again (Luke 24:1-7).

Miracles surrounded Jesus throughout His whole earthly life: at His birth (Matthew 2:1-9), His baptism (Matthew 3:16-17), the Transfiguration (Matthew 17:1-14), prayer (John 12:28-30), His death (Matthew 27:45-53), His Resurrection (Matthew 28:2), and His Ascension into heaven (Luke 24:51; Acts 1:9-11).

Jesus performed all of these miracles without fanfare. His actions were the natural, necessary outflow of a life that is creative, constructive, and compassionate, backed by infinite power and ultimate love. All of Jesus' miracles mirrored His loving and merciful character, upheld His Father's glory, and met His creation's needs.

The most ancient apologist, Quadratus, who lived some seventy years after the Ascension, wrote this to the Roman Emperor Adrian:

> The works of our Savior were always conspicuous, for *they were real;* both they that were healed and they that were raised from the dead were seen, not only when they were healed or raised, but for a long time afterwards; not only whilst He dwelled on this earth, but also after His departure, and for a good while after it; inasmuch as that some of them have reached to our times. (Eusebius, *Histories,* vol. 1, emphasis added)

Though they wanted to, even Jesus' enemies could not deny He did miracles. When they examined the blind man Jesus had healed, they were divided but could not ignore the facts, as John 9 shows. "This Man is not from God because He does not keep the Sabbath," some objected. Others said, "How can a man who is a sinner do such signs?" "What do you say about Him because He opened your eyes?" they asked the blind man. His reply? "Since the world began it has been unheard of that anyone opened the eyes of one who was born blind. If this Man were not from God, He could do nothing." When Jesus raised

Lazarus from the dead, the despairing comment of the chief priests and Pharisees was, "What shall we do? For this Man works many signs. If we *let Him alone . . . everyone will believe in Him*" (John 11:47–48, emphasis added).

The life of Jesus was a life filled with miracles. These miracles *continue* to the present day because He is the "same yesterday, today, and forever" (Hebrews 13:8).

HIS LIFE ✤ THE GREATEST

If the New Testament is clear about anything, it is this: Jesus Christ is truly God as well as truly man. He is not simply "related" to God in some vague ethical sense. If Jesus were not God as He claimed, how did He make—and how does He continue to make—such a matchless global impact for good and truth in our world? No one sane dares claim any other past great religious leader is still alive and doing what He always did for truth and life and good. Yet with Jesus millions did and still say exactly that today. Other great lives and leaders have indeed affected our world, but none of their accomplishments come even close to those of Jesus' incomparable life. Despite all the flaws and failures of His followers, despite the deviations and disguises in which we have often tried to dress Him, Jesus Christ is the greatest single spiritual figure in human history.

HIS DEATH AND RESURRECTION ✤ THE AWESOMEST

No one ever died like Jesus. Many millions have died, and thousands died the terrible death of a Roman crucifixion. Yet it is not the death on the cross that makes Jesus' death unique but that He died when He did not deserve to die and, like no one else in history, did not *have* to die. "I lay down My life," Jesus said, "that I may take it again. *No one takes it from Me,* but I lay it down of Myself. I have power to lay it down, and I have power to take it again" (John 10:17–18, emphasis added).

Jesus would not have died from old age or sickness or weakness like any other human being. He had a perfect body and perfect health, and He had never sinned. Yet He chose to die like any other sufferer of an excruciating crucifixion. His death was completely unlike any other because it was a death for the sins of the whole world.

Jesus told people He would die, but they would not believe it. They had not realized that the history taking place before their eyes those few terrible days fulfilled prophecy. Within twenty-four hours' time, twenty-nine prophecies of Jesus' trial, death, and burial were literally fulfilled. He was betrayed by a friend (Matthew 26:47–50) and sold for thirty pieces of silver (Matthew 26:15). He was accused by false witnesses (Matthew 26:59–61) but remained deliberately silent before His accusers (Matthew 26:63). He was cynically mocked (Matthew 27:31). At the Hill of the Skull, his executioners pierced His hands and His feet (John 19:37). Jesus was crucified with transgressors (Luke 23:32–33), and His clothes were gambled for (John 19:23–24).

Then three days after the Cross came an early morning earthquake and a light like the sun; terrified rumors radiated from an empty grave in the garden. Afraid, none of the disciples dared believe the confused story of the women who had visited the tomb. They had seen Jesus die with their own eyes and laid to go cold as marble on the slab of a borrowed tomb. Even so, some of the disciples returned to the tomb, half hoping for a miracle. What they witnessed—a resurrected Jesus—transformed them into people who would die rather than deny their Christ, willing to lay down their own lives with a confidence and trust in God that forever freed them from the fear of death.

HIS RETURN ✧ THE CLOSEST

The prophecies of Jesus' birth, life, and death are unique among all the world's great holy books. At least a quarter of the Bible—an estimated 8,352 verses out of its 31,124—contains detailed predictions, and twenty-seven percent of God's Word is prophetic. Consider for instance these fourteen prophecies about the Messiah, all of which came true, *to the letter,* in the baby Jesus.

1. Seed of a woman
   Prophecy: Genesis 3:15
   Fulfillment: Galatians 4:4
2. Born of a virgin
   Prophecy: Isaiah 7:14
   Matthew 1:18, 24, 25

3. Son of God
   Prophecy: Psalm 2:7 (also 1 Chronicles 17:11–14; 2 Samuel 7:12–16)
   Fulfillment: Matthew 3:17 (also 16:16; 26:63; Mark 9:7; Luke 9:35; 22:70; Acts 13:30–33; John 1:34, 49)
4. Seed of Abraham
   Prophecy: Genesis 12:2–3 (also 22:18)
   Fulfillment: Matthew 1:1 (also Galatians 3:16)
5. Son of Isaac
   Prophecy: Genesis 21:12
   Fulfillment: Luke 3:23, 34 (also Matthew 1:2)
6. Son of Jacob
   Prophecy: Numbers 24:17 (also Genesis 35:10–12)
   Fulfillment: Luke 23, 34 (also 1:33; Matthew 1:2)
7. From the tribe of Judah
   Prophecy: Genesis 49:10 (also Micah 5:2)
   Fulfillment: Luke 3:23, 33 (also Matthew 1:2; Hebrews 7:14)
8. From the family line of Jesse
   Prophecy: Isaiah 11:1 (also 11:10)
   Fulfillment: Luke 3:23, 32; (also Matthew 1:6)
9. Of the House of David
   Prophecy: Jeremiah 23:5 (also 2 Samuel 7:12–16; Psalm 132:11)
   Fulfillment: Luke 3:23, 31 (also Matthew 1:1; 9:27; 15:22; 22:41–46; Mark 9:10; Luke 18:38–39)
10. Born in Bethlehem
    Prophecy: Micah 5:2
    Fulfillment: Matthew 2:1 (also John 7:42; Luke 2:4–7)
11. Presented with gifts
    Prophecy: Psalm 72:10 (also Isaiah 60:6)
    Fulfillment: Matthew 2:1, 11
12. Herod kills children
    Prophecy: Jeremiah 31:15
    Fulfillment: Matthew 2:16
13. He shall be called Lord
    Prophecy: Psalm 110:1 (also Jeremiah 23:6)
    Fulfillment: Luke 2:11; Matthew 22:43–45
14. He shall be Immanuel (God with us)
    Prophecy: Isaiah 7:14
    Fulfillment: Matthew 1:23 (also Luke 7:16)

(Josh McDowell, *Evidence That Demands a Verdict*)

d consider this: For every prophecy of Jesus' first coming, there
ven of His second. He is not the Christ of just history, or even of
present experience; He is the coming King, the rightful owner at whose
return everything will be called into reckoning—small and great, rich or
poor, religious or not, all will face His judgment. He is not the Christ
of a long-gone past. He is the present Savior and the world's future
Judge—a future that is fast moving into present reality.

CORE Faith Versus Fatalism

The Lord Jesus Christ is the core focus of the Bible. It shows He was
no ordinary man. His birth divided history, and His life and work alone
make Him the world's greatest figure. But the thing that really counts
is the fact His tomb is *empty* (Luke 24:5-6). That deserted grave means
Jesus is alive—now! (Revelation 1:8).

A man was asked why he left his religion to be a Christian. He said,
"If you were walking along a road and saw two leaders and teachers at
the fork of that road—one dead and the other alive—which one would
you ask the way?" And that is the secret of the Gospel. We serve a
living Christ. He is not some past example. He is *actively involved* in
our world. The history of other faiths shows sad submission to
unchangeable futures and uncaring gods. But the God of the Bible is
not like that. The Creator God acts and interacts with His creation in
an ever-changing world to bring it back to His purposes. And He is
neither too small to help us nor too impersonal to care.

Fate rules the other religions of the world. The god of Islam is all
powerful but hardly personally involved with his followers. Whatever
happens in history is "Allah's will." What does Allah care about an
individual's choices? A mere human cannot change his mind. Look at
the Buddhists or Hindus, with a deep devotion powerless to affect their
destiny. Their greatest ambition is to sink into nothingness, hoping
after countless reincarnations to become part of the great, universal,
uncaring stream of time. Listen to the chanted prayers of the followers
of some Western brand of traditional, political, or rule-based religion.
Do they really love God? What more can they do to prove to God they
are worthy of salvation? How can they know what is true when only

the religious institution they serve can interpret truth for them? And how do they feel when their "infallible" religion *changes* its truths to suit the morals of the moment?

Even some Christians think of God as the Great "Fixer," pulling the strings behind everything people do. They assume we are puppets God amuses himself with. Could God possibly *care* for earth's teeming millions; does He even *want* to? If God arranged the contradictions of beauty and ugliness in our lives, if we are only pawns on His giant chessboard of triumph and tragedy, it is hard to help feeling hurt when terrible things happen to our world, no matter how much we trust God. He becomes more and more impersonal and far-off. But is God *really* like that?

The answer lies in Jesus! Into our world blazed the light of an amazing revelation. God cared for us then; He *still* cares. He is concerned about every detail of our lives. The most wonderful revelation of the Bible is the glimpse it gives us of God's nature. We see a concerned, feeling God, not One of indifferent power, but One touched with *our* hurt (Hebrews 4:15). We see a God saddened by our misery and grieved over our rebellion against Him.

We even see a God who is willing to *change* His plans when we ask Him! (Psalm 106:40–45). We see a God so personal we ache at what has happened to His world and to His heart. We see the real God thanks to the book He has given us—and we discover He is *love*!

This God made us finite, miniature likenesses to himself. His great gift to human creation is what makes us most like Him: the power to *make*, to create. He created us with the ability to *choose*, to make responsible decisions between options. While He is the only One who sees our world in its proper perspective, God can reveal to us the truths of life written on our hearts and in His Word. He frames these laws in words and ways that fit our nature. He describes and has the power to implement penalties to limit disobedience that could eventually hurt the rest of His universe. The Bible shows us that we can make only one of two core choices. We can choose to serve ourselves or to put God first in our lives and as a result live for the highest good of His universe. Our ultimate intention shapes our lives.

Time doesn't limit God. He has all eternity to accomplish His will.

Resources do not bind the Lord of the mountain—the whole earth is His. He is not held back by lack of power or of wisdom or ability. Only those who do not serve Him with a perfect heart and a willing mind think He is limited. The awesome One who can do it all is held back only by our disobedience (Psalm 78:41). He wants and calls you to choose to help carry out His mission of mercy (John 20:21).

Will *you* become His disciple—a learner—someone who will obey Him? Will you put your life completely at His disposal to do as He commands? All of our future hangs on this core choice: "Choose for yourselves this day whom you will serve" (Joshua 24:15).

Will the Lord Jesus be your heart? Will you be a part of His CORE?

And he opened his mouth and taught them. ESV

And he began to teach them. NIV

This is what he taught them. NLT

THEN HE OPENED HIS MOUTH AND TAUGHT THEM. NKJV

HE OPENED HIS MOUTH AND BEGAN TO TEACH THEM. NASB

[He] taught his climbing companions. This is what he said. THE MESSA

2

CORE
HEART

SPIRIT OF A LEARNER

Then He opened His

mouth and taught them.

MATTHEW 5:2

God equipped the human body with the amazing capacity to grow and mature. Consider a newborn baby. At birth babies can do little but suck, sleep, and scream. But as each month goes by, remarkable growth and change takes place, and before long the helpless infant is on the move, crawling, walking, and learning to talk. In fact, every living thing is created with an inbuilt system of growth that continues from birth until death. Only that which is dead ceases to grow and change.

Just as God has made our physical bodies this way, it is also true our spiritual nature is designed to grow and to mature. We are born into the kingdom of God as spiritual babies, mere infants in Christ. This birth is not the end but the beginning of the remarkable process of spiritual growth God desires to bring to completion in the life of each of His children.

Listen and Learn

Jesus speaks. We listen. We do it. This is the way the world changes. The pastor of one of the world's largest churches was asked, "What is the secret to this amazing growth?" He said, "I pray and I obey." Being CORE means being a learner. When tens of thousands meet each day in twenty-four-hour prayer, the effects of such hungry, hearing hearts radically affect the world. The same God who spoke the worlds into being wants to speak with us. His is the true creative power behind the influence of all great words and songs. If we have listening hearts, all creation can speak to us. We must guard our ears and lips so when we listen to the counsel of Christ we not only speak what He gives us to say but speak like He would say it. And it is Jesus himself who offers to sit with us and teach us.

CORE Discipleship: Following the Leader

Jesus promises to teach His disciples. He said, "My sheep hear My voice . . . and they follow Me. They will by no means follow a stranger . . . for they do not know the voice of strangers" (John 10:27, 5). God's voice is both completely normal and supernaturally natural. He speaks from the inside of our lives out, not from the outside in. By His very nature, a Person who is infinite must reveal what He says or thinks to anyone who is not. We are finite—we can never know it all and must never pretend we do. This infinite God is also a Person, not a principle. He does not *have* to speak to us unless we ask nicely.

Truth comes first by revelation, not just by study. People who know right only through research but lack a real revelation of God may never see what is wrong or, worse, never see where *they* are wrong.

Discipleship is not only about learning the right things and being disciplined. It is about listening to God's voice and doing what He says until we begin to understand both who He is and what He wants of our lives. True learning requires us to be humble, receiving like a child what Someone who loves us compassionately and unreservedly wants to share with us for our good. A true disciple of Jesus never stops being a learner.

There is wisdom from heaven and a "wisdom" from hell (James 3:13–15). The order of God's dealings with us will always be 180 degrees from the way the world teaches. If we know only how to rely on our own strength and learning, we first try to understand everything we can collect and look at; then we decide for ourselves whether or not we want to do something. It is from this limited, self-centered stand that we hope we will become more wise and good. What usually happens instead is that we become more arrogant and ugly, more proud and perverse, more cynical and careless. This is the wisdom of hell.

But when we learn from God, everything changes radically. We admit we don't know it all and never can, but He does. Like a child before a really wise and good Father, we can come without pretense and just *ask*.

God's way of teaching us wisdom from heaven is always this:

1. Revelation: God speaks

Because we are finite, an infinite God must show us what is right and real beyond what we can see or understand. We can know what is true only if it is revealed to us.

2. Practical Obedience: We serve

The infinite God not only wants to show us what is true but asks that His creation live by that truth—in the right way. Truth has practical consequence.

3. Illumination: If we obey, God might explain His revelation

After we learn to listen to God and trustingly do what He asks us, He promises to give us further understanding and truth so we may grow more and more like Him.

This is the divine order of learning. To be a disciple of Jesus we must learn from Him that truth follows humility, the purity of a good life follows from truth, and true understanding comes only to those who both *hear* and *do* what God says. It also means we cannot hope to reverse the process and get it right in either wisdom or virtue.

To learn from the divine perspective totally alters everything we do, think, and say. It encourages us to trust God and not ourselves. It results in heart change and looks for the qualities of a life rather than claims of grandeur. Its first test is not data but attitude. It measures character, not just a collection of good concepts. Most of all, it leads to a growing trust in Christ and who He is, a real friendship with God. This is the wisdom of heaven. This is the core of true discipleship.

Knowing God's Will

Every Christian asks this question at one time or another: "How can I know the will of God for my life?" Do you know how to hear from heaven?

Walk through the halls of time and study the Christians who

changed history. Often they were not especially talented people. But they all had one thing in common: They knew and did the will of God in their generation, and that made all the difference.

Scripture is the record of common people who found God's will. He spoke to people then, and He has not changed. God is still looking for people; at every crisis of history, He has found one who wants to do His will. And you can be God's man or God's woman! If you faithfully apply the Bible principles of guidance, you can know the voice of God and do His will as surely as any man or woman of God who ever lived.

GOAL AND PLAN

You are a special object of God's love! You were made to be a tiny mirror of God's own infinite personality. God has placed one awesome gift in your control that gives you the possibility to succeed or fail—the power of creative, responsive choice.

What an amazing privilege—to be made *really* free! God entrusts you with this not only for your own destiny but for that of others. Life is our time of testing. We can choose to serve Him out of love or to reject His goodness and mercy. God will not always help us unless we ask Him, and He will not stop us unless it is necessary, though He can and does step in if stupid, selfish choices try to challenge the highest good of His kingdom. But because of His gift of freedom, your destiny cannot be blueprinted!

You will not find the blueprint idea of God's will in the Bible. His work with us is more like that of a movie director. A director plans the movie's theme and purpose, guides the direction and content of his script, and has final say over the whole production. While he picks the key characters, actors get to bring their own unique gifts and talents to the role. In a similar way, each choice you make is significant; it is an act of creation, introducing new factors into His universe. Within this freedom, God works *for* or *against* our choices to accomplish His overall purpose. Christianity is unique in that the Lord God is actively involved with us. The God of the Bible is a living, moving God who has not set up history and stepped out of the picture. He cares about us and loves us. He intervenes in history at every turn and demonstrates His power to all who dare to follow His challenge.

God's will for your life is a goal, not a plan. His ultimate goal, or purpose, is to remake us in the image of His Son, the Lord Jesus (Romans 8:29). A goal is our point of aim, the star that fixes our direction and our destiny. Every Christian who follows His law of love locks into a pattern to transform his or her life into God's own image. Based on this goal is every subpurpose and lesser goal for all history and for each of His children. Some of these smaller goals are designed expressly for your life so that you can find a happy place of service in His kingdom. With each fulfillment He entrusts us with more, revealing the next goal only when the present goal is completed. These goals will always fit the purposes of Jesus during His earthly visit—seeking and saving those who are lost (Luke 19:10), destroying the works of the devil (1 John 3:8), and doing and finishing the Father's work (John 6:36–40; 17:4).

DAY-BY-DAY DISCOVERY

God hasn't left us without instruction! The Bible is His work manual—but it isn't a celestial rule book. It contains not mere points but principles. All Bible laws are descriptions of reality, relational guides intended for our highest good. With God's Word as our written foundation stone, we can build a life for God from His day-to-day guidance.

Guidance is a life-long process. God will reveal goals, help you reach them, and then set new, higher ones. God's goals never change; His overall strategy is not affected by our choices. In football, the goal is unchanging, but each side must change its game plan to reach that goal as the opposition changes its tactics. Plans are variable; dependent on our choices, they must change as often as choices do. It is for this reason God does not give us a detailed diary of our lives ahead. He wants us to make a day-by-day discovery of His revealed will. That daily discovery is guidance.

God's will for your life is an ongoing discovery of the most effective present plan to eventually reach His ultimate goal. The plans may vary with time, circumstances, and choices, but God will always work with you, daily pointing out the best course.

If you fail to consult or trust Him, not everything will be lost! An opportunity may pass that can never be regained, but with our confession and His forgiveness, He can make even failure turn to His glory! Once you are forgiven, God has the power to make even your failure into an asset—perhaps to help some other person with the same problem. In this way, "all things work together for good to those who love God . . . according to *His* purpose" (Romans 8:28, emphasis added).

HEART OF A SERVANT

As we work with God's goal for our lives, there will be exciting discoveries in seeing how choices we make and situations God arranges around those choices turn out for His glory. True freedom comes when we know we are on God's side; nothing is too difficult for Him.

Only when we make stupid or selfish choices do we come into conflict. This happens if we choose not for God but for something far less. Our purposes then clash with His, and our sense of purpose, freedom, and inner harmony disappears. This is the ultimate broken relationship, and nothing will seem to go right until it is fixed.

How can we stay in tune with God's purpose? A loving, listening heart that both hears and follows is a good description of CORE discipleship. The privileges of sonship depend to a great extent on our attitude of *servanthood*. The Son of God himself became a servant. With God, true power and authority are found only in being a servant of many. As we bend our wills and rights to God, He will give us His wisdom and strength. But self-control comes first, and we will never have it until we have the heart of a servant!

CONDITIONS OF GUIDANCE

No one will ever be guided continually unless he or she is willing to fulfill some core conditions. Check your life against these before you ask for guidance:

1. A desire to know and do all the revealed will of God. Don't ask for guidance unless you are prepared to act on it! God is always willing to make His purpose known. If you cannot find an answer, you may have some secret reservation in your heart. God will not show you His will for you to merely think about doing it. Unless you are prepared to trust His wisdom and love and do what He shows you, *don't ask Him.*

Many saying they can't get God's guidance really mean they wish He would show them an easier way. God promises to show us *only* if we are ready to *act* on His revelation (Hosea 6:3a; Matthew 7:21; John 7:17).

God will not guide those who want to run their own lives (Matthew 10:24, 37–39; Philippians 2:5–8; 3:7–8; 1 Corinthians 7:23b; Psalm 25:9).

2. A willingness to let others think you are a fool. Doing God's will often means we won't look good to the world around us. Some Christians hide noninvolvement behind a pretended fear of "uncertain guidance" or "not knowing God's will." We can't always expect a voice from the sky when the path of service is clear. God gave us common sense, and He expects us to use it. God's will is usually an area of general direction in which He leaves us relatively free to work for Him (Proverbs 3:23; 4:5–13; 6:20–22; 10:9; 11:3; Matthew 25:11–27).

Christians, in their hunger for God to speak to them about everything, often forget this. There is a tendency to equate the amount of *direct* guidance with spiritual depth. God often teaches us reliance in the big and little things of life by honoring our trusting requests for "direction" in little answers that build faith. We should never grow out of referring problems and decisions to His wise advice.

Never forget, however, that God created you *human* and not a *robot.* He gave you free will and intelligence with the check of conscience. Don't make the mistake of thinking that the closer you grow to Him, the more you will be specifically directed in all you do. Only puppets are totally dependent on the pull of a string for every move they make. Christians are often afraid to take initiative in case they step out of God's will. We forget God paints the lines of guidance with a road marker, not a drafting pencil!

This is where Christian guidance is so very personal. It is possible for us to tell God what we want to do for Him, and for God to give it to us! Sometimes God will let us choose between two possibilities; sometimes He asks us to make a choice. He is a true Father, who wants to teach us responsibility. If you have a clear picture of His general guidelines from Scripture, you do not always have to ask for special guidance. He asks only that we be instantaneously open to His redirection as we act.

> God's method in answering almost any prayer is the head-on, straight-forward approach. It calls for courage, as well as faith. It's the march-into-the-Red-Sea-and-it-divides method ... or march-up-to-the-walls-and-they-fall-down technique. He will take any promises or pledges we make to Him at their face value. He has a way of calling our bluff. (Peter Marshall, "Praying Is a Dangerous Business," *A Man Called Peter* by Catherine Marshall)

Yet sometimes the right way is not at all what we would logically expect. Some directions cut right across all limited human knowledge of the "best" thing, even contradicting it! This is direction from *intuition,* as our spirits connect in faith to the super-rationality of the Holy Spirit, who has promised to guide us into truth (John 16:13). It is sensing *in spirit* what is the desire of God. Young believers usually begin to be guided directly by their intuition and renewed conscience and can accomplish a lot for God even before they know more about His ways by studying His Word. Just as there is a danger of biblically groundless guidance, so there is also the opposite danger: that our minds will be developed at the expense of the intuitive sensitivity of conscience. This quickly kills the freshness of our Christian lives, the excitement of being prompted by the Spirit of God and being sensitive to His inner voice.

We must cultivate this sensitivity that is a hot line to His heart. It will keep us dependent on Christ's direction so we will not lose our "first love" in our love of His Word. The Holy Spirit can teach us to tune in to His promptings if we learn to obey this inner Voice.

Still, never act on a doubtful impression; it is *sin* to do so (Romans 14:5). We will feel awed, scared even, when God asks us to do some big thing for Him, but never rushed, pushed, or insecure. We need to develop our conscience until it is as sensitive as air and keep our spirit free from oppression, defilement, or too much unhealthy excitement by guarding our hearts from pride, extreme emotions, and depression. We will quickly pick up His special custom "call signs" for us if we begin with a clean heart and a clear conscience. That kind of obedience to intuition may look insane to the eyes of the world, but you will be *God's* fool, and you will see His power (Proverbs 3:5–6; 11:5; Isaiah 11:2; Matthew 11:25; Mark 3:21; Acts 26:24; 1 Corinthians 3:18–20; 2 Corinthians 5:13; Galatians 5:18).

3. A clean conscience from the past. Guidance will always be hindered or misunderstood if there are unresolved things in your life that God has urged you to make right. How can He show you more if you have disobeyed in the little things? (Luke 16:10). Every time you kneel to pray, His Spirit will point back to your clear duty to get that thing cleaned up and put right. A clear conscience is absolutely essential to distinguishing between the voice of God and the voice of the Enemy. Unconfessed sin is a prime reason why many get confused and say they do not know God's will. It is only the "pure in heart" who see Him (Matthew 5:8; 5:23–24; James 3:13–18).

4. Regular time in prayer and the Word of God. God's book is the whole basis of described divine guidance. It contains principles and guidelines to almost every avenue of serving Him. God's will is expressly revealed in His Word. Bible study shows us what God expects in daily living, and most scriptural principles of action can be directly applied to every problem situation in life. No guidance will ever break the fence of scriptural precept. Freedom in following the Lord Jesus always remains on the tracks of God's expressed descriptions of right and moral responsibility. The Bible is the broad base on which we must build daily guidance (Proverbs 6:23).

Prayer teaches us by experience what God's voice sounds like. Many people don't have a clue what God's direction is simply because they never spend long enough with Him to recognize what He is like! It is not enough to know *about* God. That is well and good, but it will never get you into His presence. This is the secret of true, core wisdom in life: knowing Jesus (1 Chronicles 28:9; Job 28:12–28; Proverbs 8:1–21). If you want to hear from God more often, how about letting *Him* hear from you more? If you want God to talk to you, spend time talking to Him (James 1:5).

WAYS GOD GUIDES US

SUPERNATURAL

1. His Voice

God has sometimes spoken in an audible *voice*. This unusual direction came to a number of both saints and sinners in the Bible. Take a look at the examples of God speaking to Moses (Exodus 3:4–6), Samuel as a boy (1 Samuel 3:1–10), Elijah (1 Kings 19:9–13), and Saul with his men (Acts 9:1–7). People later in church history have also heard that voice. Peter Marshall, chaplain to the U.S. Senate, heard God's voice, and it saved him from death in a fog in Scotland. As a result, he entered the ministry.

2. Visions and Dreams

God often spoke to people through visions and dreams to communicate an idea difficult to describe in any other way. A vision differs in only one basic way from a dream: It can occur when the person is wide-awake and not sleeping. A divine dream or vision is implanted or inspired by the Holy Spirit and can be primarily explained only by Him.

Nearly all the prophets of Scripture were given dreams or visions to instruct them. Think of Isaiah with his awesome vision of the Lord (Isaiah 6:1–8); Ezekiel, who saw the strange, science fiction–like scene near Chebar (Ezekiel 1:1–28); and Daniel, with his famous re-screening (Daniel 2:1–19) and subsequent interpretation (Daniel 2:22–47) of Nebuchadnezzar's forgotten dream. Joseph was warned and protected by two dreams at Jesus' birth (Matthew 1:20; 2:12–13). A vision at midday sent Peter to the Gentile world to preach (Acts 10:9–16). God has promised visions and dreams in the last days (Joel 2:28). It is a way He can speak to people otherwise cut off from His Word.

3. Visitations

Angels appeared to people of God in the Bible, sometimes bringing warnings from God to His servants. The Bible reveals that God has many angelic beings that serve Him in various ways (Genesis 3:24; Psalm 103:20–21; 148:2–5; Isaiah 6:1–3; Ezekiel 28:14–15; Revelation 4:6–9; 5:6–14). At times even *God himself* appeared in a physical form, a manifestation of the Word of God, the Son and second Person of the Godhead. When dealing with people in this way, He is referred to as the "Angel of the Lord."

Consider angels' earthly visits with Abraham (Genesis 18:1–33), Lot (Genesis 19:1–16), Jacob (Genesis 32:2–30), Moses (Exodus 33:19–23), Joshua (Joshua 5:13–15), the children of Israel (Judges 2:1–5), David (2 Samuel 24:16), Elijah (1 Kings 19:7), Mary (Luke 1:26–35),

Philip (Acts 8:26), Peter (Acts 12:7), and Paul (Acts 27:23). Holy angels have special powers and abilities, occupy command posts throughout God's kingdom in service to Him, and help protect and prepare people for their wonderful future in Christ (2 Kings 6:15–17; Psalm 34:7; 35:5–6; Isaiah 63:9; Matthew 26:53; Hebrews 1:14). They apparently can still visit earth, moving among people in human form (Hebrews 13:2).

THROUGH THE BODY OF CHRIST

1. Advice of Experienced Christians

Guidance is often clarified by discussion with Christians known for their close walk with God; we call it *counsel*. Much of what we ought to do can be gleaned from such kind and wise guidance, but it should *never* be used as the sole reason for any important decision. Scripture gives serious warning about just listening to others without first seeking God's face (l Kings 13:11–22; 1 Chronicles 13:1–12. Also read Proverbs 11:14; 12:15; 13:10; 15:22; 20:18; 24:6; 27:9; Acts 6:1–5; 15:1–31; 1 Thessalonians 2:11–13).

Godly guidance . . .

- fits scriptural precepts! Advice that goes against Scripture comes from the dark side.
- never goes against a previous command of God or breaks God's laws.
- confirms an already established conviction of heart given by the Spirit of God.
- leaves the heart filled with peace, joy, or spiritual conviction.
- is proven true over time (Deuteronomy 18:18–22).

Beware of people who constantly offer guidance prefaced by "God told me" or "God showed me." This is often a sign of pride or deceiving spirits. Watch out for the half truth; deception usually begins with something that is partly right, or one side of the truth, followed by a lie.

2. Direction Through the Holy Spirit

Scripture records supernatural manifestations of the Holy Spirit where God carries out through people some work normally above human ability or wisdom. These manifestations show God is really with

His people (Mark 16:15–18; John 14:12–14), edify the church (1 Corinthians 12:26; 14:3; Ephesians 4:11–13), or may deliver God's servants in times of crisis (Romans 1:11; 12:6; 1 Corinthians 12:1–12; 12:27–31; 14:12, 26; Ephesians 4:8–14).

In these cases, God has guided by a *word of knowledge*, a fragment of divine knowledge (Genesis 18:17, 19; 1 Samuel 9:19; 16:7; 1 Kings 19:18; 2 Kings 6:12; John 4:16–18, 29, 39; Acts 9:11–12; 10:5–6; 16:9); a *word of wisdom,* or the divine reasoning behind revelation (Genesis 12:1–2; 41:33–36; Exodus 31:1–4; Deuteronomy 34:9; 2 Samuel 5:23–24; 1 Kings 3:11–12, 28; Matthew 10:18–19; 22:15–33; Acts 16:6–10); and the *gift of prophecy* (Numbers 27:21; Deuteronomy 33:8; 1 Samuel 28:6; 30:7–8; Ezekiel 2:1–2; Acts 11:27–30; 16:9–10; 20:23; 21:10–13). Notice that in no case does this kind of direction take priority over the written Word of God, and every case must be tested by that Word. In the end, this kind of direction from God always involves the consent of the individual; none are "fates" from which there is no escape.

3. The Preaching and Teaching of God's Servants in Ministry

When men and women of God receive a message from God for others, we have opportunity to learn God's ways and words from their Spirit-inspired preaching or public guidance. God designed this as the core way we can learn from one another in Christian community (Acts 15:28). Take notes on these words of counsel or messages to study later. Maybe the very direction you are looking for has already been given, and you have forgotten it! Take a look at Exodus 4:10–12; Isaiah 46:10–11; John 3:27; Acts 20:27; Romans 10:14; 1 Corinthians 2:1; 1 Peter 4:11. Every message should be tested by either of the previous two sets of tests and checks.

4. Individual Direct Guidance

A. Word of God

- *Regular Bible reading*—Each time you read a section of the Bible, you fill in a portion of a "puzzle," until sliding in a key piece suddenly reveals a whole picture.

- *Open-page method*—This way of approaching God's Word is definitely not to be abused! Ask God to guide your fingers to the right

Scripture for your need. Open the Bible, trusting Him to speak to you from it (Acts 8:27–35).

- *Mental suggestion*—When you are praying, God will sometimes bring to mind a specific verse, chapter, or book. Turn to the place and read until God speaks to you.

- *Recalled memory verse*—In this case, God brings to mind a verse of Scripture that brings clear instruction in time of temptation or difficulty. This is one reason why memorizing Scripture is so important (Psalm 119:9–11, 15–16, 33–35, 65–68, 97–105; Proverbs 2:1–20; 3:1–6; 4:1–13; 2 Timothy 3:14–17).

B. Witness of the Holy Spirit

The inner voice of the Holy Spirit can let you know whether something is of God or not. Never act on a doubtful impression, especially one demanding a quick decision. God *leads,* not *pushes!* The urge to rush is usually of the Enemy. God's voice is gentle, familiar-sounding, loving, and it leaves you with a sense of spiritual uplift and rejoicing (John 3:29–30; 10:3–5, 14, 16, 27–28; 2 Timothy 1:7). Test spiritual impressions by the Word of God if you feel a sense of uneasiness or fear (John 6:36; 14:17; Romans 8:9, 14; Colossians 1:9–10; 1 John 2:27; 4:1–3, 13).

C. Waiting on God

God has three answers in guidance: (1) "Yes," (2) "No," and (3) "Wait!" Sometimes there must be delays. Our lives are bound up with others' lives, and God will often wait until they are ready before giving us the go-ahead. This is the most difficult of all answers, but it is one that is often necessary.

SEEKING GOD'S FACE

The following way of searching for divine guidance combines most guidance principles into three basic steps:

1. *Die to your own desires.* Take your desires—whether good or bad—to God in prayer and "place" them to one side for the Lord to deal with. If it helps, write them on a sheet of paper, then pray: "Lord Jesus, I take my desires and put them here. I will to die in my own mind to the things I most want to do. I want to wait for *your* desire."

2. *Resist the devil* by taking your stand in the name of the Lord

Jesus. Each child of God has a place of power with Christ (Ephesians 1:17–2:7). Standing in *His* authority, shut out the Enemy's voice by quoting to him in faith appropriate Scripture. Like a sword thrust, God's written revelation will force him into retreat (James 4:7; 1 Peter 5:6–9; 1 John 3:8b). "Satan, in the name of Jesus, I resist your suggestions, as it is written . . ." Do this clearly and simply, wholly trusting the power of Christ to back your stand against him.

3. *Listen to the voice of God.* By faith take a Christlike heart attitude (1 Corinthians 2:16). Ask God if He will now show you what to do. Any immediate, clear answer may well be His voice; take the first, definite impression. You will know if it matches what He is like. Do what He tells you to do. If nothing comes immediately, thank God for His answer of "wait" and praise Him instead.

God's Book, the Bible–CORE Word

God gave us His Son—and a book. The Bible is a book *from* God *about* God—the story of His love for humanity. Its central figure is Jesus Christ, God robed in humanity, and it records His origin, birth, life, death, and resurrection. The Bible's message is stranger than fiction: The very same God who spun the worlds in space visited earth to provide a way to heaven, and now people may share a new kingdom in His very own family. *The Bible is no ordinary book.* It stands alone because it was written by men who listened to the voice of God. The words they penned were more than human.

As a recorded revelation from an infinite mind and heart, the Bible is unlike any other book on earth. Not just a book of history, its records are accurately substantiated by modern archaeology. Not merely a book of poetry, but the inspiration of countless songs through the centuries. Not just an adventure story, yet few novels, plays, or movies can match the sheer drama of its pages. Not primarily a book of ethics or morality, though civilization's finest laws have been forged from its principles. Not a textbook, but it still astonishes scientists and scholars from fields as varied as genetics, geology, and nuclear physics. The Bible is a unique record of our problem and God's *answer,* the Good News of salvation from sin through Jesus.

Bible scholar C. A. Benham said, "What man has *produced,* man can *exhaust....* We have outgrown every other book that belongs to the past; but instead of outgrowing the Bible we have not yet grown *up to* it. The Bible is not only up-to-date, but it is always *ahead* of date" (emphasis added). Centuries of study by the most able scholarship have not begun to exhaust its riches. The profoundest study reveals unfathomable depths of wisdom. Mark Twain said, "It's not the things I don't understand in the Bible that bother me; it's the things I do understand!"

Any man or woman who wants to give an intelligent opinion or conclusion on the Bible should first spend serious time in personal, intensive research to see what it actually says. The Bible does not attempt to defend its claim to divine inspiration; it simply states it. The writers of Scripture continuously claim their message was not human opinion but divine revelation. Genesis uses the words "And God said..." nine times in the first chapter; the statement "...says the Lord" appears twenty-three times in the last Old Testament book, Malachi. "The Lord spoke..." appears 560 times in the first five Bible books; Isaiah claims at least forty times that his message was from God—Ezekiel and Jeremiah do also, sixty and one hundred times respectively. All in all, Scripture writers declared their message divine in origin at least thirty-eight hundred times!

The Lord Jesus quoted from twenty-four Old Testament books. He referred to Daniel twenty-two times, Isaiah forty times, the Pentateuch sixty times, as well as the Psalms, never implying the events or people recorded there were fables or folklore. In Luke 24:24–27, Christ claimed himself to be the subject of prophecy all through the Old Testament. Many times He stated that all things in Scripture must be fulfilled (Matthew 13:14; Luke 21:22; John 13:18; 15:25; 17:12). He claimed His own words were inspired (John 6:63; 8:42–47; 12:46–50) and that "the Scripture cannot be broken" (John 10:35). His own claims to divine origin and the claims of the Bible stand or fall together. If Jesus cannot be proved a liar or a lunatic, the Bible is God's Word.

New Testament writers who knew Christ likewise claimed divine inspiration. Paul declared his message came from God in God's power

(1 Corinthians 2:1–5; Galatians 1:11–17), and Peter says Paul wrote by "wisdom given to him" (2 Peter 3:15–16). At least six hundred Old Testament quotations and references in the New Testament interface and interlock both parts into a united whole. God says *He* called scribes to write (Matthew 23:34) and *commanded* His followers to teach what He said (Matthew 28:19–20), sending the Holy Spirit to help them beyond human observation and memory. Their understanding (Luke 1:3; John 16:13–15) of past and future records came by His Spirit's guidance and control (John 14:26). The Bible is full of data infinitely beyond its human authors' knowledge. The inspiration of Scripture is like a composer's relationship to a conductor: The composer writes a score from which the conductor produces music according to his own personality. It is like the work of a painter who selects raw materials available to him to blend and prepare colors for his masterpiece. God is the Composer and Master Painter, His author friends the "conductors" and the "colors" (2 Timothy 3:16).

UNLIKE ANY OTHER BOOK

1. ITS SURVIVAL

The Bible has survived century after century of determined persecution. No ancient book has such a vast number of surviving copies; there are thousands of Old and New Testament manuscripts. Variations between these are minor and insignificant, and great care must have been taken in copying them. Jewish scribes used a new pen each time they came to the word LORD and at that point carefully compared everything they had so far written to the original copy.

Each era brings a renewed attempt to discredit the Bible or to stamp it out, but history shows it has been impossible to destroy the Scriptures. Jesus said, "Heaven and earth will pass away, but My words will never pass away" (Matthew 24:35 NIV). God's Word is living (Hebrews 4:12). It has stood the test of centuries, critical scholarship, and the censorship of its enemies.

2. ITS STRUCTURE

Take about forty different writers over a period of about fifteen hundred years of time. Use men from many walks of life—doctors, shepherds, kings, fishermen. Pick them from miles and generations apart. Give them little or no chance to communicate. Cut many of them off from the prevailing opinions of their day. Ask them to write on religion, poetry, health, ethics, science, morality, philosophy. Ask them to make predictions of future events, the meaning of life, the mystery of existence, our final purpose. You be the editor! Collect, condense, and couch it in common language, then divide it all into books, chapters, and verses.

Now—what have you got? Literature hash! No one on earth could make sense out of such a mass of outdated ideas, wild speculations, and hopeless contradictions. The Bible was written exactly like that. Yet any honest reader who has carefully examined its message has found it one amazing whole from Genesis to Revelation, united in theme, consistent in concept, logical in development, and coherent in doctrine. In real-life illustration, parable and prophecy, recording historical people who lived and died, the Bible is the greatest love story in history, one that tells of a loving God seeking rebellious humanity.

3. Its Scientific Accuracy

The God of the Bible is the God who created the universe. *True* science and Scripture will always agree, since they both have the same Author! Science has had centuries to examine the statements of fact in Scripture. Although the opinions of people about nature and the opinions of people about the Bible have clashed, no fault has been recorded in Scripture. The Bible does not tell fairy tales. Its statements are true, able to withstand the closest tests. It is a matter of historical record that science never developed significantly anywhere except where there was a Christian influence. The scientific method and motivation for inquiry is a child of Scriptural concepts; it assumes the universe is the orderly product of a divine mind and that we can discover the secrets of His creation, since we are rational, finite miniatures of our Maker.

Before Columbus sailed around the world, Scripture recorded earth's spherical nature (Isaiah 40:21–22). When science as a baby thought the world was held up by "three elephants on the back of a tortoise," the Bible factually established its free float in space (Job 26:7). The moon is shown to act like a reflector, unlike the radiating sun (Job 25:5). The

Bible record of creation is a master example of the true harmony between geology, biology, and Scripture. Five hundred years ago, it was rediscovered that physical life resided in the blood; the Bible recorded it thirty-five hundred years ago (Leviticus 17:11). Meteorology, geology, and aeronautic principles are hinted at in Scripture (Psalm 135:5, 7; Job 28:5; 38:4). Atomic energy and radiation effects are old stuff with the God of the atom (2 Peter 3:10–12; Isaiah 13:13; Joel 2:30).

Science can tabulate for us the *what* and analyze the *how,* but it cannot tell us why the universe exists. Science is descriptive; it cannot say who you are or why you are here. It can tell us what we are able to do but not what we ought to do. Here God's revelation in science is superseded by His revelation in Scripture (Psalm 8:3–6; 19:7–14; 91:1). One shows His power, the other His purpose.

4. ITS SPAN OF TIME IN PROPHECY

If there is one thing the Bible dares to do that no other book in the world does, it is to accurately predict the future. God arranges the situations of history to bring about His glory in the lives of those who respond to His call. Working with human choices, He directs circumstances together into a preplanned series of patterns of divine purpose. The outline of many of these patterns is revealed in the Bible. There are about 3,856 verses directly or indirectly concerned with prophecy in Scripture—in other words, about one verse in six tells of future events! God's challenge to the world is "Prove Me now" (Malachi 3:10 KJV) "For I *am* the LORD. I speak, and the word which I speak will come to pass" (Ezekiel 12:25; see also 24:14; Jeremiah 28:9; Luke 21:22). Other religions have their sacred writings, but in them the element of prophecy is most noticeable by its absence. The destruction of Tyre, the invasion of Jerusalem, the fall of Babylon and Rome—each was accurately predicted in the Bible and fulfilled down to the smallest detail.

In the life of the Lord Jesus, there are over *three hundred* fulfilled prophecies. The chance these could coincide by accident in one person is laughable—one in a number followed by *181 zeroes*! To give you some idea of the size of this immense figure, think of a ball that is packed solidly with electrons (two million billion make a "line" about one inch long). Now imagine this ball expanded to the size of the universe we know—more than four billion light-years in diameter. Multiply this by five hundred quadrillion, then remove just one electron, "coloring" it red. "Stir it" in for a hundred years with the others. Then blindfold a person and send him in to pick it out on the first try. Impossible? This is the same chance Christ had of living and dying according to the Bible's prophecies by *accident*. Scripture specifically predicts events and happenings as modern as tomorrow's news release.

5. ITS SOCIAL INFLUENCE

A book's true nature is revealed by the effect it has on society. The Bible gives laws for human relationships that have never been exceeded or equaled. Whenever the Scriptures have been truly taught and lovingly lived, they transform nations. The Bible has brought consideration for others, tenderness and compassion for the old, sick, and the needy. It has dignified womanhood and guided childhood. Whenever the Scriptures have been freely circulated in the language of a people, they have released astonishing power for good, elevating society, overthrowing falsity and superstition, and opening the door to progress in the sciences, arts, and humanities.

The Bible message has delivered thousands from the chains of fear, sickness, and sin. It is without exception the most powerful book in the world for transforming lives. Practically applied, it teaches and inspires industry, fairness, and justice; it stands for the welfare of the individual, the family, the community, and the state. It has created more benevolent enterprises than any other book in history. Study for yourself the record of history. Watch what happens to a nation that honors the Bible and its Author; see what happens to progress in countries that try to suppress, reject, or misinterpret its message. *Wherever the Bible is loved and applied, the nation is exalted.* Whenever people become forgetful of its Author and ignorant of its truths, fear, war, disease, and hatred stalk the streets. The Bible is clear: "Blessed is the nation whose God is the LORD" (Psalm 33:12).

6. ITS SUPREME APPEAL

The Bible is a Book with a universal message for *all* people. It is the only volume a child and scholar may find equal delight in. Its simple, life-related principles can work in any country, transcending barriers of culture and race to bring peace, love, joy, and forgiveness. Only the Bible can make bad men good *inside*, transforming the rebel and the rotten into saints and servants of humanity.

7. Its Supernatural Salvation

The greatest proof of the Bible is the *difference* its message makes in lives. It is indeed the written revelation of the God who made us; its claims, origin, historical records, and prophetic fulfillments point unmistakably to the secret of eternal life.

God has promised to answer the earnest seeker. Bible truth must be revealed by the Holy Spirit (John 16:13; 1 Corinthians 2:11–14). Let doubters pray honestly from the heart, "God, I don't know if you are real or not, or if this is your Book or not, but if it is and you can help me, show yourself to me through its pages as I read," and God will meet them in conviction and conversion (John 20:30–31).

"And you will seek Me and find Me, when you shall search for Me with all your heart" (Jeremiah 29:13). All God requires is honesty toward Him. If anyone is willing to face the demands of truth, God is more than willing to lead them into the reality they need! (Jeremiah 3:12–13).

CORE MEANING FROM YOUR LIFE MANUAL

Your life manual, the Bible, is the most *important* book in the world. It holds the key to life and to your every problem. It is the letter from your Great Friend, your manual for miracles, your passport to power, and a textbook for triumph! Yet "devotional drop-outs" are all too common in countless Christian lives. How do you get out of the Bible what God has put into it for you?

Read

To be able to read and understand the Bible you should . . .
- desire to know God through His Word (Matthew 5:6);
- determine to seek God by His Word (Psalm 27:8);
- discipline your life to find God in His Word (John 8:31).

Read it! Soak yourself in Scripture. Carry a Bible or New Testament wherever you go. Take "bites" in spare moments—standing in a line, waiting for a friend, traveling. You cannot understand much if you do not read much. Make a habit of reading for a certain time or to cover a determined amount each day. How you treat your Bible echoes your attitude toward Christ. Your attention to its message underlines your present relationship to the Lord. Do you love God's Word? Spend time with it? It is our visible link to God's mind. Faithfulness to your Bible reflects a life faithful to the Lord Jesus Christ.

How much should you read?

By reading it about five minutes a day, you can finish the entire Bible in less than a year. It takes only seventy hours and forty minutes to read it aloud completely through. The Old Testament takes fifty-two hours and twenty minutes; the New, eighteen hours and twenty minutes. If you spend, say, on holiday, eight hours a day with it, you can finish it in just nine days!

Or perhaps you would rather read by chapter. The Bible can be completed in about eighteen weeks at just ten chapters a day. The Old Testament in fourteen weeks; the New in only twenty-seven days. The Gospels (Matthew, Mark, Luke, and John) together with Acts take just twelve days; the Epistles and Revelation only fifteen. Of course, you may not have that much time, but how much time do you have? Are five minutes or a few chapters a day too much to give back to God in Bible study and prayer?

Rules for Understanding the Bible

Use these seven simple rules as keys to unlock the secrets of Scripture. You will have no difficulty understanding the Bible with the Holy Spirit as your Guide and Teacher as long as you keep to these basic principles in interpreting God's written Word:

1. Interpret each passage or verse in the light of all other passages or verses you can find on the same subject. Failure here has troubled hundreds of otherwise sincere, searching Christians. Get plenty of perspective on verses or words by comparing them, with the help of a concordance, to others on the same subject. Use major sections to interpret minor ones, literal sections to throw light on symbolic ones, specific passages to explain general ones, and monitor verses expressing feelings and experience.

2. God's Word means exactly what it says. Whenever possible, take the

meaning of a verse exactly as it is written (literally) unless the surrounding verses (context) show clearly the language is only symbolic, a metaphor, or a word picture intended for illustration.

3. Think of each verse in the context of its surrounding verses: The *purpose* of the passage you are reading, the *message* (if any) of the entire chapter, and, if necessary, the *design* of the whole book. Never draw nonexistent meaning from a verse by pulling the verse out of its obvious meaning in its setting. "A text out of context is a pretext."

4. Texts that prove either of two theories on a Scriptural truth you are looking at prove neither. Different passages must be understood in such a way that they don't contradict each other. Truth is *never* contradictory; such verses are most usually like two sides of the same coin. Never *force* meanings into verses if they do not fit; study something else instead until God desires to show you its real meaning. Things hook-and-eye together after a while; like the final piece in a jigsaw puzzle, the difficult text might fill in a gap, letting you suddenly "see" a new picture of truth in all its beauty.

5. Use your head. God gave us common sense. He used ordinary people to write the Bible in common language. At the very least, read it like you would any other book. Keep in mind who says what: Is it human, demon, angel, sinner, saint, or God? How does that being feel when he or she says it? What resources, interest, and abilities does he or she have to carry out any promise or judgment made? Where is this being said? Why is it being said? When can I expect it to happen? Some promises are for our future life in glory with Christ; most have become due since the birth of the early church. When you find one you think might apply, ask God to make it real and use it.

6. The first time anything is mentioned in Scripture is usually the key to understanding its basic or primary meaning when it is used anywhere else in the Bible. This is true for words, phrases, things, happenings, numbers, objects, ideas, or people. Bible metaphors from Genesis to Revelation grow in richness as you read more of it, so meanings become even more wonderful as you grow in God. Also keep in mind that repetition underlines something's importance; there are no nonessentials or needless padding in God's Word. Pay special attention to those passages, words, or ideas that are

mentioned many times in Scripture; God considers them important for us.

7. Promises or judgments are conditional on our response to God's conditions. Whenever God makes a promise, He reveals a principle of universal application to everyone in like circumstances. All His promises express the great, unchanging principles of His character and government. In short, promises are not restricted in their general application to the person or persons to whom they were given but may be claimed by all people in similar circumstances. What God is at one time, He always is. What He has promised at one time to one person, He may promise at all times to all persons under similar circumstances.

RESEARCH

It's not enough to *see* what the Bible says—you should have some ways to *study* it. The Holy Spirit will guide you into truth if you ask Him (John 16:13; James 1:5), but prepare to pay a price for digging in! Put in some time and effort to search out the great truths of Scripture, or you will never grow up for God. You study for school or work. You study to improve playing skills. To be a CORE Christian, you need to study to show yourself approved unto God (2 Timothy 2:15).

Most people never get started because they don't know how. The *Ultimate CORE* Web site gives you five different ways to study the Bible, but for now here are five key helps for your study most scholars and students of God's Word have used. For any real research into the Bible, you should invest in any or all of these.

1. A good concordance. Concordances are a sort of Bible index that list where words are found in the Bible and give their meaning in the original language. Some, like *Strong's Exhaustive Concordance,* list every word in the Bible. Concordances are expensive but well worthwhile. They will help you locate verses when you can remember only a few of the words of the verse but not the reference. Simply look up a key word as you would in a dictionary and go through the list until you find the wanted verse. It saves time searching for verses you cannot place. Some Bibles have a small printed concordance in the back, and most electronic Bibles have the capability to instantly locate a verse or theme.

2. A reliable dictionary. Use a well-known dictionary, such as a version by Oxford or Webster's. With this you can look up words you don't understand and get some fresh ideas about others. A Greek or Hebrew lexicon is another specialized dictionary used in Bible word study.

3. Other Bible translations. Some versions, like the much-loved *King James Version,* use words that have long since changed their meaning. Other versions may help you understand a certain difficult passage, but be careful of those that are interpretive, giving notes or paraphrasing to tell you the "real meaning" of the verses! Often these paraphrases or comments are by fine, godly people, but you need to measure them against the Word of God. You want the Holy Spirit to be your main Teacher.

4. Other helps. A Bible atlas, Bible encyclopedia, Bible dictionary, and other study helps can be added to your library as need and funds allow. However, these are not needed for most things God can teach you from His Word. Beware of the commentaries! They can be helpful but often become a crutch, supplying a ready-made answer. The Bible can throw a lot of light on the content of many commentaries! Stay simple in your study.

5. Notebook. You need some way to record your studies. Use a well-bound, loose-leaf folder if possible, or, if funds permit, even a loose-leaf or wide-margin Bible. Computer-based Bibles usually also provide this note function. Keep a record of your journey into truth.

MEDITATE

George Mueller, a great man of faith who kept hundreds of orphan children alive by trusting God for their food and clothes, knew God and His Word. What was the secret to *his* Bible understanding? As he once said:

> It has pleased the Lord to teach me a truth I have not lost the benefit of for more than fourteen years. I saw clearly . . . the first great business of the day was to have my soul *happy in the Lord.* I saw the most important thing I had to do was to pray after dressing in the morning and give myself to the reading of the Word of God and to meditate on it. Thus my heart might be comforted, encouraged, warmed, reproved, and instructed. (emphasis added)

Search every verse for a blessing. Get *food* for your soul. Say to each text or passage—"I will not let You go unless You bless me!" (Genesis 32:26). You may be led by God's Word to confess sin, pray for others, or ask for some need, then go on and read another verse. Keep this idea of "reading as feeding" in mind as you read the Bible. It helps check wandering thoughts, straying attention, or other things that attempt to turn you from seeking the Lord's presence. Christ is in every page of Scripture—in picture, parable, and personality. Look for God's face in the book He has written for you.

Meditation helps God's Word become a vital part of us. It involves *rethinking* all our daily experiences in the expressions of Scripture, using God's own language to talk to Him. Meditation is *spiritually digesting* the Bread of Life, feeding and building the "inner man" of the spirit.

Meditation is a cleansing stream for the mind. Some will not read the Bible because they say they "don't remember any of it." But take a dirty glass. Fill it up with water and pour it out again. There may be little left in it, but the glass is different. It is *cleaner.* In the same way, thinking God's thoughts after Him purifies our thought life. The living, sacred Scriptures are guidelines for clean, clear thinking.

One of the meanings of *meditate* is to "mutter." To help grasp the meaning and fullness of a verse, read it aloud. Repeat it to yourself a number of times. This constant repetition is like dialing a familiar telephone number—remembered through habit. Many blessings come through the discipline of meditation (Joshua 1:8; Psalm 1:2-3; 1 Timothy 4:13, 15).

MEMORIZE

Memorizing Scripture should be a part of every Christian life. It is the process of hiding God's Word in the heart so we might not sin against Him (Psalm 119:11). Memorizing Scripture is like loading a spiritual weapon. It enables you to

1. Rout doubt and defeat the devil.

When the Prince of Life met the Prince of Darkness during His wilderness temptation, He didn't bother to argue or reason. Jesus met every subtle accusation with a flaming arrow of Scripture. "It is written … It is written!" It's no good learning how to use your "weapon" when the Enemy is on you! Memorizing Scripture gives ready access to the sword of the Spirit (Ephesians 6:17; Psalm 119:11).

2. Put conviction into your witness.

Great men and women of God are ordinary Christians saturated with Scripture. God blesses His Word—the more we learn and use, the *deeper* and more effective our Christianity (1 Peter 1:23; 3:15; John 6:63; Hebrews 4:12).

3. Equip for Christian service.

No one can do the work of God without a practical grasp of the Word of God. It is the building block of witness and service for Jesus Christ. You do not need to be clever, sophisticated, witty, talented, or popular—but you do need to hide God's Word in your heart (2 Timothy 2:15; 3:15–16; Psalm 119:42).

Truly the Word of God will change your life. It transforms the mind, changes, strengthens, and builds CORE character. It moves us on from grace to grace, makes all who trust in it inheritors of the very nature of God. God comes in, dwells in, walks with, talks through, and enjoys friendship with the one who opens his or her life to the Word of God and receives the Spirit who inspired it.

Read it through, write it down, pray it in, work it out, and then pass it on. God's Word's alive!

BLESSED ARE THE POOR IN SPIRIT, FOR THEIRS IS THE KINGDOM OF HEAVEN. NIV

GOD BLESSES THOSE WHO REALIZE THEIR NEED FOR HIM, FOR THE KINGDOM OF HEAVEN IS GIVEN TO THEM. NLT

Blessed are the poor in spirit, for theirs is the kingdom of heaven. NASB

Blessed are the poor in spirit, for theirs is the kingdom of heaven. NKJV

You're blessed when you're at the end of your rope. With less of you there is more of God and his rule. THE MESSAGE

BLESSED ARE THE POOR IN SPIRIT, FOR THEIRS IS THE KING-DOM OF HEAVEN. ESV

3

CORE POVERTY

THE CORE NEEDS MORE

Blessed are the poor in spirit, for theirs is the kingdom of heaven.

MATTHEW 5:3

As soon as He opened His mouth to begin to teach the crowd that had gathered on the Galilean hillside, it was clear Jesus was no ordinary man. Jesus was a remarkable teacher. He had a God-given ability to draw from what He observed and turn it around to teach the incredible truth of God.

Can you imagine Jesus, His gaze resting purposefully upon a poor woman in the crowd, smiling knowingly as He began to teach? Can you hear the murmur that rippled across the crowd in response to His first words? **Blessed are the poor**. What a paradox! What was this man thinking? To the Jews in Jesus' day, to be poor, whether financially or spiritually, was a most pitiable condition. With just His opening sentence, Jesus blew all worldly wisdom out of the water. Was He crazy? Was it really possible this kingdom of heaven was available even to the poor?

In the same way today, Jesus declares the core truth of God. His kingdom is unchanged. Blessed are the poor in spirit, for theirs is the kingdom of heaven!

CORE Trust

Just who is a poor person? People have very different ideas of what it means to be poor; what is poverty in one nation may be looked on as wealth in another. We can safely say this: Genuinely poor people have absolutely no way to meet any fundamental need out of their own resources. Air. Water. Food. Clothing. Shelter. Poor people do whatever they can in order to survive, but they have nothing to bring, buy, bargain, or trade with of their own. The truly poor live day to day in constant awareness of life's fragility, dependent for their very future on the help, mercy, or kindness of others. If the absolutely poor do not get help, they will die.

Jesus often talked about the kingdom of heaven. This is no small realm but the future from which the ruler of all worlds flows. And to whom does His kingdom belong? The answer seems shocking: the *poor*. Those with no resources of their own. Those who live, indeed *must* live, from day to day in total dependence on someone outside themselves. In short, the future kingdom belongs only to those wholly dependent on the mercy of Another. We must trust God for our very lives.

So what is faith? What does it mean to really trust God? What is the bottom line in becoming part of His great CORE kingdom? Consider the words of Jesus: "If anyone desires to come after Me, let him deny himself, and take up his cross, and follow Me. For whoever desires to save his life will lose it, and whoever loses his life for My sake will find it" (Matthew 16:24–25). "So likewise, whoever of you does not forsake all that he has cannot be My disciple" (Luke 14:33).

What is Jesus saying? *It all starts with losing it all.* Entrance begins in emptiness. God has a way of taking the losers of this life and making them the leaders of the world. But first you have to *give up* whatever you rely on to meet your deepest need and greatest desire. Jesus said poor. He did not say poor but gifted, poor but strong, poor but with potential. Poor means with *nothing*. What can you bring to the table in exchange for the greatest gift of all? What do you have to recommend you at the door? What is the talent, the skill, the qualification that will get you in? Again, nothing. Nothing at all.

Doing God's Work

Ask any deeply devoted searcher, "How do you prepare to do God's work?" The answer may at first seem as different as their cultures and circumstances, but it's invariably the same: Pray. Read the Holy Book. Fast. Study. Work. Worship. Try this. Do this. Do that.

People asked Jesus that very question, and this is what He said: "*This* is the work of God, that you *believe in Him* whom [the Father] sent" (John 6:29, emphasis added). Not try, but *trust*. Not do, but *done*.

The fact is, we all want to impress God with our lives. We hope that if we do something to get His attention by our devotion, He might give us what we think we deserve. The awful truth is that if we get from God what we *really* deserve, we are all toast. Stand before a Judge who never makes a mistake and what kind of verdict will we receive if we get what should be coming to us? All our polite words and future promises cannot undo what has already been done. "The soul who sins shall die" (Ezekiel 18:20). This is certain. And if this is true, we have no hope at all. We have nothing to bring to the table. No excuse, no circumstance, no clarification can help.

We have no chance in hell, and only one chance before it, and that is this: if someone with the power to show pity on us can step in and grant us a pardon.

> But God, who is rich in mercy, because of His great love with which He loved us, even when we were dead in trespasses, made us alive together with Christ (by grace you have been saved), and raised us up together, and made us sit together in the heavenly places in Christ Jesus, that in the ages to come He might show the exceeding riches of His grace in His kindness toward us in Christ Jesus. For *by grace you have been saved through faith,* and that not of yourselves; it is the gift of God, not of works, lest anyone should boast. (Ephesians 2:4–9, emphasis added)

Here is a simple summary of the entire message of the Bible. It is the one lesson we most need to learn and the one that we find hardest of all. *God is God, and we are not.*

What does it mean to be a disciple of Jesus? What is He looking for in those He makes and molds into His CORE? And how do you move from the outer courts to the inner holy place of His friendship? The disciples came to Jesus and He taught them. First things first: Are you really His? You want to be the best Christian you can be; are you really a Christian to begin with? The first step in His school is always the same, a simple three-part sermon combining call, challenge, and comradeship all in one: *Come, follow me.*

The Gospel Versus Legalism

Not all who use the name of Jesus are His true disciples. Some may say they are if they are expected to be Christians, because they don't want to feel left out. Some come from homes where Jesus is known by others in the family. If parents say they know Jesus, children may think they know Him, too. Many who later became famous saints of God had to first get saved from being religious. Luther, Wesley, Whitfield, and many others were officially recognized as ministers before they were even really Christians. *How can you tell if what you have is real?*

Here is one of the most searching sermons of Charles Finney, a great revivalist at the turn of the nineteenth century, condensed and paraphrased for our time. It cuts to the core on the difference between legal religion and true Gospel salvation.

People can be led in only two ways: by *force* or by *trust*. We can live by rules based on hope of reward or fear of punishment, or we can live by love based on trust in the One who leads us. Now, there is nothing wrong with God's laws. The Bible says the law is holy, just, and good (Romans 7:12). But there is a world of difference between Gospel and legal obedience to that law. Remember, law is not a *motivation* but a *description.* It works by showing us, from God's infinite perspective, the benefit of obedience or the danger of disobedience. Yet it is perfectly possible to obey for all the wrong reasons. You can do the right thing but still think of no one but yourself. You can outwardly do what is right, yet utterly fail to love God. Someone who is still selfish, motivated only by bribes or punishment, is not a real follower of Christ. But true disciples know what it means to be free from living by the rule of threats and bargains. They really do love the Lord. They are confident the Holy Spirit can direct them by God's Word, and they obey the Father because they trust Him.

Think of two brothers. One obeys his dad because he trusts and loves him. He has faith in his father. The other boy wants all he can get from his father. He obeys his father only by forced obedience because he does not really love or trust him.

The lives of the true and false disciples of Jesus are lived in the same spirit. The true child has a confidence and trust in Jesus that leads into committing everything to God and His will. The counterfeit submits only partially and still has a selfish heart. He believes and trembles (James 2:19). This person may believe Christ came into the world to save sinners and may want to be saved but never gives in at heart to be led and ruled by Christ. His "faith" is based on the selfish condition that God make him happy. It never results in the unreserved trust and love that leads God's true child to say, "No matter how tough it gets, your will be done."

False faith is a religion of law, not love. Its devotion is outward only. It is still wholly selfish and at its core totally unlike Jesus. True faith is a faith of the heart, and this is the only faith God honors. You can recognize religious people who have not yet discovered the "faith working through love" (Galatians 5:6). Here are some signs:

1. THEY SERVE GOD LIKE TAKING MEDICINE.

Legalists obey primarily to get something for themselves. They *have* to. True children of God love to do God's will because they love God. They *want* to. Love Christ for His own sake, and you will not find it a battle to do what He says (1 John 5:3; Matthew 11:30).

People who live by the religion of fear do things because they know they should. It would not do for them to say they are disciples of Jesus and not act like Christians, even though they might not enjoy living like one! When Christ and the Gospel are loved for their own sake, there is no weariness or struggle in serving (Matthew 23:4; Luke 11:46). Do you enjoy the Lord Jesus, or do you serve God only for what He can do for you?

True children of God enjoy His peace because for them heaven has already begun in their soul. They have eternal life now, not merely the prospect of it. Someone totally dependent on God's mercy is sure of God's love. If you have nothing to lose, you can relax in that love. You do not have to drive yourself to do His will. Because you enjoy God now, you need not wait until you die to taste the thrill of eternal life (John 1:12; 11:25–26; Romans 5:1; 8:1–17; Mark 12:28–34; 1 John 3:2; Revelation 3:20).

2. Their hearts are ruled by fear, not love.

Counterfeit converts are moved by their *convictions,* not affection. Their "faith" is the religion of fear. They are driven by warnings, not drawn by the love of God (2 Timothy 1:7; John 10:3–5, 14, 16, 27–28). They follow the law of God for fear that God will pass them by if they do not, but they do not love to do what God requires in His law. They know what is right but do not have a heart to do it. The more they know, the more miserable they become (Matthew 23:23). They may be very religiously active and strict and know a lot about what God asks, but if there is no love, the more they learn, the more it binds and hurts. They are filled with a spirit of fear, in case they make the wrong move or do the wrong thing. God is not a loving, compassionate heavenly Father to them but a stern, exacting taskmaster (1 Peter 2:7).

Here is a key difference. True disciples *prefer* to obey; legalists may *intend* to but usually fail because their hearts are not really in it.

3. They are more afraid of discovery or punishment than sin.

Legalists are not only afraid of hell but of punishment, judgment, and disgrace in other people's eyes. These fears keep them outwardly moral as they keep up an obedience that is formal, heartless, loveless, and completely worthless (Matthew15:1–20; 23:4, 13–33; Galatians 4:3–12; 8:4–6). People in the religion of fear keep on sinning because they are not *saved* from sin. They don't hate sin, only the punishment for it. As long as they are not found out or as long as they get away with it, they will go on sinning and live for themselves. They love the things that hurt the God they say they serve and commit the same sins again and again, telling themselves they can always repent later. True children of God are more afraid of sin than punishment. They do not ask, "If I do this, what will happen to me?" but feel, like Joseph, "How then can I do this great wickedness, and sin against *God*?" (Genesis 39:7–9, emphasis added; see also Ezekiel 8:12; Job 31:33–34; Romans 2:16–29; 2 Timothy 2:19).

People who don't really hate sin may even argue about how secure their salvation is. They *have* to, as they do not have a relaxed and real assurance. Listen to legalists pray or talk and you will soon discover their whole life *revolves around their own salvation.* They worry about it because they don't have it! True disciples enjoy salvation and do not need to convince themselves what they know by experience is already theirs. Their own salvation is not their main concern at all. Instead, their thoughts are taken up with worshiping Christ and working to see others saved (Matthew 25:41–46; Romans 14:5–8; 1 Corinthians 10:23–33).

4. THEY ARE RULED BY A SPIRIT OF GET, NOT GIVE.

True disciples enjoy helping and giving to others because they really love. Their truest, deepest, sheerest joy is to be able to do good for others (Matthew 20:28; Mark 12:42–44; Luke 3:11). But counterfeits are always looking for ways to get from others what they can. Most of their joys are those of anticipation of reward because they are not happy doing right and loving God here and now. When their hope of heaven is strengthened, they enjoy religion a great deal. Their happiness is only their hope of heaven or reward.

This desire to get marks their daily life. If selfishness rules people's conduct with others, they are selfish before God. People in this religion of fear find it hard to give anything of *theirs* to God. They may have to, to keep their reputation, but it bothers them to no end. Legalists give only if they can get something back (Luke 6:30–35; 16:11–16; 1 John 3:16–17).

God has a generous heart, and so do His true children; they love to give. Set your heart on something and you enjoy everything you save for it. The more you save from other things to give to this, the more you are pleased. Counterfeits never enjoy self-denial. They cannot understand the joy of unselfish giving to advance God's kingdom because it drains resources from their own little world, where they rule as king (Deuteronomy 15:7–11; Matthew 10:9; 13:44–46; Luke 12:13–34).

True saints are happy serving God anywhere, in anything. They are not interested in saving their own life, because they have lost it (Luke

9:23–24; 12:24–26; 14:26). They would even be *happy in hell* if they could love God and do God's will there, for they would still be doing the things that bring them happiness (Exodus 32:30–32; Romans 9:3).

5. THEIR PRAYERS AND CARES FOR OTHERS ARE BORN OF FEARS FOR THEMSELVES.

Counterfeits are chiefly afraid of hell, and when they are strongly convicted they are afraid others may go there, too. True saints pray for sinners because they have a sense of the evil of sin; counterfeits because they have a fear of the terrors of hell. The phony prays for a sinner's safety; the Christian prays for safety from sin. Christians feel compassion for the sinner but also have grieved anger on God's behalf as a result of the sinner's rebellion. People in the religion of fear feel more sorry for sinners than for God because they share their sin and sympathize with them.

Counterfeits can never understand how God could allow a loved one to go to hell. They feel more for the "loved one" than for the God whose heart the rebellious loved one has broken. Christ's words commanding supreme love of His followers over all other earthly loves have no meaning for them. They do not love Him above all else; they love themselves and everything connected with their own happiness (Matthew 6:33; 10:37–39; 22:36–40; Luke 14:25–26).

Finney concludes, "I believe you will not think me extravagant, when I say that the religion I have described, appears to be the religion of a very large mass in the church. To say the least, it is greatly to be feared that a *majority of professing Christians* are of this description" (*Lectures to Professing Christians,* emphasis added).

This religion is radically defective. There is nothing of true Christianity in it. It differs from Christianity as much as the Pharisees differed from Christ, as much as Gospel faith differs from legal religion, as much as the faith of love differs from the religion of fear. Now, to which of these two classes do you belong? Is Christ the center of your life, or are you trying to fit Him in for your own happiness? God knows if your faith is the religion of fear. Why be afraid any longer? Why try to find happiness in serving yourself? Trust Him, living no longer for yourself, but living in love for God and His glory.

It is not enough to know the right doctrine or believe the right facts. True faith means a true heart, one that finds delight in the One it loves. True faith has passion and creativity in it. True faith not only puts first things first, it loves doing it. It no more needs to be told to do what God requires than a baby needs to be told to eat or drink.

What's Core to the Poor

While the Christian life does not begin in what we do to please God, real Christianity involves a life sustained and honed by attention to fundamentals and essentials that grow out of our new relationship to Christ. In nature those things are air, water, food, clothing, and shelter. The life Jesus gives us is nourished by spiritual equivalents: of shelter and spiritual clothing, prayer, the Word of God both written and living, and the authority of God's name.

CORE SHELTER

"The name of the LORD is a strong tower; the righteous run to it and are safe" (Proverbs 18:10).

"Put on the whole armor of God, so that when the day of evil comes, you may be able to stand your ground" (Ephesians 6:13). "Stand" is a military posture. Someone who stands refuses to give ground and will not budge or back down under attack. God says you will stand, and God's promises are true. You will make it. With the armor of God in place as your shelter, you are ready to not only fight but also fight to win this spiritual war.

If you have trouble locating each piece of this armor, remember this: You need a belt of truth, and Jesus is the Way, the Truth, and the Life (John 14:6). You need a breastplate of righteousness, and Jesus the Lord is our righteousness (Jeremiah 23:6). You need shoes shod with the preparation of the Gospel of peace, and He is our Peace (Ephesians 2:14). You need a shield of faith, and He is called the Author and Finisher of our faith (Hebrews 12:2). You need the helmet of salvation for your head, and He is not only called the Captain of our salvation (Hebrews 2:10) but also the head of the church (Ephesians 5:23). And your sword of the Spirit? That is also known as the Word of God (Revelation 19:13). Jesus said if we abide in Him and His words abide in us, we can ask what we will and it will be done (John 15:7). No wonder Scripture calls us to put on Christ for everything we do! (Galatians 3:27). He is our shelter and our core weapon. He is the only way we will ever win this war.

THE ARMOR OF GOD

One of the King's great gifts to His CORE to protect them in spiritual battle is the armor of God (Ephesians 6:10-18). We get two sets of clothes from God in this life: a wedding outfit and armor. Life with Jesus is to be both a romantic, passionate adventure and a real spiritual battle. If we are going to war, we had better dress for it.

The prophet Ezekiel had a vision of a rising river. It got deeper and deeper, moving from his shoes to his waist and then to his chest until it was so high it overwhelmed his head (Ezekiel 47:1-5). The only way to stay alive was to swim. Just like that river, the waters of God get higher as we follow Him out into the depths of His purposes. At first it is rather easy to carry on in our own strength, but eventually we have to trust the water to carry us. God's dealings cover the Christian in complete armor. Shoes. Belt. Coat. Helmet. Higher and higher, until we cannot move on our own.

THE BELT OF TRUTH

The belt of truth refers not only to the truth of God's Word but also to the truth of our own lives. In this war you certainly are not as brave or wise or smart as the Captain. But if you stay real and live according to God's truth, you can fight and win.

Strength

Perhaps you've noticed how weight lifters wear wide belts. Why do they wear them? Here is one good reason: If they sneeze at the wrong time while powerlifting some megaweight, their body may give out there, at its weakest spot. Ironically, the focus of our physical strength flows right through that vulnerable area. In the Bible the "loins" represent the *focus of power* of our life or our strength: our security, our creativity or reproductive side, and the deepest emotional levels of our being.

Security

The loins are the most vulnerable area of a man's body. That's why the Roman belt alluded to in this part of the armor of God was no skinny designer creation. It was a big, strong, broad belt. It was more than a support or something to hold up the toga; it was also a protective device. The "belt" we choose represents our source of security. Sometimes it takes something as awful as a September 11 to show us the truth about the real basis of our faith.

What is the ultimate base of your security? As we grow in grace, we learn our purpose in the world. We discover areas we would consider places of power, a focus of our God-given abilities.

But our strengths can betray us. We can shift our reliance in subtle ways from trust in the *God* who gifts us to trust in His *gifts*. But when the river rises to our loins, for the first time we realize we are reaching a place where we can no longer dictate the situation.

There may come a time when everything you could once easily do is threatened by that river of God. It moves to the place of your security and promises to carry you where you never dreamed you would go.

Creativity

The loins are also the reproductive center of our lives, the focus of our sexuality, and the source of initiating new life. And it is in this area that God's rising river will touch you, threatening all that you have been good at making and initiating and bringing into being. Suddenly everything you have done so well ends instead in failure. You once were a wellspring of creativity and ideas; now, unaccountably, the spring seems to have failed.

Our strengths are often the source of our greatest weaknesses, so God must also search us out here. Outside of God himself, what we have relied on to carry us must fail so that we may learn what it is to be carried.

Emotional depth

It is not until water reaches your waist that you really notice how cold it is. In almost every culture on earth, covering is placed around the loins. To be "stripped naked" is not merely something physical. It is also mental, emotional, and spiritual, tied since the Fall of Adam and Eve to so fundamental a shame that it is given as a judgment in Scripture, one that touches us in the very deepest levels of our being (Jeremiah 13:6; Ezekiel 16:37; Hosea 2:9–10). Christian author and psychologist John White notes in his book *The Golden Cow*, "If we were to deal with sin more openly, more radically, and be less concerned with our reputations, our witness would in fact be powerful. . . . If we do not expose [sin] to be cured then to be sure God will. If we fail to deal with sin, God himself may have to deal with it publicly so that the world may know that He exists and that His standards remain unchanged. He may shock the world and shame us by revealing our nakedness for all to see."

God is not threatened by the fact that His people can fall. Christians are not exempt from the consequences of sin. "For the time has come," the Bible says, "for judgment to begin at the house of God" (1 Peter 4:17). The same God who is going to call the world into account will certainly start first with those who claim to bear His name. We have this "treasure in earthen vessels" (2 Corinthians 4:7). Everything we have of value to give to our poor world is only borrowed from Another. We have relied too long on good things, even God-given good things, and taken our eyes off Jesus himself. If we find ourselves exposed and threatened and challenged in everything we thought safe and secure, we should know this will not stop until God uncovers everything we have kept from Him.

THE BREASTPLATE OF RIGHTEOUSNESS

The breastplate protects the heart, the most vital organ of our body. We all know that the heart in Scripture represents pretty much what it does today: the fundamental intent, preference, and focus of our lives. But the heart is also the seat of passion, of affection, of real reaction. When a guy says to a girl, "I love you *with all my heart*," she hopes he does not just mean, "I pick you first."

In the big battle, God gives His righteousness to protect our heart. This is especially important in today's world, where we are continually exposed to the constant clamor of sophisticated media.

Faced with a constant barrage of demanding, exciting, scary, sad, painful, and frightening images, we learn in a way to live like someone in a war. If we have a choice, we remove ourselves from the danger by switching off or disconnecting the source. If we don't, we try to some-how dull our response, steeling ourselves to what is going on all the time and trying to ignore our feelings. Those who have been badly shaken one too many times can go over the edge into the rigid irre-sponsiveness we call "emotional shell shock." Either we turn off or limit the input, or learn to turn off or limit our response.

This stream of media has affected the church in the West. We are not deeply moved by much. We have learned to carry our filters and screens around with us, to protect our deep levels of feeling from any-thing that may affect us profoundly. In consequence, we are often emotionally and in other ways shallow. We feel few things deeply. We are sheltered, secure, protected. We carry our defense against medi-ated, secondhand feelings into the sanctuary and even into the inner court of God. We will not be affected, even by real events that demand real feelings. We are never caught naked and we are never ashamed. But that is going to change if we are serious with God. The river is rising, and it is reaching for the depths of our emotions, and we will again experience reality firsthand.

Shoes: Preparation of the Gospel of Peace

These are no ordinary Nikes. They are armor for ground-based assaults, the ancient equivalents of mines and spikes designed to slow down and hobble a soldier so he could no longer keep up with the troops and could be picked off from behind. You cannot fight long without armored feet.

People with well-shod feet fear no future trail. They walk through fire and flood, stones and straw alike and do not shrink or stop. As the feet carry the body, the will carries the soul. One thing we can say of people with such shoes: They are always ready to fight.

Paul said, "I am ready to preach the gospel" (Romans 1:15). There are different words in the Bible for "ready." One means to have train-ing in place so your responses are automatic in an emergency. Like a martial arts master who has practiced so long that reply to threat is automatic, we need automatic responses to temptation and sin that are swift and strong to answer the attack.

But the word Paul uses here is different. It means to *have a future mind.* It means he is always facing and looking forward to the future and is not taken by surprise when it comes. We know how powerful and all-transforming the Gospel is. Knowing what it can do to a world is a powerful incentive to go through trials and snares laid by Enemy hands and treat them all as temporary before we take the field and win the prize. But the preparation that looks forward to what is to come, ready for the long and if necessary hard or disappointing haul, is the best preparation of all.

We are in this for the King, however long He tarries and no matter what the expectation of others.

The story of the shoes is this: Knowing that the Gospel can bring not only peace to the heart but future peace on earth, *prepare* for that future. Trust God from day to day, but always think about and plan for what you can do tomorrow.

THE SHIELD OF FAITH

Shields are the only defensive provision for mobile frontal assault from any angle, since they can be shifted to any angle of fire. Anointed above all else, the shield of faith is the grace of graces in our life with Jesus. Long and large as a door, it can cover the whole body. We have already seen the absolute core essence of faith, but it is justifying faith that provides this shield. What can cover you in the many attacks the Enemy may launch?

To it all, we have only one answer: *Jesus Christ.* Whatever may come and whatever the Enemy of our soul may do, Jesus is the core reason we are in this battle. We fight for *His sake,* as He died for ours. We do not rely on our own strength or power or wisdom but His. The battle is not ours but the Lord's. We not only trust God or die—if need be we will trust God *and* die (Romans 4:17–5:11).

Last note on the shield: There is no armor for your rear. Don't turn your back to the Enemy. Never retreat, only advance. There is rest but no retreat in this spiritual battle.

THE HELMET OF SALVATION

Helmets guard the head (Philippians 4:7). To win wars takes more than strength; it takes strategy. War has its needless casualties and deaths from friendly fire. People do dumb things and die or get in the line of fire of their own troops. All battles are first won or lost in the mind. Soldiers cannot fight well unless they are sure the fight is worth it and that they will finally win. When we fight God's war, we know the battle is real and that even good soldiers can be wounded or killed. But we know salvation is worth it. If we don't fight for the world's souls, they will be lost.

Why do we stay in the battle when the odds against us sometimes seem so great? We have cheated; we have read the end of the book. We know who wins!

THE SWORD OF THE SPIRIT: THE WORD OF GOD

It was just a love letter you found lying on the ground. Curiosity got the better of you, so you opened it up and began to read. No, you didn't know who wrote it, nor to whom it was written, but you understood the words and knew what it was talking about. Yet it didn't seem to mean very much to you.

Why didn't you understand the letter? You knew the language. You understood the words. You could read the writing. Your problem? You didn't know the writer, and it wasn't written to you. The letter's message might as well have been in code.

The Bible is like that. If you have not given yourself to the Lord Jesus as your Savior and Master, the Bible is largely a sealed book. It won't speak much to you if you don't know the Author. But when you are on real speaking terms with God, it starts to add up.

Our first step in understanding the Bible is to begin to read it. Christians are people of His Book. It is basic food, fresh water, and weaponry. There is no way to follow Jesus without also knowing and loving the Book He gave us. It is no accident that both Jesus and the Bible are called "the Word of God" (John 1:1; Revelation 19:13; Isaiah 8:20). Both speak with divine power and authority. Both are fully true and trustworthy. The world needs Someone to know and something to study. God gave us both a Book and His Son. We must obey both.

We do not love Jesus more than we love His Word. We do not obey Jesus more than we obey His Word. We do not know God any more than we want to know His Word. Now, how much do you read the Bible?

Jesus said, "*If you abide in My word,* you are My disciples indeed. And you shall know the truth, and the truth shall make you free" (John 8:31–32, emphasis added).

The Word is the sword of the Spirit. It is not you who is going to swing it but Another. All you have to do is carry it into the conflict and keep it sharp and ready.

CORE PRAYER

"More things are wrought by prayer than this world dreams of," writes Alfred Lord Tennyson. "Wherefore, let thy voice rise like a fountain both day and night" (*Idylls of the King*).

Prayer is life breath to the CORE. Prayer is the vast, little-known, and little-explored power that moves God's arm, shakes nations, blinds hell, and accomplishes the impossible. Battle prayer is for desperate people in dangerous times. When communication links to the Commander go down, the troops can lose the fight: How can you really pray—and see miracles happen?

1. Don't pretend with God. Tell Him exactly what you think and feel. If you have screwed up, admit it honestly.

2. Be natural. Don't try to force yourself to speak in a funny way. Remember, as well as being your Lord and Master, He is also your Father and Friend. The Bible does not tell us a particular set of words to say but rather gives us an *attitude,* one of reverence, respect, gratitude, and reality. Don't use God's name as a punctuation mark: "*Oh, Father, I thank you, Father, that You, Father, can hear, Father...*" Better to say nothing for a while than to push on mindlessly and use words just to fill in space.

3. Don't talk too much! What would you think of someone who phones you, pours out a list of things he wants, asks for a large number of favors, perhaps even tacks on a quick word of thanks for things you have done in the past, and then hangs up before you can say a word? Some prayer is like that! Take time to *listen* to God, to let Him speak to your heart and to your mind. Learn to wait on Him.

4. Pray specifically. What's the use of asking God to "bless the world and all the people in it"? How would you know if He did? If you want to see your prayers answered, why not pray for specific things? "Faith

in a prayer-answering God makes a prayer-loving Christian" (Andrew Murray, *The Ministry of Intercession*). Make definite, faith-sized requests. Pray only for things that you can really believe God for. When you have seen those prayers answered, take another larger faith-sized "bite." This is the way to help you grow both in faith and prayer.

5. Pray always. This sounds like an impossibility, but it really means to always be in an attitude of prayer. It means to never get in a place where you can't pray readily and easily. If you have to "change gears" inside, then you are in the wrong place with God. Christians who "pray always" live in miracles and know real joy and guidance.

You don't have to say long prayers—Peter's prayer wasn't! (Matthew 14:30).

You don't have to take a particular position—God isn't as concerned about your body kneeling as He is about your heart kneeling. You can pray at a desk, on a playing field, walking along the road, or driving a car. You don't even have to close your eyes. Doing so helps keep your mind on God, of course, but with practice you can often pray without it. Jesus often "lifted up His eyes to Heaven" to pray (John 17:1).

6. Thank God. Too often our prayers are just request sessions. Does a "friend" who only asks you for things all the time really care about you? Should it be any different with your heavenly Father? Spend at least a good ten minutes just thanking God.

7. Fight the temptation to rush through or miss out on a scheduled prayer time. Realize it is an attack on your spiritual life. If Satan can block our prayers, he can ruin our effectiveness. Keep the channels open and don't let the frequency get jammed.

Here is a helpful thing to think about with prayer: Prayer is *work*, spiritual work. It is not easy; it takes discipline and determination. But it is just as necessary as Bible study or any of the other Christian disciplines you want to do.

If wandering thoughts come drifting into your mind during prayer, pray about them. Your biggest battles will come when you are tired or sleepy. Try to plan prayer sessions so that you will be fresh when you begin. Remember, *prayer is work*. But it is the holiest and highest work we can do in the kingdom of God.

8. Pray with others. When you pray with other Christians, you are

talking over your problems with one another and sharing them with the Lord. Try this next time: Put out a chair for God. Keep it empty for Him and imagine Him sitting there listening to you as you talk with one another in your prayer circle. How would you speak to Him? How would you speak to one another? He says, "Where two or three are gathered together in My name, I am there in the midst of them" (Matthew 18:20). Pray first that God will let you know what to pray about. Then share it with others in your circle and pray together about it until you feel God has it in His hands and is going to answer.

Keep each prayer short and don't be full of words. Nineteenth-century evangelist D. L. Moody said, "I never pray longer than five minutes; but I never go more than five minutes without praying." It is not the length of your prayers but their strength that counts with God.

9. Jesus prays for us. Here is something *amazing* to remember: We can ask friends to pray for us. We can be put on an intercessory prayer list so that others can pray for us in our ventures and battles. But did you know that *Jesus himself* is praying for us? (John 17:9, 20). You may face a time when no one else can help. In that time, remember Jesus *always gets His prayers answered.* Have you ever asked Jesus to pray for you?

CORE SIMPLICITY

A final word for the poor in spirit: Poor people must make do with what they have and get creative with what is available. When you are poor, life becomes very simple and reduces to bare essentials. Margin is the space between what you actually can do and what everyone wants you to do. For some it is dangerously thin. To get some margin back into your life do these:

1. Focus. What are you called to do right now in life? What will it take? Write a list of absolute bottom-liners—*If I don't learn or do this, it can't or won't be done.* Check your list and cross off *anything* that isn't truly essential to do. "Do you not know that those who run in a race all run," said Paul, "but [only] one receives the prize? Run in such a way that you may obtain it" (1 Corinthians 9:24).

2. Eliminate. Cut out from your life anything you can live without right now. What you need is not all the things you *might* do, but like

Paul, "But *[this] one thing I do*" (Philippians 3:13b, emphasis added). Think of your life as a mountain climb. Don't leave anything behind you really need, but don't carry any dead weight, either.

3. Simplify. Possessions are to be used, not loved. Cut back on *things* to buy more time for the key things like *relationships*. Eat less. Buy less. Make do with what you have or need, not what you merely like. Use equipment less to make it last longer. Share, loan, or borrow. Forget the latest fashion. Fast from some things—food, fun, fellowship—to make time for the critical. "Use it up. Wear it out. Do without." Turn off the ads and tune out the lies. Make a list of all you think you need and then start crossing things off. It may terrify you at first, but then it may be fun. Give things away.

As to reducing your options, the Bible makes it simple: "Narrow is the gate and difficult is the way which leads to life, and there are few who find it" (Matthew 7:14). "If the LORD is God, follow Him" (1 Kings 18:21). "He who is not with Me is against Me" (Matthew 12:30). "There is no other name under heaven given among men by which we must be saved" (Acts 4:12). All or nothing obedience. Be full CORE— or there's the door!

CORE THANKFULNESS

Above all, a truly poor person can appreciate generosity and genuine charity. In all your dealings with God, stay thankful and grateful. The Bible tells us we are to give thanks *always,* for this is the will of God (1 Thessalonians 5:18, emphasis added). God's will is not revealed to the ungrateful heart. Giving thanks is not a routine or ritual but the right response to Someone who has intervened to save our very lives. How much do we owe the Son of God? C. T. Studd, the famous British superstar of a previous century who gave up his professional sports career for the Gospel, said, "If Jesus Christ be God and died for me, no sacrifice I make can be too big for Him." One of the saddest sayings of the Son of God is what happened after He cleansed the ten lepers and only one came back to thank Him. He said, "Where are the [other] nine?" (Luke 17:12–19). Jesus *notices* when we are careful to honor Him. And those who honor Him, He will honor (1 Samuel 2:30; John 12:26).

Blessed are the poor in spirit! Can you see it now? Those who are blessed are those with open access to the kingdom of God. Riches are not necessary. The right family or the best education are not prerequisites. Talent, skill, or giftedness won't guarantee entrance into God's kingdom. The kingdom of God is available to all those who recognize their need, realize they have nothing, and are prepared to empty themselves so God might fill them with His fullness. Remember: God is God, and you are not. As long as you are truly His, you have all you need.

Blessed are those
who mourn, for they
shall be comforted NIV

EMBRACED BY THE ONE MOST DEAR TO YOU. ONLY THEN CAN YOU BE

IS MOST DEAR TO YOU. ONLY THEN CAN YOU BE

YOU'RE BLESSED WHEN YOU FEEL YOU'VE LOST WHAT

DEAR TO YOU. THE MESSAGE

Blessed
are those
who mourn,
for they
shall be
comforted. ESV

God

blesses

those

who mourn,

for they

will be

comforted. NLT

Blessed are
those who
mourn, for they
shall be
comforted. NASB

BLESSED ARE THOSE WHO
MOURN, FOR THEY WILL
BE COMFORTED. NIV

4

CORE PREPARATION

LIFE FROM DEATH

Blessed are those who
mourn, for they shall
be comforted.

MATTHEW 5:4

It seems impossible: How can we be **blessed** when we mourn?
Losing someone precious hardly seems an occasion for being
blessed! All the emotions that go with a death seem so ugly: shock,
numbness, hurt, anger, loss, guilt. We go into a kind of daze and
can't believe it happened. We feel hurt and angry—at the disease,
the drunk driver, the drugs, old age. We feel guilty—"If only I had
said that, or done that, or known this!" We get mad—at others for
not being there, at ourselves, even at God. Then, finally, we miss
the deceased person. Little things trigger old memories, and we
feel sad and lonely all over again. Death is an awful thing. But
there is more than one kind of death, and to die **rightly**
is the door to life.

Death Is Ugly

What does Jesus say about death? You won't find a funeral sermon
from Jesus. He felt like what we feel when someone we love dies. He
hated death (John 11:33). When He saw what death had done to people He loved, He was not only moved—He was angry.

What words of comfort did Jesus give to mourners at a funeral? Not
many. He ruined every funeral He attended. He sent away the profes-
sionals paid to help. He stopped the sadness by raising the corpse from
the dead and restoring the victim to his or her relatives (Mark 5:38–42;
Luke 7:12-16).

God treats death as an enemy (1 Corinthians 15:26). Anyone who
has felt the hurt, sadness, anger, or loss that comes with the death of
someone or something we knew or loved has felt in a small way the

way *God* feels about it happening in His world.

It is right to feel like this. Every loss of life—whether from war or terrorism, sickness or disease, age or accident, crazy mishap to calculated murder—terribly hurts not only people but, even more, our Maker. The good news is it will not always be like this. God never planned for us to die. He has no pleasure even in the death of the wicked (Ezekiel 33:11). In the purposes of God, one day there will be no more crying and no more death. Death, so final to us, itself dies when it meets His resurrection power. In His new world, people will never get sick or old or die again (Revelation 21:4). One day He will wipe all tears away. Sorrow and sadness will end because there will be no more need to cry (1 Corinthians 15:26, 55; Revelation 20:14). *The last enemy to be destroyed is death.*

But for now death is a sad reality of our hurt and fallen world. We never should get over the shock of what it is and what it does. It is the worst thing that can happen. Yet God can still redeem something precious from death (Psalm 116:15). The God who tasted death himself for our sakes can bring blessing even out of our brokenness.

Broken Things

Have you ever felt completely broken? God has. Experiencing suffering love for another is a central theme of Scripture. God uses *brokenness* to save the world. Broken vessels in the hands of a band of Gideon (Judges 7:19), broken bread from a boy's lunch that fed the hungry (Matthew 8:19–20; 14:19), a broken bottle of perfume (Mark 14:3). Ultimately, an infinitely precious Body was broken for us on a tree (1 Corinthians 11:24). These are the elements of true redemption.

There is much in the Bible on brokenness. Through it all, God hears the prayer of the broken and destitute and promises to bind up their hearts and draw near to them in their hour of emptiness and grief (Psalm 34:10; 51:17).

GOD'S BROKEN HEART

This generation knows all about brokenness. People don't feel threatened by the thought of damnation when they are already living through it in their homes, streets, and schools. You, too, may have been shamed by your culture and blamed for your failure. You may understand pain and hurt if you have been hurt over and over again. You may even know what you have done to bring suffering to others. What you may not know is the great divine grief over your hurt and brokenness over your lostness. It is the goodness of God and His suffering over our world's sin that can lead us to repentance. One often-missing theme in Christian ministry today is the broken heart of God over the sin of the world.

A core topic of past powerful revival preaching was not *our* brokenness but *God's*. People are always so quick to take the attention off God in order to focus on ourselves, expecting life to conform to our complaints and expectations. We quickly point to the "poor non-Christians" who lack so much in their lives, who "miss out on so much blessing," and who face the danger of a terrible future outside the eternal care of Christ. And all of this is true but not central. *Christianity is not primarily about us but about God.*

WHY HAVE WE FORGOTTEN GOD'S HURT?

1. Our own hurts swallow us up and mean more to us than anything else in the world. This is part of the pain that drives the piercing and burning so popular today, as well as the widespread use of drugs and alcohol. We make our pain the central hurt of the world.

2. We have internalized Eastern assumptions and ancient Greek presuppositions about God that damage our ability to sympathize with His cause. Impassibility becomes uncaring, high and holy, alien and cold. Adoption is looked on as a secondary rescue attempt by a stranger with an agenda, and unconditional love is seen as calculating, needy, and patently self-serving.

3. We are not intimate with God. We rarely feel the passion of His heart. *We become like the God we worship,* and for many the god of the Pharisee is no different than the God of the Bible.

4. We think the focus of worship is us. We are like medieval people who thought the sun revolved around the earth and could not get out of the rut by trusting divine revelation. We forget it's not what He does *for us,* but what *He is*—the most amazing, lovely, terrifying, funny, wisest, kindest Being in the universe. Why do the angels around the throne never get tired of singing the same song—"Holy, Holy Holy"? God is intrinsically valuable. He is worth it all, worth incomparably more than anything or anyone else.

CORE Repentance

The answer to a terrible life is a radical death. The only death *more* radical than physical death is the death of all we have given ourselves to that has made our lives a living hell on earth. That is why Jesus said we must deny ourselves, take up our crosses, and follow him (Luke 9:23). The old self *must* die. We must be willing to really see what our sin and our selfishness have done to us, to others, and most of all to God, who loves us and made us.

That is what the Bible means by "repentance." People who repent are those who by the power of the Holy Spirit see, know, and hate what they have done to themselves, to others, and to God. "Taking up your cross" does not mean wearing a symbol around your neck or on your ear. In Bible times, a cross was something you died on. When a man in Bible days took up his cross, he said good-bye forever to his friends and family. He was not coming back. And when the cross had finished its awful work, everything he had done and said and been had come to an end.

We have one chance to give up our lost lives to the One who can "put us to death" in the only way that wipes out all that is awful and evil and ugly in our lives.

Jesus put it like this: "Whoever desires to save his life will lose it, but whoever loses his life for My sake will save it" (Luke 9:24). When we come to feel we can no longer stand life as it is anymore, death is indeed the answer.

FOUR KINDS OF DEATH

The Bible talks about four kinds of death:

1. Physical death, when our bodies can no longer sustain our essential inner selves and we lose hold of our place in this world for the next. Death marks our mortality.

2. Spiritual death, which is the state we live in when we try to live our lives outside of the life that is in Jesus Christ. Another word for spiritual death is sin, which kills everything.

3. Endless death is the awful penalty of sin, the *result* of living a life cut off from life with God in heaven. Endless death is a place of such emptiness, agony, and misery it can only be described by terrifying metaphors like thirst, worms, and fire.

4. Death to sin through Jesus. This death opens the door to life, because Jesus died and rose to take away the sin of the world, and the power of His finished sacrifice goes on forever.

In everyone's life there are things that need to die. If you want to follow Jesus, new life begins here: "If anyone desires to come after Me, let him deny himself, and take up his cross daily, and follow Me."

The hardest death to die is *death to self.* It is incredibly difficult to admit wrong and clean up the past. Is there something in *your* life you wish had never happened? Do you remember something you would much rather forget? Did anything happen once to you that you wish you could now change? Then there is probably some work for you to do in this next section. You could have an unforgiven past that needs the cleansing of *confession* and *restitution.*

Clean to the Core

God has designed our memory to record the past. When our conscience is clear, the mind is undisturbed by guilt and free from uneasiness. But past sin is also recorded in the mind. These "guilt deposits" must be dealt with; otherwise every time a similar temptation takes place, our minds will refer to that past surrender of will to selfishness for guidance. Failure and defeat will automatically crowd our thoughts, preparing us to sin again the same way. This is the reason so many people cannot seem to resist temptations.

Although this "law of sin" has terrible strength (Romans 7:14–24), God has given us two powerful tools to overcome it. *Confession,* which brings self-honesty and forgiveness, and *restitution,* or righting wherever possible the harm that has been done by selfishness.

The purpose of confession is to restore a ruptured relationship. Too many Christians overlook the fact that when we hurt both God and people, it is necessary to make things right with both. We ignore what we have done to harm *others* by our selfishness and wonder why we do not feel justified after asking only *God* for forgiveness. No wonder so many of us lead such miserable lives! Without confession and restitution we can never . . .

1. Overcome temptation.

Satan uses the memory of unforgiven sin to remind us of past failure and prepare us for still more terrible defeats. He "trades" on the past, using unerased sin to drive people deeper and deeper into bondage (Psalm 32:1–5; Acts 23:1; Hebrews 9:14; 10:12; 1 John 3:21–22).

2. Obey God.

Unforgiven sin blocks faith. When sin is constantly brought to mind, we lose sight of God's purposes and fall into despair. The promises of God no longer seem rich. Multitudes of young people fall by the wayside in universities and colleges because of *dirty pasts* that corrode faith. Clean consciences help us face anything in the confidence that there are no secret weeds of unrighteousness that have not been rooted out and burned. Conquering past failure gives us present power to beat temptation (1 Timothy 1:5–6, 18–19; 3:9; 1 Peter 3:15–16).

3. Overflow with joy.

A sure sign of an unclean conscience is a loss of joy. Unforgiven sin strips away freedom from the spirit, and life becomes obviously miserable. An uneasy and restless conscience will not let our mind be at peace. A forgiven past is a vital source of rejoicing for the liberated Christian (Acts 24:16; Hebrews 10:22).

4. Overcome the world.

"He who covers his sins will not prosper, but whoever confesses and forsakes them will have mercy" (Proverbs 28:13). If we do not right the sin we have done against even one person, then to that person we are not truly a Christian. Every time we try to speak for God, our past can testify against us. When previous selfishness is confessed to those you've wronged, you can speak boldly and surely of the power of Christ Jesus to completely deliver from sin.

CLOSET CLEANING TIME!

How do you get rid of the skeletons in your closet? God's method is the only really effective one—face each wrong with its full load of guilt, but *don't* hold on to it! Bring it out into the open before the Lord Jesus, confess it to Him (and to those others involved), then receive healing forgiveness. This will not be easy, but if you want to live a normal, happy, guilt-free life as God wants you to, you need to do this to gain a clear conscience. To confess your wrong will kill your pride stone dead. It may hurt, make no mistake! But try to live in peace without making your past right, and you'll never do it.

First, get a paper and pencil. Next, find a place where you can be truly alone, where no one will interrupt. If possible, go out into the country somewhere or lock yourself in a quiet room where you can meet with God. This is a special moment—make a special time and place for it.

Spend a little time at first just quietly waiting in His presence. Don't say anything. Wait there in the stillness until you begin to feel God there with you. As you sense His holiness you may start to feel your own worthlessness, but this is good preparation.

Now ask Him to start digging! Ask the Lord to search your memories and to bring to your mind unconfessed past sin. As they come to your mind, do not give in to the temptation to ignore them and look for something else. *Admit them* one by one as God shows them to you and, most important, write them down!

And they *will* come, one by sordid one, drifting reluctantly through the fog of your consciousness. These may be things you have run away from for a long, long time. Strangely enough, you will find yourself remembering a lot more of an unforgiven past than you ever had thought possible. Write everything down, using if you like the spiritual diagnosis sheets found on the *Ultimate CORE* Web site. After rereading your list, add any other things that come to your mind.

Go over it a *third* time, and you will find still other sins connected with the first. You will remember things you didn't think you would remember in eternity. Go over the list slowly, thoroughly, and carefully, *just as if* you were about to die and stand before the Judgment Bar of God himself.

Take each sin slowly and carefully. Check each area that is a sore spot and write out what you will have to do to make it right. Confess them to God one by one as He shows them to you. Don't give in to the temptation to pass quickly over any area because it hurts to think about. Take courage; face your sin. *This first part will be painful.* Let God break up the hardness formed by unconfessed sin. If tears begin to come, let them. "Godly sorrow produces repentance," and tears may soften your heart so that God can work with it (2 Corinthians 7:10; see also Psalm 34:6, 18; 147:3; Ecclesiastes 7:3; Ezekiel 34:16).

Deal with your sin in true repentance. This means to *see* it, *hate* it, and *forsake* it. Your sins were committed one by one; think over them one by one. This is the way to feel and see your guilt before God; this is the way the Holy Spirit can open your eyes to the deadly work sin has done. *Feeling sorry* is not enough; you must decide now to make a total turn from these hateful things that hurt God. You must choose to give up every filthy habit, selfish ambition, bitter feeling, and ungodly friend and to get right everything on your list! Until you do, you will never have lasting peace with God. Do not dare allow yourself any excuses; it is your life at stake.

THE NUTS AND BOLTS OF CONFESSION

NAME YOUR SIN

Most difficulties in confessing past wrong to others start right here. Until you are totally honest with yourself (and that means being willing to name why you did what you did), when you actually do go to ask forgiveness, you won't get it. Envy, for instance, might make you gossip or talk behind someone's back. Later that person finds out that you have been saying things about him or her. These are the result of your sin of envy. Can you see that it won't be much help to say, "I'm sorry for saying things about you"? You can't change the results of what you've done. A spiteful word, an unloving action, a hasty judgment all make their black mark on history. You cannot undo these any more than you can recall time. Don't ask forgiveness, then, for gossip but for envy. Confess the sin that *caused* your words or actions. If you don't confess this *basic* sin (God will show you exactly what it is if you ask Him), you may only deepen the split between you and the other person. Now, be brutally frank with yourself. What was the root wrong you committed? Write it down so you can see it.

Just as important, when you confess, make sure the way you ask forgiveness is right. Wrong attitudes cause half-hearted and worse-than-useless confessions that may quite probably only aggravate the wrong. Such "confessions" as these show that a root of pride has not been exposed or dealt with:

- "I was wrong—but you were, too!" Pride and bitterness underlie this weak attempt at apology, and it is worse than useless. Go before God and ask Him to conquer your pride and hurt.
- "Forgive me—*if* I have wronged you." This one misses on humility. Say this kind of thing, and you show you haven't yet seen your wrong in God's light. Be honest!
- "I'm sorry, but it wasn't all my fault, you know." This apology doesn't blame the person wronged (not directly), but it shows you don't want to shoulder blame, either! Take on your guilt squarely and honestly. Be brave—face it.
- "I'm sorry..." or "I apologize..." Some tries at confession get only as far as this. That last step of self-humbling is always the hardest, and our pride may cause us to try this as a last-ditch effort to escape. The problem is that our sin is not named. Until it is, forgiveness can never be real or total. *Name it!*

THE RIGHT WAY AND THE RIGHT MOMENT

Here are three basic approaches to correct confession that contain all the elements of a proper, pride-humbling step for forgiveness: (1) "God has convicted me of something I did against you.... (2) I've been wrong in . . . (being envious, stealing, etc.). (3) I know I've wronged you in this . . . (here, add any steps you want to make in paying back where necessary) and I want to ask you—will you forgive me?" Spoken in the right attitude, these kinds of confessions are sure to get results. Don't talk too much—the more you say, the greater the danger you will start to shift the blame off yourself. Focus on what needs to be said and when.

How do you know when the moment for confession is right?

1. Time

- Do you know the *sin* you have to confess?
- Have you *thought through* what you must say?
- Is it *convenient* for the person to see you? (Don't go if he or she is busy or still angry.)
- Can you be *alone* for a few moments when you ask?

In most cases, privacy is best in confession to avoid any embarrassment the person wronged may feel. If others are there when you go, ask if you can see the person alone for just a minute.

2. Attitude

- Is *your* attitude right? If the other person senses insincerity, bitterness, or pride, your words will mean almost nothing. Think of all the real hurt and loss your sin has caused. As you think about this deeply, asking God to reveal its results, the proper feelings will come. Your attitude in confessing will show in a sincere tone of voice as you ask quietly for forgiveness with a bowed head.
- Is the person you are approaching in the right frame of mind? Is he or she in a reasonably good mood to forgive? Don't try to confess to someone still in a state of bad feeling who will not listen to reason. If the person gets angry when you try to talk to him or her, wait quietly and humbly in a repentant attitude. Ask forgiveness again when that person's temper is more under control (Proverbs 22:24).

WHAT TO WATCH OUT FOR

1. Don't set the person you've wronged off again! Any words you use to take blame or attention off yourself will surely relight the other person's anger or bad feelings.

2. Don't involve others. If you are asked to, simply point out that *you* are the one to blame, and it would mean a lot to you if the person you hurt would forgive you.

3. Don't wait too long. Make a special time for it. Don't try to fit it in.

4. Don't try to witness, as well. Never witness during confession or restitution, unless you are actually and specifically questioned about salvation. Your act of restitution is witness enough for the time being.

Later you may be able to tell that person more about the why of your confession. First things first!

5. Don't play down your own guilt. If you don't fully realize your own wrong, the one you are asking to forgive you may think you are insincere. This happens because of the following:

- Our *conscience* becomes "seared" and weakened in sin (1 Timothy 4:2). After a while, wrong does not appear to *us* to be as bad as it actually is.

- The *other* person we have hurt tends to think more of our wrong than we do. That person feels strongly offended; *you* were to blame. Remember it.

SETTING BOUNDARIES

1. "How far do confession and restitution go?" As a general rule, you should confess *only as far as the extent of your sin.* If you have sinned only before and against God, confess only to Him. Sin against another and you confess it alone *to that person.* If you have sinned against a group, the group should hear your confession. There is no point in confessing sin to others who are not concerned in it. Such confessions are morbid, self-centered, and will hinder your testimony, not help it. If you do this foolishly, you will do more harm to yourself than good.

Restitution can only go as far as a person can humanly repay. You will never be able to undo all your wrong. God expects you to do all in your power to restore what you have taken from others—no more, but certainly no less. We must be totally committed to restore what was before our sin. God asks of us the willingness to go, if need be, to a hundred people to restore a relationship. True and total repentance is doing what is right up to the *full limit* of our ability. It concerns only that known and recognized sin by the repentant one. Often others, seeing your sincerity, may make exceptions to any claims they have for restitution, but it is your task to trust your case to the hands of God, who does all things well.

2. "I don't really feel sorry for my sin. How can I repent?" If this is the case, you haven't really seen your sin as God has. Have you asked Him to show you your sin—as He views it? Be ready for the shock of your life—if you can stand it!

However, you cannot create feelings by simply wanting them. The Holy Spirit will convict you by recalling from your memory in detail all the results of your wrong. Go over your sin in detail, never in general. General repentance is usually no repentance at all. As you think deeply about the effect of your sin, feelings will properly equal your wrong.

3. "What if I fail and do the same thing all over again?" This will rarely happen if your repentance is real and deep enough the first time, but if it does, then you must humble yourself and confess it again. Jesus taught and the disciples practiced this principle, building it into their lives (Matthew 6:15). Confession is God's all-covering method of taking responsibility for our sin and throwing up a block to future wrong.

4. "What happens if those I confess to don't forgive me?" Again, this will be a rare exception if the initial confession is deep and sincere. Should it occur, you must prove by your changed life and attitude that you really meant what you asked. Your good works will convince others of the truth of your confession. You will need to ask God for much patience and lots of love (Romans 12:20–21).

5. "Those who are in authority over me won't let me ask forgiveness." If, for instance, a parent or boss stops you from making something right, you can ask God to change that person's attitude. "The king's [the authority figure's] heart is in the hand of the Lord—He turns it whatever way He wants to" (Proverbs 21:1). God can change people's minds, but you must not defy God-given authority and take matters involving them into your own hands. The only permitted defiance of authority is against a command to deny the Lord himself or to commit an obviously sinful act. In all other situations, you must rest your case in the hands of God and wait patiently for an opportunity to make things right when the time comes (Numbers 30:2–16; 1 Corinthians 10:23, 27–33).

6. "Why is it so important to add restitution to confession?" Society is disintegrated and destroyed through sin; restitution is the reverse process of integrating and restoring, and nothing makes a more powerful impact on a selfish world! It is the best way of testifying to the world of the change that Christ can make; it gives the new Christian a good start in the lessons of humility and unselfish peace-making. It is

actually the Bible way of taking "revenge" on sin. If this was taught as part of every new believer's responsibility, *Christian* social revolution would catch like fire (2 Corinthians 7:10–11).

Leaving the Prison of Guilt

Forgiveness is always costly, but it tears down the wall of a stubborn, proud will. Once you have asked forgiveness from God and others and confession has been made to all concerned, the promises of God for complete and total deliverance from the accusing finger of past sin are yours.

Wrong actions cannot be wiped from our minds. But we can *exchange* them for the memory of forgiveness! Every time Satan attempts to remind you of past darkness to discourage you, you will be able to recall a bright memory of confession and forgiveness to turn the shadow of accusation into happiness. Words of pardon from others who accept our confession and forgive can put wings on our hearts and move us to praise God for His forgiveness. Joy and peace flow like a river through a soul cleansed by the blood of Christ.

1. The inward look

Pray for a heart-search by the Holy Spirit whenever you feel doubt or discouragement. Revealing selfishness is His job. He searches our inner lives, dredging up all that is not of God. We must not always morbidly look inward for faults; this feeds selfishness, not kills it! But self-searching is a valuable tool if you sense the warning of spiritual depression; doubt of God's presence, love, or assurance; or lack of power. Sometimes some of these things may be present in your life even when there is no known sin. In times like those, ask God for further insight, hold to His promises by faith, and learn to smile out the gray days that are sent to teach us obedience in difficulty. However, if sin has clouded your relationship with God, a deep heart-search by the Spirit will reveal the cause so that we can bring it to the light of God's judgment.

2. The backward look

If the Holy Spirit shows you sin, you must go back to the place where the Lord first met you: *the Cross.* You see the Lord Jesus crucified—for that sin—bearing your penalty. The sight shocks you and grieves you, and you see the awfulness of God's judgment. This is not the *law*—God armed with holy anger and determined to punish the sinner without hope or help—but love demonstrated in the infinite sacrifice God was willing to give in order to save you from sin. If we sin, we again nail Christ to the cross. We again tear open the wounds of the Savior and make a joke of His redemption.

3. The forward look

Remember—God has called you for a purpose. Don't let failure make you lose hope. Never let yourself be discouraged from your core calling. Failure to *overcome* is simply a step toward maturity. Like a runner that stumbles in a race, you cannot afford to stop and cry over a fall that costs you lost time or opportunity. Confessed and repented-of sin is forgiven sin! God help you to forgive *yourself* when He has forgiven you! Shouldn't you be satisfied when *God* is? Learn from failure, but then get it right and forget it. Begin the sprint for the victory tape.

Today many millions are jailed in their own guilt, not knowing what to do or whom to turn to. Minds are snapping under the terrible load of guilt from a filthy past. It is up to *you* to put into practice what you know must be done. Your testimony of complete and total deliverance from both the penalty and power of sin through the grace and mercy of Christ Jesus can be the means of opening up the prisons of guilt for at least some who are on the pathway to a lost, bitter eternity. Don't just read this—go and *do* it! This is the *only way* you can be free to love with God's love so that others may see and believe that Jesus is the Christ, the Son of God, and that He can truly save His people from their sins.

"Blessed are they that mourn," Jesus said. You cannot know the power of His resurrection until you, too, have shared in His sufferings, identified with His own death, and attended your own "funeral." There's room on the cross for you. Once you've accepted that place, you will be able to say with Paul, "For to me, to live is Christ, and to die is gain" (Philippians 1:21).

You're blessed when you're content with just who you are—no more, no less. That's the moment you find yourselves proud owners of every-thing that can't be bought.

THE MESSAGE

GOD BLESSES THOSE WHO ARE GENTLE AND LOWLY, FOR THE WHOLE EARTH WILL BELONG TO THEM. NLT

Blessed are the meek, for they shall inherit the earth. NKJV

BLESSED ARE THE MEEK, FOR THEY WILL INHERIT THE EARTH.

Blessed are the gentle, for they shall inherit the earth. NASB

Blessed are the meek, for they shall inherit the earth. ESV

5

CORE ATTITUDE

BE A WORLD CHANGER

Blessed are the meek,

for they shall inherit

the earth.

MATTHEW 5:5

To change the world we must first concede that we need to change ourselves. This is core: An internal refit is vital. We cannot take shortcuts. One of the tools required for this overhaul is **meekness**. What is this humble servant heart that trembles before God? Humility like this hears and obeys when God speaks. Only when we obey even God's whisper do we gain CORE character and the freedom to grow and mature.

CORE Rights

In the end, Jesus says, the meek get the earth. The word *meek* can give a misleading picture. Who in heaven's name wants to live in a world run by wimps? Someone meek must surely be someone without any passion or drive. No fire, no adventure, just a boring person with only a little more personality than a houseplant. To have the earth belong to people who at best might be called "nice" might make for a safe but not exciting world.

Yet Jesus, the meekest man who ever lived, wasn't nice. Holy, yes. Good, certainly. But nice? Ask the money changers in the temple if meek meant nice when Jesus made a whip, turned over their tables, and drove them all out of His Father's house. In God's new world, the lion does lie down with the lamb, but the world still has lions. Meekness isn't weakness.

Our world now is anything but nice or safe. It seems that on every side people are hunted, hurt, and homeless. There is much anger, worry, and greed. People are so bound up and enslaved that we hear a constant cry for *freedom*—more liberty, more rights. But more than two hundred years ago the great statesman Edmund Burke penned this warning: "Men qualify for freedom in exact proportion to their disposition to put moral chains on their own appetites. Society cannot exist unless a controlling power is put somewhere on will and appetite, and the less of it there is within, the more there must be without. It is ordained in the eternal constitution of things that *men of intemperate minds cannot be free. Their passions forge their fetters*" (emphasis added).

Contemporary history is filled with movements for human rights. But we can't change the world until we ourselves have been changed. We can't free others until we are truly free. Emphasize rights and you encourage rebellion; emphasize responsibility, and you open the door for revival.

Nearly two thousand years ago, the apostle Paul wrote to a small group of people living in the capital of the world's greatest civilization. Some were rulers, some servants. Yet together all of them had been freed from one form of slavery and gladly surrendered to a new kind. Fresh power now gripped their lives, and a transforming faith had altered their destinies. In the midst of a world filled with slavery, they carried a brave new message that struck off peoples' past shackles to give them peace and power in the midst of a chained society.

Paul had some astonishing, perhaps even disturbing things to say about the kind of life that results in true freedom. Part of his message was this:

> You are the slaves of the power you have chosen to obey. All men have a choice of two masters: sin, leading to death, or obedience to God, bringing a life of right. Thank God that you, who were once enslaved to sin, have followed from the heart the challenge given to you. Having been delivered from the mastery of sin, you have now willingly become the slaves of Christ and His righteousness ... now, being free from sin and being enslaved to God, your lives have begun to show holiness and you are on the path of life that never ends. (Romans 6:16–22, authors' paraphrase)

It's hard to imagine anything good might be learned from slavery. But perhaps Paul and the early Christian church knew something about the nature of slavery lost on us today. While slavery to earthly masters can very often be harsh, slavery to Christ will set us free. If we really want to change our world, even our world of personal relationships, we need to ask ourselves whether we are concerned with our "rights" or whether we are "love slaves" of Christ. Each of us must settle this core question: *Who has the right to rule my life?* The answer is not only simple, it is logical.

The one who has a *right* to rule people is the one *best qualified* to rule. And who is better qualified than God? He made us. He has the wisdom, the understanding, and the love. He has the power to direct and control, the justice to be perfectly fair, and the mercy to be kind. God has the ultimate right to our lives. He has the first right to be loved, the right to be worshiped, the right to be obeyed. He has the right to be King. Who is marching for the rights of God?

Long ago a party of powerful religious leaders came to speak to a quiet Carpenter. These leaders had a problem with the man because He said He had the right and authority to forgive sins. And so they asked him, "Master, we know you teach and say what is right and don't play favorites. So we have a question for you. Is it lawful for us to give tribute to Caesar or not?"

Jesus lifted up his eyes. "Show me a penny," He said. They gave Him one. "Whose image and name are stamped on this?" He asked. "Caesar's," they replied. "Then give to Caesar the things that are Caesar's, and give to God the things that are God's" (Matthew 22:17–21, paraphrased and condensed).

As a child of God, you are stamped with God's own image. Have you consciously handed back what is really His? Have you given Him what is His right?

CORE Freedom

Why did the early Christians all happily call themselves "slaves of Christ"? In Greek, there are words for hired servants or slaves taken in war. But this is a special word for a servant: *doulos,* someone who *chooses* to be a slave. To understand what it means to be a love slave of Christ, we must see what such servanthood meant in the first disciples' day.

The disciples clearly understood that a Christian was a person delivered from the service of sin to become a love slave of Jesus. No true Christian refused Jesus as Lord of all known areas of life. The same is true today: If Jesus is not our Master, then we are not truly Christians (Romans 10:9). Deliberately withholding obedience to God and refusing to surrender sins are signs of a false faith, because it is impossible to let both God and sin control our life at the same time (Matthew 6:24; 7:16-23; James 3:11-13). The Bible does not condone moral mixtures of bad and good. You are either a love slave of Christ or a bondslave of sin (Romans 6:12-22).

At the same time, we are given freedom to *choose* the power we will obey—either selfishness or the Savior. We will be a slave to one or the other. Our hearts are ultimately fixed on pleasing *Christ* or pleasing *ourselves*. If we do not really belong to Him, His laws seem tiresome, His demands extreme, and we will resent and rebel against His commands. But once we give Him our love and become His, God opens the door to His family and we enter the path to true freedom. God is a loving Master! He is not harsh or unfair or overbearing. His yoke is easy and His burden is light (Matthew 11:29; 19:29).

Remember, like legal bondage, slavery to sin is marked by fear of punishment and hope of reward, as well as guilt and emptiness. Slavery to Jesus has the mark of *love*—unselfish choices for the highest good of God and His creation. This is the sign of CORE Christians. We love Christ. We love others. And we do what our Master asks us to do.

PEOPLE WITHOUT RIGHTS

When people became slaves they ceased to have any say in their lives. Bought with a price, they belonged absolutely to their master. All that a slave had and was lay under the control of that owner. They were called to serve and to go on serving regardless of praise or blame, weariness or sickness, thanks or disgrace.

When we are slaves to sin, the only way out of that slavery is death, sin's final payback. Death is still the only way out. But the Lord Jesus offers a new kind of service and an alternate way of dying. Christ challenges us to die to our old way of life, allow Him to bury our selfish past, and live as His love slave. Under His control we will not suffer the wages of sin, because He paid the price in full. But if He is to be Boss,

He must be absolute Boss. This involves totally surrendering *all* of our rights to Jesus. Until this happens, He is not our real Master and Lord (Matthew 10:24-39; Philippians 2:5-8; 3:7-8).

DISCIPLES ARE LEARNERS

Today we know the love slaves of Christ as His *disciples.* All disciples are learners. It's possible you didn't understand what becoming a Christian really meant when you first gave your life to God. You acted on all the spiritual insight you had, and God met you graciously in His love. Since then, no doubt, you may have wondered why it can seem so difficult to be a servant of Christ and why it often seems impossible to serve others as He commands you to do. Perhaps you have thought, "If it weren't for the irritating things other people do, I could be a better disciple." How often do we react in anger because we feel someone has hurt us and violated our rights?

There is one basic lesson you must learn as a true disciple—the core lesson of meekness. You must know *now* that the Lord Jesus wants *all* of you, and He is not going to stop dealing with you until He has it! To grow spiritually, you must learn to be meek (Proverbs 22:4; James 1:1, 21).

Meekness simply means *having a will that is yielded to God.* It should be our core response to the claims of Christ. When we truly surrender to God, our lives will show the fruit of the Holy Spirit (Galatians 5:22-23). Our response to God's shared love, joy, and peace will be marked by faith, meekness, and self-control. Meekness is *vital*! Without it there can be no true discipleship (Psalm 149:4; Colossians 3:12; James 1:21). It is a key to getting guidance and instruction from God (Psalm 25:9), and without it we cannot inherit what God has for us (Matthew 5:5; 1 Peter 3:4). Lack of meekness results in worry or failure to get along with others (Galatians 6:1; 2 Timothy 2:25; Titus 3:2).

CORE Problems

ANGER

One of the most destructive results of an unyielded will is anger. Selfish anger is among the most damaging of sins—in fact, God lists it with murder! (Matthew 5:21–22; Colossians 3:5-8; James 1:19-20). Selfish anger results from personal resentment and damaged pride. It ruins our personality by fanning the flames of bitterness, envy, and jealousy to damage our character (Proverbs 16:32; 19:11; Ephesians 4:30-32). It damages our body by filling our system with stress and tension, causing heart attacks, ulcers, and other physical ailments. It ruins our relationships with others socially, blasting friendships, family relations, and testimony (Proverbs 21:19; 25:24). The Bible warns against selfish anger in no uncertain terms. Christians are instructed not to befriend or be seen with an angry person (Proverbs 22:24). People who are selfishly angry at their brother are in danger of judgment.

Surprising as it may seem, Moses was once "God's angry man." As a young man, he did not learn meekness. He knew his place of responsibility in God's deliverance plan but was not ready to be used. His unyielded rights blew up in murder, and God let him flee to a desert. There, tending stubborn sheep for forty years taught him to obey God! Moses finally yielded to God so completely that he was called "meek, above all the men which were upon the face of the earth" (Numbers 12:3). Very rarely did he lose his temper again.

We must distinguish selfish anger from *holy anger*. There is a holy anger in Scripture. God gets angry, and God does not sin. Holy anger is a righteous wrath for the *rights of God*. It is sin to feel anger due to personal resentment and damaged pride; that kind of anger is marked by resentment and destructive, unloving choices. But holy anger is a right reaction to wrong done against others, especially to *God*. It is always marked by some constructive action taken to end the wrong that created the anger, and includes feeling sorry for the one who caused it, choosing a way to help that person wherever possible, so he or she does not do the same thing again. Holy anger will be as stern as the depth of love we have for God. The Lord Jesus had it, and a Christian who does not have it is not really following in His steps. It is a Bible command that we "be angry, and do not sin" (Ephesians 4:26).

NERVE GRATERS

Irritation often sparks selfish anger. An *irritant* is something frustrating you have no control over. Each day can bring us irritation. It

CORE ATTITUDE

can come from circumstances, people, or even ourselves. Our failure to respond correctly to it is sin. Each trial and cause for complaint is actually a test of dedication, revealing character or the lack of it. What can you do when you become so irritated you are tempted to blow it by blowing up? If you react in love, these obstacles can be stepping-stones to power with God. React to them selfishly, and they will be barriers instead. We must learn how to handle irritations in Christ.

When Rage Rushes Up

1. *Don't explode.* Getting mad like an overheated pressure cooker is both useless and dangerous. If you *are* in the right, you don't need to lose your temper; if you are wrong, you can't afford to! (Ecclesiastes 7:9; Proverbs 29:8).
2. *Don't explain.* Trying to justify or defend yourself if you are angry with someone only makes it worse. Throw up a wall to protect your rights, and you block the chance to conquer anger (Proverbs 19:11; 29:22).
3. *Don't excuse.* Shifting the blame onto the one you feel was the cause of your anger irritates that person! Result—two problems instead of one; two angry people instead of one (Proverbs 15:1).
4. *Don't enclose it.* "Anger rests in the bosom of fools" (Ecclesiastes 7:9). The one who nurses anger is a fool in Scripture. Holding anger inside and silently fuming will only make it worse. "Don't let the sun go down on your wrath," warns Scripture. Don't hold on to rage (Ephesians 4:26).

You can respond to irritations in the right way! First examine the irritation that provokes you to anger. God has allowed this to happen to test your meekness. Thank Him for this irritation! This is one of the ways God will try your spirituality.

Next you must *expose* any hidden heart attitude or sin. Ask yourself, "What kind of person did this irritation uncover? Has something been revealed in my heart that would not please Jesus?" Irritation is like a flame playing on a sample of gold. Under intense heat, never-before-recognized impurities come to the surface. God, the Master Goldsmith, keeps playing the flame until His gold is refined. This is one of the purposes of a trial. A "scum-skimming" process of confession and asking forgiveness will quickly bring you to maturity if you learn to seek *His* face in it.

Unless you deal with the scum as God brings it to the surface, you will never see the same problems in others. An important principle for you to recognize in this can be summed up in Peter's words to the lame man: "What I do have I give you" (Acts 3:6). Want to help others into a better place with God? You can't lead them any farther than you have gone yourself. Disgusted at the way someone you have spent time with behaved? Check your own life for seeds of the same sin. *You can't give it if you haven't got it!*

Finally, you can empty out bad attitudes by confessing discovered sin to God (recognition), apologizing for embarrassing Him (repenting), and receiving His loving forgiveness. Then ask yourself, "What sort of godly attitude should I have instead? How would Jesus have behaved in that situation?" Ask God to help you respond rightly to the next similar trial with patience, self-control, and meekness.

When you treat trials this way, they can actually *help* instead of hinder. Did you give yourself to God to be His disciple? Then don't complain about the training! You are like a rough block of stone needing to be chipped, chiseled, and sanded. Every cut at the old shape will hurt! The more you spare yourself from these, the less useful you will be to Christ.

This is what is meant by "rejoicing in tribulation." Each trial, cause for complaint, and irritation gives you another chance to prove your devotion to Christ. If your motives are for His honor, obstacles are stepping stones; if not, they are barriers. Active faith clings to God in the face of discouragement. God may try your faith to the breaking point, but never beyond. And each time a *test* gets tougher, so does your *faith*.

WORRY

It is only natural that people trying to run their *own* lives will worry. They have no heavenly Father's promise of provision and must ensure they can meet all these needs themselves. To assume a responsibility not rightfully ours cannot fail to produce worry. Can you see this destructive force stems, too, from unyielded rights? Yet occasions for worry may also become *opportunities* for you to discover the faithfulness of our Father. There are six basic essentials for living:

1. *Acceptance:* a sense of belonging, being thought well of, feeling loved and cared for by someone.
2. *Accomplishment:* a longing to do something worthwhile, leave a mark in history or society and make the most of time, talents, and opportunity.
3. *Provision:* having food, housing, clothes, and money to meet needs and pay bills, rent, and taxes.
4. *Possessions:* having things we can call our own—goods, possessions, or belongings we can use in the business of living.
5. *Safety:* being guarded against illness, incapacity, or disability; being in good health, protected from hurt, danger, or disaster.
6. *Security:* assurance of the future, whatever "tomorrow" may bring; a sense of guidance as we venture into the unknown.

Greed and Addictions

Perhaps the most dangerous consequence of not yielding our rights is the door they open to greed and addiction. Listed by some early Christians as one of the seven deadly sins (they called it *gluttony*), greed is when something good or even necessary becomes a controlling power in our lives. Over 360 verses of the Bible warn us of the dangers of *covetousness,* of desiring something that is not legitimately ours. To covet is to selfishly want something we have no right to or are not authorized to have. It involves always wanting more power or property at another's expense. To covet is idolatry because we are controlled by what we want.

But an even greater danger is desiring something *legitimate* in an illegitimate way. This is the root of enslaving addictions: Something good, pleasant, or even important becomes the central focus of our lives. These can be God-given things or structures like family, learning, sex, money, friendship, or adventure.

A classic example is food. Hundreds of thousands of young people, especially girls, are trapped by dangerous eating habits. A glutton is not always fat. You can be skinny and be a glutton. *Gluttons make a god out of food.* They center their whole lives around what they eat, making food the most important thing in the world to them. In the Bible, people who made a god out of food and drink actually courted death (Deuteronomy 21:20; Proverbs 23:2).

All addictions—gambling, drugs, sexual addictions, pornography, theft, violence, slavery to others' opinions and whims—have their roots in our desire for *good* things like adventure, pleasure, companionship, approval, security, family. Unless those same good things are fully given back to God's control, they can become dangerous or even deadly, turning into ever-worsening cycles of addiction as we chase after what we feel entitled to.

The Solution—CORE Surrender

The following steps can be used to surrender rights to rid your life of worry, anger, or greed. If you will carefully and prayerfully follow these now, you will be free!

1. Find your "right." What happened or has taken place that made you angry or worried? What actually causes your strong feelings? Perhaps it is the right to do what you want with your own time, money, or things; the right to dress or act the way you want to; the right to be thought well of by someone you like a lot who has shown no interest in you; the right to a certain activity, friend, etc.

2. Write down your right on a slip of paper. Write it out in full if it will help you see what you are hanging on to.

3. Build a small fire, either outside where you can be alone with God or in the secret place of your heart. Use this fire as an "altar" where you can offer up in prayer this right to the Lord (Genesis 22:1–18). This will be your secret sacrifice, known only to yourself and God. Here, you give it back to Him. From this moment on, it will be His right, not yours.

4. Expect God to take His right! Let Him test your sincerity. If the right has been truly given to Him (as it should have been in the first place), it is no longer yours to worry about or get angry over. Expect God to test you within the next ten days. Your motto can now be, "If the Lord is glorified, the servant is satisfied!"

It is significant that the gospel of Mark, which most shows Jesus in

His absolute power and strength, is the gospel that depicts Him as the great Servant. The young Roman Mark was impressed with the crowds that followed Jesus and the speed with which His miracles happened. Mark's account is filled with authority and power, yet in it Jesus' favorite term for himself is the *Son of Man,* a simple name that speaks worlds of who He is. He who brought galaxies into being with a word never had to lift up His voice. True power never has to make a big noise (Isaiah 42:1–7). God never has to show off, He just shows up. A meek and quiet spirit is of *great value* in the sight of God (1 Peter 3:4).

To live like Jesus is to walk in a world that rightfully belongs to Him and His family. "The earth is the LORD's, and all its fullness, the world and those who dwell therein" (Psalm 24:1). The One who owns it all is our Father and our Friend. We are called to be His ambassadors, His representatives to the world. Wherever we walk on earth, we will be both servants to the people there yet co-owners under its ultimate Ruler. We live in the strange paradox of the CORE: We have nothing yet possess all things. In God's upside-down kingdom, the CORE turns things right-side-up by starting at the bottom. Only the meek qualify to rule the world. Only a kingdom of servant hearts can save it.

Blessed are those who hunger and thirst for righteousness, for they shall be filled. NKJV

You're blessed when you've worked up a good appetite for God. He's food and drink in the best meal you'll ever eat. THE MESSAGE

BLESSED ARE THOSE WHO HUNGER AND THIRST FOR RIGHTEOUSNESS, FOR THEY SHALL BE SATISFIED. ESV

God blesses those who are hungry and thirsty for justice, for they will receive it in full. NLT

Blessed are those who hunger and thirst for righteousness, for they shall be satisfied. NASB

Blessed are those who hunger and thirst for righteousness, for they will be filled. NIV

6

CORE SPIRIT

HUNGERING FOR GOD'S POWER

Blessed are those who

hunger and thirst for

righteousness, for they

shall be filled.

MATTHEW 5:6

An insatiable appetite for God is a rare jewel not often found in the life of modern-day Christians. To seek God is our core quest, and prayer is the central way we can do that. The true measure of any Christian can be found in the passionate depth of his or her prayer life. Scottish evangelist Robert Murray McCheyne once said, "A holy man is an awesome weapon in the hands of a Holy God." The tragedy of our generation is that we want power without prayer, solutions without seeking Him, and to rule without relationship. God has more in store for us than that: His very will is escorted to earth through our hunger and thirst for His righteousness, and if we ask, God will give us His power so that we can honor Him.

CORE Prayer—Hot Line to God

God knows everything going on in His world. He knows your need and that of all His children. Why, then, do we need to pray? Isn't God willing to do what needs doing? Will God only work when He hears from our lips what He already knows?

Prayer is a chosen awareness of God. To pray is to begin to hear God's voice and see as God sees. Prayer is a focused intent that fixes and centers the whole heart on God. Prayer is sought God-consciousness. As we pray, we become aware of need, of failure. We begin to understand spiritual realities. We *feel* as God feels.

Prayer times are *growth* times—you cannot afford to skip them or your spiritual growth will be stunted. Prayer puts us in a place where we can understand and work with God. It is *awareness,* not distance, that separates us from Him. Prayer is not a tool to get God in touch with us but to put us in touch with *Him!*

Prayer connects a circuit of power: God himself is the source of energy, we are the transmission wires, the object of prayer the thing to be energized, and prayer the switch. Through God's intervening gift of mercy, faith-based prayer actually calls into being the circumstances and material realities we need for His service. Prayer is as mighty as God is!

Prayer that unites to ignite is real prayer. Before the world is changed, *we* must be changed! Prayer teaches and transforms, developing a picture of Jesus in our "negative" lives. Prayer has no rival in teaching us God-dependence. Only by awareness of Him will we grow to be like Him. When the Lord Jesus prayed on the mountain with Peter, James, and John, He changed (Luke 9:28–29). He actually shone like light. This simple object lesson in the supernatural taught the disciples what prayer really does. It transfigures those who use it and makes them the "light of the world."

THE KINDS OF PRAYER

When we pray with needs in mind, it is called *supplication,* a dependent awareness of God. *Intercession* is awareness of God with another's need on our hearts. *To wait on God*—a powerful, silent form of prayer—is a reverent awareness of His presence. The prayer of *praise* is a joyful, worshipful awareness of the One who loves us (Jeremiah 33:3; Psalm 62:5; 9:1–2; Isaiah 40:31; Hebrews 4:16).

It's easy to be self-centered in prayer. Why do you pray? Is it to prove you belong to God? If it is simply out of idle curiosity to see what He can do, why should He answer?

But if you pray to honor *His* name, then pray! God will surely hear and answer. When we put His glory first in prayer, we will surely see results.

There is no limit to what God can do with you as long as you don't try to steal His glory. Many seekers miss God's answer because they want to be the stars of the show. The Father shares anything with His children—*except* His glory. "I am the LORD, that is My Name; and My glory I will not give to another" (Isaiah 42:8).

THE PRAYER OF POWER

As your prayer life deepens, you will discover some of the key principles that lead to powerful prayer. Here are a few to help you make your prayer life more effective for the Lord Jesus and His kingdom.

1. Faith

It's important that we really believe God for what we are asking. If we are sure it is in His will, by His Word, and by His Spirit, then we should be bold about praying in faith. God will answer no matter how difficult or even impossible it may seem to us as humans. Jesus said, "Have faith in God. For assuredly, I say to you, whoever says to this mountain, 'Be removed and be cast into the sea' and does not doubt in his heart, but believes that those things he says will be done, he will have whatever he says. Therefore I say to you, whatever things you ask when you pray, believe that you receive them, and you will have them" (Mark 11:22–24; see also Matthew 21:21–22). "If you have faith . . . nothing will be impossible for you" (Matthew 17:20).

2. God's Spirit

We need to ask for the help of the Holy Spirit for *direction* in prayer. Often we do not know how we should pray or what we should ask for, and it is His gracious ministry to lead us into what we should ask from our heavenly Father. As Romans 8:26 says, "Likewise the Spirit also helps in our weaknesses. For we do not know what we should pray for as we ought, but the Spirit Himself makes intercession for us with groanings which cannot be uttered."

3. God's Word

One of the best ways of praying is to fulfill the conditions of a biblical promise and "remind" the Lord about it. God has promised to honor and back up His Word—you can pray with confidence! "Now this is the confidence that we have in Him, that if we ask anything according to His will, He hears us. And if we know that He hears us, whatsoever we ask, we know that we have the petitions that we have asked of Him" (1 John 5:14–15).

4. Fasting

If you really want an answer from God, link prayer with fasting. Prayer and fasting, when done together, signal to God that we really mean business. As you will see later in this chapter, in a fast, we give up things we need in order to give ourselves more to God and to prayer. As a result, fasting intensifies our prayer lives by enabling us to concentrate more wholly on the Lord Jesus. Try missing a meal or two and spend the time in which you normally eat praying. At times God may lead you to fast by taking away your appetite for food before a big test or prayer battle. When the disciples failed to cast out a demon from a boy, Jesus said, "This kind can come out by nothing but prayer and fasting" (Mark 9:29).

5. If all else fails, try tears!

Sometimes it helps to go somewhere where you can be alone with God without anyone to disturb you or where you cannot be distracted. Go to the woods or a lonely hill or an empty house and lock yourself away with God. Learn to cry to Him, to pour out your soul in honest prayer, to really express your needs in a holy *shout* to heaven. If you are in great need, cry to God. "The eyes of the LORD are on the righteous, and His ears are open to their cry. . . . The righteous cry out, and the LORD hears, and delivers them out of all their troubles. The LORD is near to those who have a broken heart" (Psalm 34:15, 17–18). "[Christ], in the days of His flesh, when He had offered up prayers and supplications, with vehement cries and tears . . . was heard because of His godly fear" (Hebrews 5:7).

6. Intercede

Pray for others. Put yourself in their place. When you pray for them, feel their problems and difficulties. One rule of intercession is this: Always pray when God brings a person or group to mind. Never disobey the voice of God. Continue to pray for people until God lifts the need to pray for them from you. Intercession has been called "the highest and holiest ministry." It is the highest form of prayer and forms the backbone of every real move of God in a nation. "[God] desires all men to be saved and to come to the knowledge of the truth" (1 Timothy 2:1–4).

WHEN PRAYER DOESN'T GET ANSWERS

Have you ever wondered why God doesn't seem to answer some prayers? Check your prayer life for any of these answer blockers:

1. The wicked prayer

Prayer for something God has forbidden will not be answered. To pray, we must stay within God's promises and laws. If we pray for something outside of these, God will not regard our requests. The Bible says, "You ask and do not receive, because you ask amiss, that you may spend it on your pleasures" (James 4:3).

2. The unforgiving prayer

If you try to pray with bitterness in your heart, God cannot answer until you are willing to repent. The only time we can expect answers from God to prayer is when we have forgiven all the wrongs others have done to us and have been forgiven all our own wrongs. "And whenever you stand praying, if you have anything against anyone, forgive him, that your Father in Heaven may also forgive you your trespasses. But if you do not forgive, neither will your Father in Heaven forgive your trespasses" (Mark 11:25–26).

3. The selfish prayer

Selfish prayer has only our personal small interests in mind, not God's honor and glory. We are to pray "in the name of Jesus." This means that we are to come to the Father as Jesus himself would come. To come in the "name" of a country is to come with its best interests at heart and with all its rights and powers represented in your request. To come to the Father and pray in Jesus' name is to come with the best interests of God at heart and to come representing the Lord Jesus. And Jesus did not pray just for himself so that He could be happier but that His Father and the whole of heaven could be pleased.

4. The clueless prayer

Sometimes we do not understand what we are praying for, and we do not know enough of the Word of God to pray wisely. Paul asked God three times to take away his "thorn in the flesh," but the Lord left it there as a safeguard to protect His apostle from becoming too proud of what God had done in his life. "Concerning this thing I sought the Lord three times that it might depart from me" (2 Corinthians 12:8). And He said, "My grace is sufficient for you, for My strength is made perfect in weakness" (12:7–9).

5. The self-righteous prayer

Self-righteous prayer secretly compares us to others in a way that is more favorable to ourselves. This kind of prayer only bounces off heaven's ceiling. We can never come to God on the basis of "how far" we have advanced in the Christian life. We can come only on the basis of the cross and blood of Christ, as people whom He has brought back from sin and death by His grace. "He spoke this parable to some who trusted in themselves that they were righteous, and despised others. . . . The Pharisee stood and prayed thus with himself, 'God, I thank You that I am not like other men—extortioners, unjust, adulterers, or even as this tax collector'" (Luke 18:9–11).

6. The shamed prayer

Shame is one of the greatest of all hindrances to prayer. When the disciples asked Jesus how to pray, He gave them the story of the man who went to his friend, asking for bread. Unfortunately, the friend had already closed up shop. How did the man get his request? He made a terrible racket outside in the street and did not take no for an answer. He was embarrassing in his persistence; to put it simply, *he had no shame.* After telling this story, Jesus said, "Ask, and it will be given to you; seek, and you will find; knock, and it will be opened to you" (Luke 11:9). Jesus died not only to take our sin, but our shame. When we let God lift shame off our lives and get to know Him in His awesome greatness, we will get real answers to prayer (Psalm 25:2; Isaiah 5:7).

7. The doubting prayer and *8. The wordy prayer* are other prayers that won't receive answers. To pray and get answers, don't pray unless you really believe God can and will answer (James 1:6–7). Then pray until you can see with spiritual assurance you have been heard. And strip your prayer life of all wordy, foolish talk just for the sake of hearing yourself speak. If all *you* do is speak, that's all you will hear (Matthew 6:7).

CONDITIONS FOR PRAYER THAT WORKS

God will answer our prayers when we are careful to meet His conditions. Catherine Booth, one of the cofounders of the Salvation Army, gave these basic conditions as the "golden links" by which prayer connects with heaven's switchboard:

1. Living in daily unity with Christ. "If you abide in Me," Jesus said, "and My Words abide in you, you will ask what you desire and it shall be done for you" (John 15:7).

2. Systematic obedience to the teachings of the Word and the Spirit of God. "Beloved, if our heart does not condemn us, we have confidence toward God. And whatever we ask we receive from Him, because we keep His commandments and do those things that are pleasing in His sight" (1 John 3:21–22).

3. Unwavering faith in the truthfulness and faithfulness of God. "But let him ask in faith, with no doubting, for he who doubts is like a wave of the sea driven and tossed by the wind. For let not that man suppose that he will receive anything from the Lord" (James 1:6–7).

4. Pray in Jesus' name. Praying in Christ's name is not just a charm or a nice Christian way to end a prayer. It gives us the authority and right to speak with a Holy God and a seal that ensures all we pray for is in line with the will of God and is for His final glory. Jesus' name even has power over the Enemy and his evil hosts, and in that name we can command evil forces to release their holds! (John 16:23–24; Acts 3:6; 4:30; Philippians 2:10).

When we learn to live in these promises of the Bible, we will learn what it means to have our prayers answered. "Whatever things you ask in prayer, believing, you will receive" (Matthew 21:22). God's Word is true; if your experience does not match the promises, you know that there is probably something wrong with your experience. Examine yourself. Repent from all known sin. Be willing to be part of the answer to prayer. Then pray, and you will know what it means to have power with God. You will know how to pray and get answers.

CORE Fasting

Little is said about fasting today. Yet there are fifty-five references in the Bible to fasts and fasting, and the early church considered it one of the pillars of the faith. All those God used in Scripture held strict control over their eating. Elijah, Moses, and John the Baptist lived on scanty rations and fasted long periods. Jesus himself fasted forty days before His miracle ministry began, and He was often reproached by His disciples for not eating. The apostle Paul said he was "in fastings often" (2 Corinthians 11:27), beginning his ministry with a three-day fast. Jesus said when He was taken away, "Then they [His disciples] will fast"! (Luke 5:35). Almost every great move of God is born on the wings of fasting and prayer.

WHAT FASTING IS

1. Fasting is a voluntary missing of a life need—food, drink, rest, sleep, spending time with others, etc. It is a sacrifice for physical or spiritual benefit.

2. Fasting is beneficial. Physically, a fast from food cleanses the body, sharpening the mind and the feelings as toxins stored by poor eating habits are burned away. Spiritually, when coupled with prayer and Bible reading, fasts can build devotion and deeper faith in God.

3. Fasts can be long or short. Fasting may be practiced daily by restricting food or other intake or by a complete sacrifice of meals for a certain period of time. Provided someone does not have a medical condition that prevents it, little harm and much good can result from missing a meal or two.

WHAT FASTING IS NOT

1. Fasting from food is not starvation. Hunger and appetite are two different things. Appetite is simply a habit craving for food. When a few meals are missed, stomach pains are the demand of appetite for satisfaction. True hunger doesn't begin until all waste tissues are used up by the body. In a normal, healthy person, this can take many weeks!

2. Fasting does not bring spiritual merit in itself. It is a tool and when used intelligently is a key to power. But fasting brings no spiritual benefit if it is misused or boasted about to others.

3. Fasts are not impossible to do. Most of the discomfort or difficulties of even a long fast are over in a few days as we become used to our new routine. Before starting a long fast from food, seek reputable advice on how to do it properly. Fasting is a great way to grow in your spiritual life, but long fasts from food are a science, with definite physical and spiritual rules that must not be broken (Matthew 6:16).

BENEFITS OF FASTING

1. Fasting is an effective tool for helping to reduce strong physical desires. A fast diminishes natural desires to a low level, helping us bring these under control.

2. Fasting can be used in times of special temptation when we must depend on God for deliverance or for carrying out difficult but important tasks (Acts 1:3; 14:23).

3. Fasting can help us to make decisive, critical choices. Fasting, prayer, and reading God's Word boost spiritual sensitivity and can put us in a place of extraordinary mental clarity and perception or prepare us for mighty acts with God (Matthew 17:20–21).

4. In times of crisis or sickness, fasting can be a help. In fact, our body may automatically shut down our appetite, helping us to rest. When this happens, fasting and prayer can carry us close to God for healing restoration.

CORE Bible

We have already seen that God has at great cost given us His Book to tell us what He is like and how He deals with us to bring us back to himself. What is also of core significance is the power of God's Word to bring life, health, and healing to our lives. The One it speaks about has power to do what is beyond our ability to do.

The Word of God is both written and living. When kept before our eyes and close to our heart, what God says to His family is literally "life to those who find them, and health to all their flesh" (Proverbs 4:21–22). The same God who spoke creation into being uses His Word to both re-create and renew the entire spectrum of our lives. All of the great structures and situations of life are dealt with by the universal truth and power of the Bible.

Out of its 31,102 verses, one half of the Bible is devoted to four great themes. They are truths of salvation (7,670, or nearly one verse in four), temporal blessings (3,003, or one in nine), prophecy (3,856 Old Testament verses, 1,499 New Testament verses, or one verse in six), and the work of the Holy Spirit (511 Old Testament verses, 664 New Testament verses). In the Old Testament, one verse in forty-five is about the Spirit, but in the New Testament it amplifies to one in twelve. God wants us to be saved for eternity, to be blessed here and now, to know what is coming. And He wants us to know the One Person who has come to make all of this possible.

The CORE Director

The most mysterious figure in the Trinity is the divine director of operations, the Holy Spirit. The Holy Spirit is core to Christian life.

The Old Testament talks mostly about the work of God the *Father;* in the Gospels we see the work of God the *Son;* but from the Resurrection through to today's generation, it is the *Holy Spirit* who directs the church through the Word of God. The Bible shows us that the Holy Spirit is distinct from the Father and the Son but is also God. He is a divine Person with intelligence, feeling, and will. The Father is the *source* from which divine work begins; the Son, the *medium* through which it is performed; the Holy Spirit is the *executive* who makes it happen. He acts to personally teach, lead, guide, and glorify Christ in the lives of disciples (Isaiah 11:2; Matthew 28:19; John 14:26; 15:26; Acts 8:29; 15:28; Romans 8:9; 1 Corinthians 12:11; 2 Corinthians 13:14; Galatians 4:6).

SPIRIT NEEDED

Even a quick reading of revival history will convince you: Among all God's servants that have deeply affected their generations, there is a *harmony of deeper experience* with God. Terms used to describe this power have been as different as their denominations, conversion experiences, and educations, but the *experience itself* has always been essentially the same. Just as there is practical agreement among evangelical Christians about the way of salvation, so there is a practical agreement among those who believe in a deeper Christian experience than conversion: the empowering of the Holy Spirit. And the evidence of history is this: No man or woman has ever been used of God until they first discovered the secret of power with Him.

Christians have called this experience by many different names. Men like D. L. Moody, R. A. Torrey, C. G. Finney, William Booth, Andrew Murray, George Whitfield, A. B. Simpson, and others have called it "the baptism of the Holy Spirit." Others, like G. Campbell Morgan, Robert Murray McCheyne, Praying Hyde, and C. H. Spurgeon preferred "the filling with the Holy Spirit." Some have called it "empowering"; others, "the anointing of God." But the question is not "can you name it?" but "do you have it?"

Billy Graham, perhaps history's best-known evangelist, put it this way in his message "How to Be Filled With the Spirit":

> Everywhere I go, I find God's people lack something; God's people are hungry for something. Many of us say that our Christian experience is not all that we expected; we have oft recurring defeat in our lives, and as a result across the country from coast to coast there are hundreds of Christian people hungry for something we do not have. . . . I am persuaded that our desperate need tonight is not a new organization or a new movement—nor a new method. We have enough of these. *I believe the greatest need tonight is that men and women who profess the Name of Jesus Christ be filled with the Spirit!* We are trying to do the work of God without supernatural power. It cannot be done! When God told us to go and preach the Gospel to "every creature" and to evangelize the world, He provided *supernatural power* for us. That power is given to us by the Holy Spirit. It is more powerful than atomic power. . . . It is more potent than any explosive made by man."
> ("Revival In Our Time," Greater L.A. Crusade, 1949, emphasis added)

This gift of power is *not* receiving the Holy Spirit in salvation. When people are born again, their conversion is dependent on and effected by the Holy Spirit in response to their repentance and commitment to Christ (John 3:5–6; 7:37–39; Romans 5:5; 8:9–16; 1 Corinthians 2:10–12; 12:3; 2 Corinthians 5:5; 6:16; Galatians 4:6; 5:25; Ephesians 1:13–14). The Holy Spirit, God's own agency in salvation, draws people (Proverbs 1:23; John 16:7–11), convicting them of sin (Psalm 51:12–13; Micah 3:8; John 16:8–11), then pointing them to Jesus and making His sacrificial death real. The Holy Spirit then enters people's lives (Romans 8:9, 11; 1 Corinthians 3:16) and baptizes them into the Body of Christ, the church (1 Corinthians 12:13). But this conversion *to* Christ is not to be confused with the gift of power to carry out the task of world evangelism.

The disciples were saved before the day of Pentecost (Luke 10:20; John 15:3, 15–16; 17:6–9). They had already renounced any idea of living for themselves and devoted their lives to reaching the world as the Lord Jesus had commissioned them (Matthew 28:19). But they still lacked the promised *power* to fulfill their task! The Lord's last promise to them was "You shall receive power when the Holy Spirit has come upon you; and you shall be witnesses to Me" (Acts 1:8). They were told to wait until they were given power "from on high" before beginning their work (Luke 24:29). They had met Christ and they knew Him as Savior, but they did *not yet* have the power of the Holy Spirit to do His work.

R. A. Torrey, a world-renowned evangelist and Bible teacher of the early twentieth century, explained it this way:

> The baptism of the Holy Spirit is a definite experience of which one may and *ought* to know whether he has received it or not.... The baptism of the Holy Spirit is an operation of the Holy Spirit *distinct from* and *subsequent* and *additional to* His *regenerating* work. In regeneration, there is an impartation of life, and the one who receives it is *saved;* in the baptism of the Holy Spirit there is an impartation of *power,* and the one who receives it is filled for service. (*What the Bible Teaches,* emphasis added)

The church must make two great rediscoveries if we are going to make an impact on this millennium. We must realize with burning conviction that the vision and commission for world evangelism are not just reserved for faithful ministers and pastors, missionaries, and evangelists but given to *each of Christ's disciples* as his or her life work. All of us are responsible for the souls of men and women who pass into eternity all around us. Whatever our vocation, our calling, whether we preach or pray, write or print, trade or travel, work with our hands, keep house or state, our whole lives and every influence must tell of the Lord Jesus Christ and His kingdom.

The second great conviction that must burn itself into our hearts is the *absolute necessity* of the Spirit's gift of power for the CORE to carry out this task. Many people today talk about our dependence on the Holy Spirit, but few live as if this is the case. Without the promised power of the Holy Spirit, no one who wants to work for Christ can ever be truly effective. We cannot do the work of God with human wisdom and strength. We have the same task and promise as the early disciples, and the Holy Spirit will give us the power to do it.

HIS DANGEROUS DISCIPLES

The book of Acts is a book of *revolution*—full of people of boldness, daring, and almost incredible power with God. Wherever they went there was either revival or revolt. This was holy "madness"—what looked like madness to the world was a cool-headed, clear-eyed sanity to God! Paul was accused before Festus and Agrippa of being mad (Acts 26:24). When the Gadarean maniac was restored to his right mind, the men of the Gadarea region were afraid! (Matthew 8:28-34).

The world has always been afraid of people in their right minds. Sin is a kind of insanity. When people live holy lives, it is only natural that the world will accuse them of being fools. Even the Son of God himself was said to be "out of His mind" (Mark 3:21). This is not wide-eyed fanaticism or uncontrolled extravagance. This holy madness—obeying God rather than people's opinions and feelings—can grip the heart of the simplest children of God and transform them. They may be called eccentric, illogical, or even fools, but they will be *God's fools,* and they will change the world (1 Corinthians 4:9-10).

The 120 gathered expectantly in the Upper Room on the day of Pentecost knew what they were waiting for. This energizing experience would give them an overwhelming sense of God's presence. It would give them more intimate, loving communion with God than the physical presence of Jesus had on earth. Jesus had been with them, but by this anointing of the Holy Spirit, He would seem to be welling up *inside* them and all *around* them! They had already been given one "power"—that of legal right or authority to become the children of God (John 1:12). Now they were to have power—energizing, explosive, enabling power—to act, think, and live like their Lord with the out-poured energy of heaven! (Luke 24:49; Romans 15:13; 1 Corinthians 2:4; 1 Thessalonians 1:5).

In this empowering, our souls are introduced by the Lord Jesus to the Holy Spirit. The role of Christ and the Spirit are *reversed* from those in salvation. The Holy Spirit has introduced the soul to Christ; now Christ makes the indwelling presence of His *Spirit* real to the believer. The climax of this energizing process is the flooding up of God's reality in the soul like a fountain, until the believer is utterly immersed in His power and love. Once initially experienced, this is to be the *continuous experience* of each believer—deeper and deeper "baptisms" or "fillings" with the Holy Spirit as we look to Him in faith for delivering and transforming power (Acts 2:4; 4:8, 31; 7:55; 9:17; 11:24; 13:52; Ephesians 3:19).

RECEIVING POWER

The Holy Spirit is the *gift* of the risen Christ. His anointing, filling, empowering work is a baptism of love; the soul is overwhelmed by the love of God. It is a baptism of love that gives *power;* God is God and we are not, and we cannot do a heavenly task without heaven's help. The most impressive evidence of this power is the *ability to make the things of God real to you and to others;* a man or woman filled with the Spirit of God becomes deeply, intensely *believable.* The Holy Spirit works to impress the heart and convict with the preached Word of God. When empowered people speak or pray, their words strike fire. This gift is offered to *every* child of God who is willing to meet these conditions:

1. HONESTY

Do you really want God's power? God will not give His gifts for self-glory or selfish pride (to make you a "great" man or woman or to "build up your church," etc.) (Acts 8:18–24; James 4:3). He does not empower to free from trouble, to make you happy, or even to make you holy; although, of course, these things often go hand in hand with a Spirit-filled life. He fills for His glory, and *that* must be your motive.

2. CLEANLINESS

Is your heart clean and right before God? Can you talk to Him freely about anything? The gift of the Holy Spirit is neither earned nor deserved. He is not given on the basis of "special attainment" in holiness. The gift of the Holy Spirit is primarily for power; people who receive this gift have no more Christian character immediately *after* their experience than they had *before.* Being filled with the Spirit is a source of help to build a Christian character and does not happen *because* of a person's high degree of devotion to Christ.

God answers the cry to energize your life only on the condition that all obvious sin is forsaken (Galatians 3:2). Scripture shows the Lord is more than willing to give the Holy Spirit to His children. The very fact that He not only promises but *commands* us to be "filled with the Spirit" (Ephesians 5:18) is the highest possible evidence that we *can* receive it, for He does not command unless we have power to obey. Once the dams of conscious obstacles are swept away, you may not even have to ask God to fill you. In fact, you will probably not be able to keep Him from doing so!

3. OBEDIENCE

When you have dealt with all obstacles, you must receive *by faith* from the hand of God. There is nothing to be afraid of in receiving God's power. The Lord Jesus said, "If you then, being evil, know how to give good gifts to your children, how much more will your Father give the Holy Spirit to those who ask Him?" (Luke 11:13). The Holy Spirit's power is a love gift for every child of God. Don't be afraid to fully open your life to His love. If there is something you are not willing to have happen, some personal point of pride you hold, or some right you don't think God will ask you to surrender, be sure that *very thing* is the reason why you still have no power with God or others. *Obedience* is better than sacrifice (1 Samuel 15:22).

RECOGNIZING THE CHANGE

The experiences of every Christian differ. God has His own means of meeting your need; never try to copy someone else's experience. Get an experience from God, and you will know what you have is real.

A God-powered saint becomes *intense.* When people live in the Spirit of God, they have power to *make Christ real* to others and bring them to His feet. They glorify the Giver. The Holy Spirit reveals the Lord Jesus to the soul. His love and goodness take on a new freshness and life. The Spirit-filled person is *Christlike.*

The CORE is under responsibility to ask for this holy energy. However they experience this volcanic encounter, they can be sure of one thing: they will see and feel and know the difference in their lives. Any "filling by faith" that does not include a *definite change* in power with God and people is nonsense.

Pastor and author A. W. Tozer once wrote these words: "Nowhere in the Scriptures nor in Christian biography was anyone ever filled with the Spirit who did not *know* that he had been, and nowhere was anyone filled who did not know *when*" (*Man, the Dwelling-Place of God,* emphasis added).

WHAT THE SPIRIT GIVES

PEACE

Even in a storm of persecution, you will be at peace with God. People may attack your character, your reputation, or even your life, but they will never be able to shake "the peace of God, which surpasses all understanding" (Philippians 4:7). With a conscience "without offense toward God and man" (Acts 24:16), your life says clearly, "Through the grace of God, I have real victory." The Lord Jesus walks with you. God keeps you in the hollow of His hand. The Holy Spirit gives your life and words the good gifts of God and the fruit of righteousness. "If God is for us, who can be against us?" (Romans 8:31).

PURPOSE

Life will no longer be a meaningless search. Consciousness of God's presence and of His purposes will dredge out your past shallowness. You live no longer to please people but your heavenly Father (Matthew 6:18). For His sake, you gladly suffer anything—counting your life as His to use.

POWER

Above all, you become *useful* to God. Where there was emptiness, there is blessing. The love of Christ radiates out from your heart to light a tinsel world with reality. Others sense you are in touch with reality whether they admit it or not. The Lord Jesus takes first place in your conversation. He becomes number one in your affections.

Staying Full

The filling of the Holy Spirit is not a one-time experience but something you need on a daily basis. In order to keep yourself open to this gift, there are some new habits you should create.

1. Keep up daily devotion to God. Search and surrender, rejoice, rest, seek heaven, and surrender again. Take stock when you need to, turn from or turn out what you have to, trust always and only in Him. Dedication is a *life-long process* (Hebrews 12:14; 2 Corinthians 7:1; 1 Thessalonians 3:13; Acts 4:31).

2. Live in the present moment. Trust God *now;* do God's will *now;*

do not offend God *now*. Do the next thing He shows you (Philippians 4:6; Colossians 4:5).

3. Avoid emotional extremes. Be cheerful, but not light; be serious minded, but not morose. Do everything in the name of the Lord Jesus (Titus 2:12–13; 1 Corinthians 10:31). The safest way we can think of ourselves is as forgiven children of God.

4. Cultivate deep humility and reverence in your approach to God. Never allow yourself to be irreverent toward Him or His great work, however joyful or ecstatic you may be. Be sensitive and respectful of who He is. Walk softly before God (Genesis 17:1; Micah 6:8).

5. Be vigilant. Absolutely refuse to give in to temptation under any circumstance or to any degree. In the strength of God you must say a firm no every time, or you may lose in an unguarded moment what has taken you years of work and what you may never be able to regain (1 Thessalonians 5:6; James 4:7).

6. Never dwell on one subject, excluding others of equal importance. Never let *one* topic of Christian life become all-important. Don't make a god of your own present interests. Some danger signs: avoiding experiences falling short of God's best, distrusting the faith of those who make no special efforts to be holy, having no desire to study more than one or two Bible topics, lessening interest in work that aims to bring others the Good News of Christ (Colossians 1:10).

7. Avoid being conspicuous. Don't try to "pull rank" because of your learning, talents, holiness, person, or possessions. Your testimony should be simple and honest, *exalting Jesus* and *humbling you.* Cultivate a sense of childlike confidence and gratefulness to God. Even the way you *dress* shouldn't be attention getting. Stay out of the limelight (Colossians 4:6; James 4:10; 1 Peter 5:5).

8. Don't faultfind. Never talk about the faults of an absent person. Do not dwell on persecution by others in thought, word, or prayer, especially in public. Avoid finding fault with everyone and everything; you may feel sorrow at the condition of things, but do not scold (Philippians 4:8; 1 Thessalonians 5:14; James 4:11).

God's Spiritual Gifts

Some think spiritual gifts ceased with the completion of the Bible. They correctly point out that Jesus finished His work on the cross and that we need nothing more than Christ to do the work of the Gospel. They are right: We *do* need Jesus, and we need Him even more than the first-century Christians did. And we need nothing more than Christ, for without Him we can do nothing (John 15:5).

But the disciples with Jesus in ministry were promised and given gifts by Jesus even when He was right there with them. Spiritual gifts were given by God *before* Jesus died and rose again, and spiritual gifts were given throughout the New Testament *after* Jesus died and rose again. The record of history is that in times of revival and spiritual awakening, God still does wonders. "Jesus Christ is the *same* yesterday, today, and forever" (Hebrews 13:8, emphasis added). These gifts are the graces of Christ himself.

There are three sets of spiritual gifts detailed in the New Testament:

1. Motivational gifts: There are seven of these—prophecy, ministry, teaching, exhortation, giving, ruling, showing mercy (Romans 12:4-9).

Motivational gifts are the internal heart of our approach to all ministry and reflect our unique desires. If we have a prophet's heart, we will always see how far the church is from its days of great purity and power. If we are motivated to teach, we enjoy study and preparation. If we are encouragers, we will exhort or encourage people to praise God. Givers quietly give, and administrators try to keep everything shipshape. Mercy ministries encourage others to care and to empathize.

We recognize our motivational gift by the way we try to develop it in others. Over time we will find ourselves in situations where we have to carry out one or more of the other six motivational ministry tasks. Maximum power and grace come from doing each through our own gift: The teacher teaches by declaring God's standards, by encouraging others, by giving, by showing mercy. Find the way you like to go about God's work, and you will probably find your motivational gift.

2. Ministry gifts: There are eight of these—apostles (church planters and founders), prophets, teacher-pastors, miracles, gifts of healings, helps, governments, languages (1 Corinthians 12:28-31). We can call these gifts the calling gifts, and they help define the particular kind of work God wants us to do for Him in the world. Many times we will not know our particular calling for Jesus until we have been tried and passed many character tests.

One of the ways you can recognize a particular calling of God is by the excitement or interest you feel when someone who matches your gift ministers to you. If you find yourself "lighting up" inside every time you meet someone with a particular kind of calling, it could be yours, too. Don't worry if at first you can't define how you are to minister. God will show you when it is time.

3. Gifts of power: Nine of these are listed—word of wisdom, word of knowledge, faith, gifts of healing, the working of miracles, prophecy, discerning spirits, speaking in tongues, interpretation of tongues (1 Corinthians 12:4–11). The purpose of these gifts is to show people something that is not possible without God in order to make them conscious of their sin and convert them to Christ. Regular time in prayer and the Word of God develops your sensitivity to what God is doing in you and through you, but don't forget that these gifts operate only *in ministry situations.*

All three sets of gifts—motivational, ministry, and power—can be combined by the Holy Spirit in different ways with your personality, talents, training, and life experiences to give you a unique calling and ministry unlike anyone else's in history. Seek God's face, and He will gift you in ways that will bring Him the greatest glory through your life.

ENHANCING YOUR GIFT

All of God's gifts are great. Some may seem more useful than others, but all of us are given something. Scripture says, "Eagerly desire the greater gifts" (1 Corinthians 12:31), but if He has no bad gifts, which gifts are best? The best gift for you is the one God can give you for your own particular calling and ministry.

God has a purpose for everyone, and *being in His will* allows Him to do with us as He would. Gifts are not the Giver. Many gifts are given for the sole purpose of contributing directly to His awesome kingdom. All of them are expressions of the nature, character, and power of God and all can be weapons of the Spirit. Some gifts seem more indirect in their application to evangelism or missions, but all display facets of the character of Christ.

There is nothing in the world like seeing God use a spiritual gift to do something quite beyond your ability or power in the life of someone else who needs Him. It is a source of real joy, wonder, and excitement, both for the one receiving the gift and the one through whom the gift from God was given.

No matter what your gift, ask yourself some questions:

1. Am I using the gift to the glory of God?
2. Am I developing this gift to the max?
3. Is it being utilized in the many aspects of my life?

A simple point: Follow in the footsteps of Jesus to the detail, and your life will be how it was intended to be. Disobey, and you could lose more than your gift. When you are given something precious from God, it must be used and practiced as often as possible. Be honored in what His power in you can do for Him without being proud. Enjoy your gift. And ask Him for whatever else you need to do the work He's given you.

PERSPECTIVE OF A PROPHET

Spiritual growth comes only from obeying God. Only He can give us the spirit of prophecy and the heart of a prophet. But we can learn to be better able to hear the voice of the Lord by doing the following:

1. *Stay sensitive to the prompting of the Holy Spirit.* The prophets of Scripture spoke not only to general circumstances but in special emergencies. They usually spoke spontaneously to people or situations they needed to warn or encourage. The best example of this is how Jesus drew His parables from the people and scenes immediately around Him (2 Peter 1:21).

2. *Cultivate the sense of the presence of God.* With this comes the close connection between our thoughts and Scripture words that strike to the heart. When you are moved by God, you will move people (1 Corinthians 14:24–25).

3. *Love people and the nation.* Often in Scripture we cannot distinguish between the prophet and the people for whom he speaks. Prophets don't behave like disappointed politicians or disillusioned leaders.

Christ wept over His country. Paul loved the Jewish people like Moses did and was ready to die in their place if it would save them (Romans 9:3; 10:1; Exodus 32:32).

4. *Promote national unity.* The prophets' goal in revealing people's fault was to bring the nation back to God. The sense of common origin and ultimate worship overcame the sense of their separation and alienation (2 Chronicles 28:10).

5. *Change themes as fast as God gives them to you.* In different times different abuses attracted the prophets' attention. They never got stuck with a pet slogan. What was prophetically right in one time might be wrong the next (Isaiah 1:1 versus Malachi 1:8). Stick with simple faith in the few great principles; everything else will change.

6. *Don't back off on truth.* Some prophets were persecuted, some were briefly popular. But in all there was the same divine spirit of revelation that rose above the passions, prejudices, and petty distractions of life. "Do not be afraid of them or their words. . . . Do not be afraid of what they say or terrified by them. . . . Speak My words to them, whether they will listen or fail to listen" (Ezekiel 2:6–7; see also 3:8–9). What is called for here is neither weirdness nor independence, nor useless opposition to the existing framework of the world and the church in which we find ourselves.

7. *Look beyond the limits of your time.* The prophetic heart sometimes sees the past in the present, the future in the past, or the future in the present. The walls of time fall, and the prophet's vision leaps over the boundaries of immediate surroundings. Learn to listen, *really listen,* to the Holy Spirit by Scripture and the whole world will speak to you. Prophets are messengers of hope. They know "Jesus Christ is the same, yesterday, today, and forever" (Hebrews 13:8).

The Power That Deceives

"The Spirit clearly says that in later times some will abandon the faith and follow deceiving spirits and things taught by demons" (1 Timothy 4:1).

The Bible says that God's "Spirit Himself bears witness with our spirit that we are children of God" (Romans 8:16). Our own spirits can put us in touch with the Lord if we know and love Him. But if we do not serve the Bible Jesus, we are open to attack from the enemy of our souls—the devil and his demons. The Bible reveals that these dark destroyers are not just figments of our imagination. They are not states of mind but real, personal spirit beings that have great power and intelligence. They have knowledge (Matthew 4:6; Mark 1:24; Acts 19:15; 2 Corinthians 2:11; Ephesians 6:11), emotions (Mark 3:11; 5:7; Luke 8:31; James 2:19; Revelation 12:12), the power of choice or will (Isaiah 14:12–13), and have personal names (Mark 5:9).

Because the members of the demonic and dark angelic race are at war with our minds and souls, we must be aware of their tactics and tricks. Unless you learn to stay away from their traps by staying close to God and to His Word, you can get into real trouble with them. Even some very clever people have been taken in by thinking they can use these spirit beings' powers for their own purposes, but these secrets are just bait for the trap. Satan does not care what he gives as long as he can get people to serve him and not the true God. He will promise people anything as long as they will worship him.

Sometimes people experiment with the occult for the thrill of the forbidden. Astrology and horoscopes, séances, ouija boards, tarot cards, and psychic practices like fortune-telling are a few seemingly harmless ways in which many people are introduced to the occult. These things are not to be taken lightly; the Bible is gravely clear in warning us of the deadly dangers of these practices (Leviticus 19:31; Isaiah 47:10–14). No true disciple of Jesus has the right to take part in any of these since they can open us to occult deception and demonic attack. If you have tried any of these before giving your life to God, you must take steps to break free from them. (See the *Ultimate CORE* Web site for details on breaking free from the occult.) Continuing with them is an open invitation to invasion.

Three things make us susceptible to occult deception:

1. Sin. Any form of sin can be a platform for demonic attack (2 Corinthians 4:4). The twin roots of *pride* and *unbelief* are the base of the devil's invasions. (Pride is the refusal to be known for what we really are; unbelief is deliberately rejecting what God says is true.) To protect ourselves from these sins, every Christian must be open and honest before God. We must trust His Word as our guide.

2. The untamed mind. Almost all of the devil's attacks have to do with the mind; he makes thoughts his battleground. Satanic-inspired thoughts can be revealed by some of the following signs: sudden thoughts that are unclean or blasphemous to God; ideas that pop into our heads without any relationship to the train of thinking; a running commentary in the mind; thoughts that depress or puff up the believer into forms of depression or pride. Such thoughts must be rejected in the power of Jesus. We must check all new incoming thoughts with care, comparing them to what God has said in His Word to be true.

And we must never allow our minds to go blank. God never told us to stop thinking; in fact, we are to love Him with *all* our minds (Matthew 22:37). This rules out for the Christian every practice or tool that asks us to turn off our minds or thoughts or surrender our thinking, such as the ouija board, drugs, telepathic experiments, astral projection, levitation, and hypnotism. Only God has the right to guide our thoughts.

3. Ignorance. We will not be kept from the Enemy by being sincere. God has promised safety only if we walk carefully in His Word and humbly before His eyes. Some people think that guidance and protection from deception come automatically with being a Christian, but the Bible does not tell us that Christians are immune to deception without conditions being met on their part. We are told to "test everything. Hold on to the good" (1 Thessalonians 5:21). The Bible and prayer and God's own Spirit will help us not to be ignorant of the ways of the devil.

When people begin to obey God and live as God wants them to, God will show them everything they need to know to live happily. No one on earth is wise enough to tell the difference between the true and false in the spirit world on their own. To search for spiritual knowledge or power outside of God or His Word is both deadly and wrong. Only God is qualified to give us the true facts about the spiritual world. Only His power will not harm our lives or those of others.

Keeping Your Spirit CORE

There are ways to keep the heart set on seeking God. We become what we think about. We need to become closer to Christ. In order to do that, we need to feed our minds and spirits with things that point us toward Him. Those things of God will keep us CORE.

1. *Read biographies of God's great men and women.* Try to read at least one book a month. Time proves a Christian's work. Study the lives of those who had and have power with God and prevailed. Look for the secrets of their Christian lives. What did these men and women have that *you* can develop?

2. *Take notes on Spirit-touched messages from servants of God.* Every sermon or teaching of truth that stirs and draws you closer to God can become a part of your life. Careful notes may recall their spirit and feeling, as well as the teaching itself. File these neatly in loose-leaf folders or on a computer, retyping as needed for clarity and readability.

3. *Spend as much time as possible with people who are used of God.* The essence of fellowship is the presence of the Holy Spirit making Christ real between believers. To be with those who exalt the Lord Jesus in their lives is to sense something of the heart of God. Jesus called the disciples first of all to be with Him. His own strong spiritual communion with the Father inspired the disciples to greater heights of faith and love (Mark 3:14; Acts 2:42; Hebrews 10:25).

4. *Guard your tongue.* Don't sin with your mouth. God has promised to fill believers' words with power, but not if we can't watch our tongue. Too much talk signals the sin of foolishness (Proverbs 10:19). Jesus never wasted a word. Even His longest messages are masterpieces of condensed power. We are told we will be judged for every idle word we speak. Only God can tame a person's tongue. It is the expression of what we are. Let your words be few (Ecclesiastes 5:1–7; Proverbs 13:3; Matthew 5:37; 12:36–37; James 1:26).

5. *Go to the "Desert Bible School."* This is simply a place of solitude. Moses, Paul, Elijah, and even Jesus learned lessons of power there. Too many words, too much mixing with people takes the edge off spirituality. Great eagles fly alone; great saints of God can walk alone. Solitude gives us the chance to face reality and be tested. Don't be so busy *doing* that you can't *be*! The deepest rivers of God run silently (Psalm 91:1; Matthew 6:18; Luke 1:80; Galatians 1:15–18).

Building on the foundation of prayer, fasting, and the empower-
ment of the Holy Spirit will bring Jesus Christ in you and the world
face-to-face in a dynamic, Spirit-inspired way. It will see you functioning at a level of power and integrity you previously may have thought
unattainable. Build carefully, build diligently, and build sensibly. You
are a part of the Church on the Radical Edge, and you are making
history!

Blessed are the merciful,
for they shall receive mercy.

NASB

You're blessed when you
care. At the moment
of being "care-full," you find
yourselves cared for.

THE MESSAGE

GOD
BLESSES
THOSE
WHO ARE
MERCIFUL,
FOR THEY
WILL BE
SHOWN
MERCY. NLT

Blessed
are the
merciful,
for they
shall
obtain
mercy.

NKJV

Blessed are
the merciful,
for they shall
receive mercy. ESV

BLESSED ARE THE MERCIFUL, FOR
THEY WILL BE SHOWN MERCY. NIV

7

CORE
FUSION

CREATING CRITICAL MASS

Blessed are the

merciful, for they

shall obtain mercy.

MATTHEW 5:7

The love of God is the greatest force in the universe. God's love shook the world to its foundations. The early disciples were not tied together by organization, sworn together by doctrine, or frozen together by tradition. They were **melted** together in love.

God's core purpose is to **unite His children with himself**. His love can move a world. This is the core of all ministry. There is nothing more powerful in heaven. Love is our **greatest single weapon** for world conquest.

God is love. A loveless Christian is an impossible contradiction. "He who does not love God does not know God, for God is love" (1 John 4:8). It is the love that draws the lost.

In the soul-searching "Lord's prayer" of John 17, Jesus relates love to **unity**. Purposely He allowed His disciples to hear Him pray this. It was His last request before the cross. God wants us to be one. The **means** of doing this is not by plans or programs but by loving Jesus. This oneness will show visibly on earth what is already true in heaven—that the CORE is a single body with Christ as the Head. If the Church lives like a love-linked family, the world will see God's reality.

What Is Love Like?

Love is neither a state of mind nor a feeling. The love God asks of us is based on His heart-written law. It is an intuitively known direction for life. It is the rule of *unselfishly willing the highest good of God and His universe.* It says: "Don't play God. Don't live as if you are the only one in the world. Don't be selfish." Love is the law of right choice, of unselfish action, a standard all understand and assume everywhere.

The Ten Commandments are one core expression of this moral law in word form. The first four act *vertically:* from people to God; the last six *horizontally:* from people to people. They each describe a temptation or blessing and what general course we ought to take. Every other Bible command does the same. God has not given us a detailed rule book, but a *description* of the way things really are. The Ten Commandments God gave Moses are a revealed, written expression of the *spirit* of the moral law. These ten general descriptions of moral reality can never be broken or disobeyed without hurt. They are bare minimums to build on and can never be "done away with" (Matthew 5:16–20).

Jesus summed that expressed law into two simpler, more searching ones (Mark 12:30-31):

1. Love the Lord your God with all your
- *HEART* (will),
- *SOUL* (feelings),
- *MIND* (reason),
- *STRENGTH* (body).

God simply asks us to put Him first in all we choose, feel, think, or do. We are to purpose His highest good in every situation. We do what is right as far as we are capable of seeing: God asks us to do only what we *know* we should and to use our lives wisely for His glory. We will never be tempted more than we are able to handle, but God will always make a way of escape that we can bear it (1 Corinthians 10:13).

2. Love your neighbor as yourself.

Did you know you don't even have to feel good about people to love them like God does? Loving people like Jesus does never means ignoring or excusing their sin. God doesn't. We are to love them "as we love our self." How do you do that? To love yourself is to want to be cared for and happy, to be treated right and fairly. Self-love is not sin, but *selfishness* is. Selfish people take care of the self no matter how others feel or are concerned. They disregard the rights and happiness of others unless these can be linked to their own. Even then, they always put their own interests first. We all need self-love, but selfishness is sin.

Loving your neighbor as yourself, then, means to do good to others just as you would care for your own happiness and well-being. A "neighbor" may be very nasty or may do things to you that not only make you hurt or angry but are completely wrong. To love neighbors like that doesn't mean you must pretend they weren't really as bad as they seemed or what they did didn't really happen. It means to will them good *despite* your own natural feelings—to conquer bitterness and revenge and be as concerned that they be cared for as you are for yourself. To do this is to love as God loves (Matthew 5:44–48; Romans 13:8–10).

Christ's two commandments are further condensed in the church letters to a single word: *love.* Love is the fulfilling of the law (Romans 13:10). It is the basis of right and goodness—the inbuilt law of decency and honor—to intend and prefer the highest good for God and His creatures as the ultimate goal of life.

This love is a free, intelligent choice of the will. It chooses right in *itself,* whether this brings personal gain or not. It enjoys everyone's good things. It shows as much care and concern for a stranger as a friend. Choosing the highest good for all in any situation produces clean lives and good actions. Love is just and firm, not weak or sentimental; it flames up to oppose wrong. It holds up under pressure and longs to forgive or show mercy whenever justly possible. Love is honest and does not pretend; willing to help even the dirtiest people, "love has a hem to its garment that touches the very dust" (Anonymous). Love self-sacrifices, even the right to not do good to others who need God (Romans 5:5–9; 8:28; John 13:1; 15:17; 1 John 4:7).

To follow God's law of love is to be perfect in His eyes. It is to do all we know we can and must do to live up to all the truth God gives us. Love is not a *feeling* or a *thought* but a *choice* made with intelligence and consideration. It is to "do to others as we would have them do to us." It asks us to use only what we have when it is needed, demanding no more than what we are able to give. God's commands are never beyond what we can handle.

Causes of Disunity

Disunity caused by sin is the headache of heaven.

Fellowship is the presence of the Holy Spirit between Christians. Sin cuts off this spiritual communion. The uniting love of God is today's desperately needed dynamic for world impact. Jesus said the world would believe He is real if they could see how those who follow Him really love one another. It is core, yet sometimes Christians cut off one another and pull away from the one thing that counts. Why?

CORE FORGIVENESS

Failure to forgive is the greatest cause of this disunity. Jesus linked love with forgiveness. *His* pardon from the cross is what calls from us a loving response.

Forgiveness is God's way of dealing with the guilt of sin. It means giving up all just claims against those who injured us without any further thought of compensation or "paying back." Anyone who will not do this cannot expect *God's* pardon.

Even Christians can be offended and disappointed by one another and nurse a poisonous grudge in their hearts. When this happens barriers go up, usually *felt* rather than spoken. Without forgiveness we cannot pray and work together as a family like we used to. It doesn't seem the same anymore. The whole business seems less like a joyful adventure than a silly game. Bitterness is deadly.

Forgiveness is essential for core fusion. Jesus said, "If you bring a gift to me and remember that you have something against your brother—first go and fix it up with him. When you've got that right—then come and offer your gift" (Matthew 5:23–24, authors' paraphrase). Don't bring a gift to God when you first ought to forgive a former friend and make things right with him or her. Do the first thing first.

"Forgive us . . . *as we forgive those* who trespass against us" (Matthew 6:9–13, emphasis added). Ever prayed that prayer? Do you believe God answers prayer? The whole Christian life is about being forgiven, forsaking sin, and forgiving others. True forgiveness is putting a problem to rest and freeing others involved to have a chance to

CORE FUSION

live once again in harmony. Without forgiveness, we would have no real relationship with God.

The parable of the debtor in Matthew 18:23–35 tells us three things:

1. Some things can *never* be paid back no matter how hard you try;

2. God's preferred way to deal with our bad debt is not payment (by exacting strict justice or demanding the last penny out of hurt and desire for revenge) but to freely forgive; and

3. He expects those who follow Him to take on His *same* spirit and attitude.

This merciful approach is why some people despise Christians. They see our lives and know what a mess we were before we met God ... and then we met Him and are changed and what happens in our lives after that may not be what we deserve. They know the outcome isn't really fair, and they are utterly right. *With God, it's not about fairness; it's about forgiveness. It's not about justice; it's about mercy.* Justice is what we deserve. Mercy is what we don't deserve and have no right to ask for. So what would you rather have from God—what you really deserve or mercy?

THE CURSE AND CAUSE OF BITTERNESS

Bitterness is a "wounded spirit," a keen disappointment in someone. It is a natural response to wrong done by someone else. It can be real or imaginary, a reaction to one big thing or a whole lot of little things. Bitterness is like drinking poison and hoping someone else will die. Why does God condemn bitterness?

All of us change by the way we think. God plans to make us like Jesus. When we think of Him we become like Him, and the more we do this, the greater the change from "glory to glory." But what happens if we let someone else deeply affect our lives?

Harbored hurt messes up a whole life. Few people realize how much bitterness can change a person's entire appearance. If we don't learn how to forgive and instead choose to retaliate with evil when someone wrongs us, it will mark our face as well as our heart and make us ugly both inside and out.

What if what happened wasn't our fault? Think of Jesus: He was hurt even though He never did anything wrong. It is always harder to forgive when we know we are right and the other person is really wrong. The temptation is to get back somehow at the one who hurt us. But that is not what God wants us to do (Romans 12:19). It is okay for God to avenge His servants; it is *not* okay for us to try to do it for ourselves. The way we respond when we are hurt is one of the greatest, hardest tests we ever have to pass if we are going to be all the man or woman God wants us to be.

When we are disappointed by someone, our thoughts turn away from God. We begin to think instead over and over again of that person's offending actions and attitudes. Our minds feed on bitterness. The poison seeps into the soul—and our very thoughts begin to destroy us.

"As he thinks in his heart, so is he" (Proverbs 23:7). It's all about focus. What gets our attention gets our hearts. Think long on an enemy, and, even dead, that person will change us to become *just like him or her.* We *become like* the one we despise. We re-create that person's faults until there is not one but *two* hateful people—our enemy and us! (James 5:9). Bitterness is like an aching tooth: The more we bite down on it, the better it feels.

If we lose sight of God's standards and focus instead on those of someone else, our own standards cannot fail to change. Comparing ourselves with that person leads to pride. You can excuse yourself and say, "At least I don't do the same *things* as that person does." Yet when you hold on to a grudge, the damage is done—you have the *same attitude.* Bitterness is one of the characteristics of Satan, but it can infect even people who claim to belong to God.

Bitterness can lead into all kinds of rebellion and hardness. If you recognize bitterness in your own life, you must confess it to God. When it has been thoroughly repented of and dealt with, you must then forgive the one who hurt you. "Therefore, as the elect of God, holy and beloved, put on tender mercies, kindness, humility, meekness, longsuffering; bearing with one another, and forgiving one another, if anyone has a complaint against another; even as Christ forgave you, so you also must do" (Colossians 3:12–13).

When people hurt us, God can give us power to forgive. This turns our hurt into a chance to help them. Self says "get revenge" instead. At the moment of being hurt, we can choose either way. We have power to choose how to respond but no power to change the consequences if we make the wrong decision. If we forgive people as God asks, we begin a great force for good in their lives as well as our own.

CORE FORGIVENESS

Have you been hurt by your friends or family?

Bitterness is deadly. It takes us deeper and deeper into trouble, sending more people to death than any other sin.

We trust someone; that person betrays our trust. He or she shuns, disgraces, and rejects us. Now that horrible betrayal is still painfully burned on our mind, and that hurt makes us want to hit back. Other bitter people have done exactly that; they left behind them a trail of more wrecked lives.

Bitterness makes us blind to others' needs. It wraps us up totally in ourselves. It poisons everything and makes everything we do poisonous. We lose all our friends except those who feel as hurt and mad as we do. Hurt kills love dead. Up goes an ice wall around us that no one can break through with love. Proverbs 14:10 says, "The heart knows its own bitterness, and no stranger shares its joy" (RSV). Bitterness starts us blaming everything and everyone else for problems. We get the idea that if we point long enough at others, people won't look too hard at us.

Bitterness attracts rotten "friends" like dung gathers flies. Bitterness wipes out our trust for any authority. Lives that once trusted can burn with the acid of revenge and come out in protest against all rule or control.

In the face of all this, God *commands* us to forgive!

Now, maybe you feel like joining the crowd of people who laugh at this very idea. It is a cynical laugh, compounded by a hundred thousand hurts and betrayed trusts. It comes from both the old and young—flag-waving sixty-year-old patriots and angry sixteen-year-old terrorists, street kids and church kids—people with thin lips and unsmiling eyes. They say, "Forgive? Them? What for? You don't know. You just don't know."

But God *does* know. That is why He commands us to forgive. We ignore this law at the cost of our lives. Forgiveness breaks the vicious cycle. God never says to forgive *as long as* the other person repents or *as soon as* things get better. When we give our lives to Jesus, we give up the right to retaliate for ourselves. We let Him fight our battles. We clear out the files of hurt done to us.

Peter said, "Lord, how often shall my brother sin against me and I forgive him? Up to seven times?" Jesus said, "Up to *seventy times seven*" (Matthew 18:21–22, emphasis added). What did He mean? *Lose count.* Let go and let God. Burn the list of what wrongs people have done to you and let them go.

HOW TO FORGIVE

Forgiveness is God's way to spare our happiness. Look at your life. See what bitterness has done. Think back over all the things you have said and done because someone, sometime hurt you. Was getting even worth what it has done to you? Look in the mirror. See what you are becoming—a walking grudge against the world. If you do not forgive, bitterness will destroy you. Yes, the hurt *is* their fault. But being bitter is always your own. And you must forgive or you will change, step by step, until you become like the ones you most despise.

If you have been hurt by your family or by others you know you must forgive, here is what you must do to be free. It will be hard, but you can do it. Take God's help and do these things:

1. Make a list of all those who have hurt you. Take your time and leave plenty of space under each name. You won't have any trouble remembering them.

2. Under each name, list the wrong things that person has done to hurt you. You have held on to wounded feelings long enough. Perhaps your parents failed to give you the kind of example you wanted. They told you not to do things you saw them do, and the word *hypocrite* was an easy response. Or perhaps they expected too much from you, harping on how good your brother or sister was and "why can't you be like them?" Or maybe your parents couldn't care less what happened to you, or maybe your friend stole your girlfriend and left you broken, bruised, and bewildered. Write them all down. These are the poisons that have eaten your life.

3. Now make another list. On it, write down the things you did to hurt *others*! It is strange how your normally excellent memory might fail you about now. But ask God to bring to light all you did to wrong family, friends, and others and write it down. You smoked grass because Dad drank; you did cocaine because Mom couldn't sleep without her tranquilizers. Your best friend hurt you, so you never forgave him no matter how much he tried to make it up, just to show him you couldn't care less.

How many lies have you told yourself because of your hurt? How many times have you punished your own body and mind because of something someone else did to wrong you? How many others have you hurt because someone hurt you? Write it all down as honestly as you can. Put on your paper all you have done to hurt your family and friends.

It is not easy to see it all brought back to you as if it were Judgment Day, but as you do it, you will discover a strange and terrible thing: A lot of what you have on your list is exactly the same as what you have on your parents' or friends' list. You have judged and condemned them, but you have done the same things!

4. The next step is to get on your knees and ask God to show you how much the things you have done have hurt *Him.* Your work is not over until you glimpse what has happened to His heart. Remember: In every hurt you ever felt, in every hurt your family has felt, in every case where your bitterness hurt someone else, God felt it all. He who has total experience has been put through the sum total of all that pain. Isn't it time you stopped hurting yourself? Isn't it time you quit infecting others? And isn't it high time you stopped hurting God?

No excuses. Everything you have felt in all your deepest hurts is only a tiny fraction of what God has felt for you, yet there is healing in His heart. If with all this He can forgive you, you can draw on His grace to forgive. Deeply repent of what you have done. The way of bitterness is a street that dead-ends in hell. Hurt put you on that street, but you were not made to be its slave.

You must let God set you free, but freedom is impossible if you hold on to the very thing that is changing you into the kind of person you hate. Bring your list to Him, and ask His forgiveness. Ask for it to be made as clean as you would want it on the Day of Judgment. Apologize to God for what you have done. Say, "Oh, Lord, I have been hurt, and I hit back in horrible ways. I have been just like the ones who hurt me. I have become filled with bitterness and callousness and pride. Forgive me for my rotten attitude and my sin. I know I couldn't help being hurt and that you understand that. But I could help what I did to hurt back. Wash me and make me clean again. Take away my bitterness over these feelings, these grudges I have in my heart."

5. Next, get off your knees and take the list of what *others* have done to you. Pick it up and *rip* it up. This is the last time you are going to think about it. Tell God as you do this, "I forgive them, Lord, right now. I refuse to hold these hurts that have bound my life any longer. I will not be the slave to others' wrongs. I choose not to hold these things in my heart or mind any longer." Then take a match and burn your torn list. As you burn it, see those old resentments going up in smoke. See the past turn into ashes. When the fire is dead and cold, blow the ashes away in the wind. Let your grudges, your hurt, your whole ugly past go with them.

6. Now comes the hardest part. Call, write, or go to see the people on the list of those you've hurt as soon as you can, as long as you know what to say and if you can speak with them for a minute without interruption. (Write only if seeing them or phoning them is impossible.) You have to apologize to them for what you have done to hurt *them*. Take the worst thing on your list and apologize for that. Do it humbly, sincerely, with a broken heart. Do not mind their reactions. They may be surprised; they may be embarrassed; they may be so convicted they become angry with you. Leave this in God's hands. If they are open to it, God will be able to heal in seconds a breach that has taken years to split. Do this for your own and God's sake, if not for theirs.

When you have done this, you will open a channel on your side for healing to begin. Many others may even be healed from hurt. Now you must begin the process of living in love toward them. It will be a challenge. You must prove by your life that you really feel differently toward them now. Bitterness causes suspicion, indifference, ingratitude. You understand all this because you have been there yourself.

It may take months for the breach to heal. But God will do things in your life that you never would have believed possible.

Through it all, *pray* for the ones who have hurt you. The Bible says, "Bless those who curse you, do good to those who hate you, and pray for those who spitefully use you and persecute you, that you may be sons of your Father in heaven; for He makes His sun rise on the evil and on the good, and sends rain on the just and unjust" (Matthew 5:44–45).

7. The final step for you to take in forgiving people who wrong you is to begin to list ways in which you can help the ones who hurt you. Are there things that they need that you can work to buy for them? Are there jobs around your parents', siblings', or friends' homes that no one likes doing that you can do for them? Are there things that they have asked you to do that you have not done before? Then *do* them in the name of Jesus! Then you will find something strange happening to your heart. As you do these things, step by step God can restore the love that you once might have had for them. It may even bring them to Jesus. After all, if you can't be an effective testimony to those you know about the wonderful change the Lord Jesus can make in a life, who can?

CORE Christians follow a Leader who more than any man knows what it means to stand in the gap for a broken world. When first asked the crucial question "How much can you love people who really, really hurt you?" He held out His arms wide, only to have them *nailed* open. And in that, He said to the world that broke His heart, *"This much,"* before dying. Jesus went through it all first. Now that He has shown us the way, we can choose to humbly follow His forgiving example.

Blessed are
the pure in heart, for they
shall see God. ES

Blessed are the pure in heart, for
they shall see God. NASB

Blessed are the
pure in heart, for
they shall see God.
NKJV

BLESSED
ARE THE
PURE IN
HEART,
FOR THEY
WILL SEE
GOD. NIV

GOD IN THE OUTSIDE WORLD. THE MESSAGE
YOUR MIND AND HEART—PUT RIGHT. THEN YOU CAN SEE
YOU'RE BLESSED WHEN YOU GET YOUR INSIDE WORLD—

God
blesses
those
whose
hearts
are pure,
for they
will see
God. NLT

8

CORE
PURITY

PASSION FOR THE DIVINE

Blessed are the pure

in heart, for they

shall see God.

MATTHEW 5:8

"Who may ascend into the hill of the LORD? Or who may stand in His holy place? He who has clean hands and a pure heart . . . He shall receive blessing from the LORD, and righteousness from the God of his salvation" (Psalm 24:3–5).

The God who owns the world and everything in it is looking for a generation with a pure heart. The pure in heart see God; not so much greater **faith** but **clearer vision** is required. The pure heart sees all of life in His light (Titus 1:15). "We would see Jesus," and when we do, the light of His glory will penetrate our hearts, exposing even what we may consider the smallest sin.

A pure, penetrating light shone through a small lens projects a large picture on a screen. The slightest blemish on the film or lens is magnified multiple thousand times for all to see. Core purity keeps our life a clean lens, letting us intensify God's light and shine forth unrestrained, unblamable, and unashamed.

Purity is the one element that brings fire and passion into any life that would give itself to greatness. It is an irreducible requirement for a free and unfettered friendship that transforms all it touches into beauty and newness. It is what makes us intensely **real** in our love to Jesus and utterly **genuine** with others. Heart purity empowers a life to conquer sin and to lock in to what is true, right, beautiful, and world changing.

ULTIMATE CORE

The Pressure of Media Madness

How does the lens of a life get dirty?

Once we commit our will to indulge desire in spite of God's law, no form of self-denial is holy. If our will surrenders to desire, the choice is as wrong as the act itself in God's eyes. Perhaps the only reason we do not carry out an actual act may be out of fear for ourselves, not God's law of love. Many things may bring a stop to outward immorality: fear of criminal or cultural consequence, fear of discovery, social disapproval, or strict social standards. While unfavorable or uncomfortable circumstances may prevent outward sin, millions of hearts are still inwardly nothing but sewers (Matthew 5:27–28; Mark 7:20–23). A sure sign of a life's conquest by violence, lust, envy, sloth, and other forms of immorality is a steady mental diet of media that glorifies those things. You can tell people's character by what they like to look at.

TV, MOVIES, AND THE INTERNET

You live in a visual world. You are one of the first generations to grow up in a culture with access to total media exposure. Your world communicates its ideas and lifestyles largely through pictures.

Television and the Internet have given us instant access to what is going on around the world. Conflicts and concerts, disaster and triumph, the good, the bad, and the ugly all connect those who live in the wired nations of the world. Movies have become the popular dramatic form of our time, the way the culture tells its stories and makes its heroes. Computers provide vast information bases, and video games entertain us.

Movies that uphold family values or draw from biblical truth consistently draw more people and make more money than any others. But the morals of the many moguls who create media entertainment rarely match the life of ordinary people. Their own sick, sensualized, or shocking fantasies are held up as norms for a culture to follow. If Jesus sat down with you to watch TV or a movie, what could you watch that would not embarrass you?

What wrong have you learned from the world's media? You may be surprised at how it affects you. For instance, think about your language. Is your speech seasoned by God's Spirit and controlled by the law of love? Does it flow from a kind heart and a clean mind? Swear not at all, says Scripture. Though some may try to convince you it isn't a big concern, cursing never marks the speech of the CORE (Matthew 5:34; Colossians 4:6; Romans 12:14).

People who do not know how to respond to this media force will lose their place in this world, yet people who surrender to its power may lose their place in the next. No one else will ultimately be able to keep you from situations where you could fall into hurtful flights of fantasy or scar places in your mind that cripple your life. Only you can guard your mind and heart against the dangers of such a strong influence. Remember that Jesus knows what you listen to, what you watch, what you think about—and why.

THE POWER OF MUSIC

Music is another key avenue that affects our heart purity. There are as many flavors of music as there are people-groups in the world. Much music comes down to personal opinion and taste. *If you don't like it, don't listen.*

But as the single greatest and most powerful force affecting young adults today, music is often shamelessly marketed in the lowest common denominator. Advertisers say that what we watch or listen to can't affect us, but they spend billions assuming it will do just that.

While a lot of music is neutral and highlights common truths about life, there really is such a thing as evil music. Evil in music is not just about certain lyrics (although such lyrics can abnormally affect us) or a particular sound or arrangement of notes and beats that can adversely affect the soul, but the *heart motive* in which the music was created and the intention of the listener's heart. Music cannot *create* evil, but it can flow out of an evil atmosphere or help to create an atmosphere where evil can flourish.

Say you hear a song you initially like very much. But let's say an occult band created this piece. If you have no idea what the song was written about, you might consider it neutral or even feel drawn closer to God when you hear it. People have been converted listening to songs where a writer had no intention of influencing any such outcome. God can make even people's anger praise Him (Psalm 76:10).

But if others listen to that same song with a heart of rebellion, selfishness, hate, lust, or any other sinful attitude, the song *for them* is not the same. They continue to listen for pleasure knowing something is wrong and choose, consciously or subconsciously, to allow that evil to burn into their minds. Music can amplify and reinforce a rebel heart.

Any song ever written can be used in an idolatrous way if our hearts are set on sin. The religious person who criticizes a barely dressed, sewer-mouthed stage star may also make an idol of a godly Christian singer. The Christian critic who searches for hidden evil lyrics inserted backward into an occult song may miss the obvious *forward* ones in a supposedly religious song that promotes a lifestyle of selfishness, pleasure seeking, and greed.

In his letter to the Philippians, Paul wrote, "Whatever things are true, whatever things are noble, whatever things are just, whatever things are pure, whatever things are lovely, whatever things are of good report, if there is any virtue and if there is anything praiseworthy, meditate on these things" (4:8). When your heart is pure and clean before God, you will listen to your conscience and make wise choices about what you expose yourself to. The early Christians didn't live by sets of rules. They knew what God said about life and listened to the voice of the Holy Spirit, who can show us right and wrong even when we don't yet know all the details (Acts 15:28; 24:16; Romans 2:15; 9:1). God can speak to you and show you what to do when you are unsure. And remember, if you are not sure if something's wrong for you, it *is* already. "Whatever is not from faith is sin" (Romans 14:23).

A Passion for Sexual Purity

Sexual purity is so central to our core strength it is a subject of special focus in Scripture. God has given us the power to re-create life as a sacred gift—one key reason why sex seems so significant to us and why God has so much to say about it in the Bible. It is core that sex be kept sacred and special. It is *not* "evil" or unholy. The Bible does not hesitate to praise the joys of a God-given, God-honoring sexual love in marriage. Symbol of some of the most sacred relationships of Scripture, Christian marriage represents on earth the passionate love the heavenly Bridegroom, Jesus Christ, has for His body, the church (1 Corinthians 6:18–20). In its heaven-designed place, sexual love is the most beautiful relationship on earth. This great gift signifies God's ultimate purpose for us: Living in love through eternity in God's family (1 John 3:1–2).

Because God made us to have such a unique relationship with Him, He made definite differences between animal and human sex drives. Automatic laws of instinct spark animal reproduction. There is no love in these sexual couplings, just blind instinctual desire. Human desire for sexual love and children is quite different. Placed by our Creator at the focused direction of human will and thought, He designed sex to both awaken and function under the control of our personality. In our early years this force sleeps, hidden from our attention, but as we begin to mature it makes itself felt in our lives.

The Lord gave us sexual desire for two major physical reasons: *re-creation* of the race by having children (Genesis 1:27–28; Psalm 127:3–5) and as a source of *recreation*—deep spiritual and physical pleasure between husband and wife (Genesis 2:24–25; 24:67; Ecclesiastes 9:9; Matthew 19:4–6; 1 Corinthians 7:2–5). The same Bible that gives serious warnings about the misuse of sex (Proverbs 5:1–8, 20) clearly describes how sexual needs may be met to bring us great happiness (Proverbs 5:15, 18–19). A husband is to be "intoxicated" with his wife's love; this is not only described by the Holy Spirit as a part of wisdom (Proverbs 5:1), but God approves of this sexual union (Proverbs 5:21). God made sex to be surprising, a life-long, beautiful adventure.

CORE RELATIONSHIPS

So what has gone wrong? We have more books on sex than ever before, more tips on "making love" that somehow still leave us lonely. In all our learning we have left out God and are paying the price for it! Sex for so many has become cheap, perverse, and empty. Precious things are not to be overused or made a part of every mealtime conversation but treasured for special times. We must learn God's way to direct our desire's power to preserve sex in purity, or we will join the ranks of the lonely, shamed, and bitter.

Sex is like a fire. A fire is amoral; the same flame that warms a home can burn it down. There is no difference between the fire that comforts and the fire that kills; each burns the same way. But in one case it burns in its proper place and time, and in the second, it burns out of limits and out of control. The same built-in joys God gave sex can instead become raging fires of destruction.

Sex goes wrong for the same reasons a fire can destroy. It can be (1) *lit too soon* (getting emotionally involved before God's time) and (2) *go out of control in the wrong place* (premarital or extramarital sex). To avoid the first, follow these rules of thumb:

1. Avoid any "steady" relationship until God's time. The biggest problem with the dating culture is that if you spend too much exclusive time with another person you can become too familiar with each other. Things can happen you never planned. You let down your guard, ignore the warning of your conscience, and invite trouble. Hundreds of thousands of young people have avoided this trap by making voluntary vows to God to lay aside dating games and commit themselves to being content to wait for God's time and person.

2. Keep busy and active. King David fell into sexual sin through laziness. If he had been out on the field with his men doing the job God had called him to do, he wouldn't have been sitting around his palace with too much time on his hands. Fill your life with activities you can enjoy under God, and you will spare yourself a lot of pressure to date.

3. Avoid tempting situations. A tempting situation can be defined as any place that allows two people who like each other a lot to be secluded from the eyes of others. Set up some boundaries with an accountability partner or perhaps even one or both of your parents to help you set and maintain a safety zone. Watch out for being "home alone."

4. Don't get serious with anyone until you are ready for marriage emotionally, vocationally, financially, and above all spiritually. No one should say "I love you" in any romantic context until that person is prepared to say, with all its implications, in the next breath, "Will you marry me?" If you can't make the second statement, don't bother making the first.

5. Don't let yourself get seriously emotionally involved with anyone until your wedding date is set, and save all physical involvement for marriage alone. Courtship is to be a *spiritual* experience! In courting, the couple take up personal and social responsibilities they will later share with sexual privileges should they marry. If you cannot be satisfied with godly togetherness and conversation, with the desire to keep your lives and time together holy and pure before God, you are *not* in love! Lust can wait only five minutes; *love* can wait for five years. Give any deepening affection a good time and separation test. If you can maintain what you think is God's direction over some serious distance and months without physical contact, it is more likely to be love than infatuation.

6. It can be good to be single! To choose not to marry because your calling, vocation, or lifestyle points in a different direction, or because you haven't found someone you want to spend the rest of your life with, can be to choose God's best for you. Some of God's most core servants never married.

To be single and to have the grace to live single without sexual involvement is a gift God can give to those who make the choice to share their deepest and most intimate love with Him alone (Luke 18:29). Christian singles can feel lonely at times, but they are never alone. Jesus is the true source of all love and friendship, and they are freed up to pay undivided attention to a world without His love (Isaiah 56:3–5). There are places singles can go that are out of range for those with the responsibility of a family. In difficult or dangerous times or situations, someone single can do things and dare things that would put someone married at unnecessary risk. At the edge of the end of time, many will choose to remain unmarried for the kingdom's sake. As Paul, the single who became one of the greatest figures in the early church, put it:

> I wish everyone could get along without marrying, just as I do. But we are not all the same. God gives some the gift of a husband or wife, and others he gives the gift of being able to stay happily unmarried.

So I say to those who aren't married and to widows—better to stay unmarried if you can, just as I am. But if you can't control yourselves, go ahead and marry. It is better to marry than to burn with lust. Nevertheless, each one should retain the place in life that the Lord assigned to him and to which God has called him. (1 Corinthians 7:7–9 TLB, 17 NIV)

KEEP HIS TEMPLE CLEAN

Sex is never just sex. God says sexual sin is like *nothing else.* It cuts to the core. It can hurt us physically, mentally, emotionally, and spiritually. It can screw our life up in ways we would never dream. "If we persist in sexual sin with the thought that one day we will get right with God, we should remind ourselves that God may still be there to forgive and restore . . . but *we* may not be. . . . *You cannot compensate by sacrifice what you lose through disobedience"* (Ed Cole, purity counselor and author of *Maximized Manhood,* emphasis added).

When confused with true love, sexual desire can strike so quickly that irreparable damage is done before a person realizes it. Sexual desire is a tremendously powerful physical and emotional force. No one is old enough to date until he or she fully understands both the purpose of courtship and the dangers of physical involvement. Unless each member of a dating or courting couple is committed to the total lordship of Jesus Christ so that they "glorify God in [their bodies] and [their] spirit[s], which are God's," they should not have the freedom to hang out for long together (1 Corinthians 6:20). Millions of scarred lives and shattered dreams are terrible testimonials to the reality of dating dangers.

Getting physically involved is like igniting a built-in bomb. The trouble with sexual stimulation *outside* of marriage is that it was designed by God to lead into sexual intercourse *in* marriage. Don't start experimenting, no matter how close your friendship, or you will set the fuse burning down to the end God designed it for before you are ready for it or can afford it.

HOW FAR IS TOO FAR?

Moral freedom may be defined as "Not the *right* to do what you want, but the *power to do* what is right." As temptation presents itself, we Christians face a choice between simply pleasuring ourselves or waiting for real love. Surrendering to God's way gives us true sexual freedom; surrendering to selfish desire enslaves the heart in lust and moral bondage.

Our culture has degenerated to such a level that God's guidelines may be met with incredulous stares and protests. But to follow God's love rules for sex is neither old-fashioned nor outdated. Moral purity is a rare gem that must not be bartered for the approval of a God-rejecting society. *One night of stolen pleasure is not worth a lifetime of regret!* (Judges 16:4–31). Results of disobedience to God's protections are painfully obvious—moral filth and perversion are at an all-time high! It is time God's CORE sets an example of purity and holiness worthy of the Name by which it is called (Job 31:1; 1 Corinthians 6:18–20; 10:31; 1 Timothy 2:9–10).

NINE REASONS TO SAVE SEX FOR MARRIAGE

God made sex to bring fulfillment in a total harmony of body, soul, and spirit. The sexual love God gave us was made to be an *outward* expression of an *inner* submission. All kinds of difficulties and problems are created by premature sexual involvement, such as

1. Guilt

God has placed the alarm of *conscience* in our souls to warn us of impending danger. Our conscience alarm can protect us from emotional upheavals and insecurity because it safeguards us from losing trust in ourselves or others. No Christian wants to bring to a marriage altar guilty hands and a soiled mind.

2. Fear

We can't love someone we are afraid of. Love without fear means being able to fully trust the one we want to love. If you experiment with sex with a future spouse before publicly committing yourself to each other in marriage, how can you be sure either of you will remain faithful *after* marriage? Self-trust and trust of each other is vital to a successful marriage. Sexual sin destroys trust.

3. Dilution

Every sexual act is a *giving away of ourselves.* Do it with a dozen, and you tear away twelve parts of your inner self that you will never get back. Sex *always* involves a mutual sharing. Why do you think so many people with multiple sexual partners feel so empty and disappointed that they move on to someone else? What you in the CORE are looking for is *more*. God designed sex to be an investment in each other's lives forever. To love someone is to care for that person's highest good. Sex in a loving marriage builds long-term wholeness and is God's way of making two people one (Genesis 4:1). The Bible word for sexual intimacy is to "know" another: to be close and share on the most deep and lasting level a man and woman can experience (Ephesians 5:20–32). You *can* love and be loved forever! But every sexual act with a stranger strains or shatters the bond you wish to build with the love of your life (Proverbs 5:16–20). The *less* you have given of your inner self to others, the *more* you will have to share with someone who will reward your investment with love and trust.

4. Debt

Over a million teen girls get pregnant every year. Each baby born to a teen outside of marriage demands more than $100,000 in government welfare. The cost of teen childbearing in the U.S. alone in a single year is over $16.5 BILLION! But the cost is much higher than that. What price do you put on a hurt heart? Who counts the cost of a shattered and shamed self, a lost trust, ruined respect, or a broken dream? What does it really cost to bring an unwanted baby into the world or, worse, to take its little life because it interferes with someone's personal pursuit of pleasure? Free sex is never free. Someone always pays. Promiscuity has an awful price. "You are not your own" (1 Corinthians 6:19a).

5. Disease

Decades ago there were two sexually transmitted diseases. Now in the twenty-first century there are twenty-nine, and every nine months researchers seem to find a new one. Twelve million people contract a sexual disease every year in America alone—thirty-three thousand a day. Some diseases, like AIDS, can kill in just a couple of years. Some just make people *wish* they were dead. Some will hurt their children. There is only one way to be sure you don't get a dangerous disease through sex, but no one in a world without God or God's laws wants to say it: *Marry a virgin as a virgin yourself and live with the same love all your life.* That's God's plan. If you take a long look at the ugly alternatives, it looks like He knows what He's talking about (Proverbs 5:15–20).

6. Disappointment

She did it because he said he "loved" her. He pushed her into it because he wanted to prove he was a "real man." Her friends said it was all right as long as she really loved him. His friends told him everybody else had done it, so what was he waiting for? It was no big deal. It was only casual. *All were utterly wrong.*

Sex is never casual. Sex is God's gift, and *nothing* God gives is casual. Because sex itself is so deep, sexual hurt isn't shallow. What we do and what we learn in sex builds a pattern and burns a memory that will last us for life. Short of the healing hand of Jesus, scars from sexual sin never go away. Each time we link our body and our soul to someone else, the reruns of everything we have done before with anyone else start to play.

7. Distrust

What's wrong with giving in before marriage? What difference does a piece of paper make? If you love someone enough to get engaged, what harm can it be to have sex a little early? After all, how else will you know you are compatible? If you love someone, why wait?

One thing is sure: The very best way to hurt a growing friendship is to violate the rules that underlie your trust. *Over half of all engagements break up.* Many shatter precisely because the couple didn't think early sex would make that much difference. A broken engagement without sexual involvement may mean pain and sadness but rarely a loss of friendship and certainly no sense of sin. The guilt, anger, mutual loss of respect, and embarrassment that go with broken engagements triggered by premarital sex are a hurt few want to live with.

Think of God's love laws as a *shelter* within which you will share together the best friendship, the best spiritual life, and the best sex possible. Only in marriage can you build a home for real trust and total openness to each other. Only in marriage can you create the kind of life-long commitment you give to each other "in sickness and health, for richer or poorer, till death do us part." Only in marriage can you be totally open and vulnerable to someone else knowing they will never leave you, laugh at you, or let you down. *The reward of the trustworthy is more trust.* Living together outside of marriage is a commitment not to make a commitment. You never really take off your mask and get real before each other and God.

Keep your gate locked from all others and from each other until God gives you the key in your public, sacred vows. But open that gate early, and you violate that trust. You will always live with the secret question: *If we couldn't trust ourselves to hold back before marriage, how can we ever be sure it can't happen to either of us after marriage?* And that fear hurts love (1 John 4:18).

8. Dependency

Sexual sin *addicts.* Sex divorced from commitment and care carries an inbuilt emotional black hole. Addictions form when we try to derive lasting pleasure from something that cannot in its very nature satisfy, and sexual adventure outside of God's loving laws can never fully satisfy. Go the wrong way on this from the start, and you will find that sex can hook you worse than any drug, and with as dangerous consequences as any chemical (Ephesians 5:3–9).

Sexual addiction doesn't have to involve someone else. You can become sexually addicted by masturbation or virtual, visual, or audio pornography. Sexual sin is not always *fornication,* or sex with an unmarried person (1 Corinthians 6:18). Sexual sin can be adultery (Matthew 5:27–28), same-sex sodomy, or lesbianism (Leviticus 18:22; Romans 1:24–32), and any form of near sex allowing anything except actual intercourse (Romans 13:13–14).

Let God show you what He sees when He calls sexual wrong *sin.* We learn only by revelation or results. Sex is so powerful and fundamental in life that, misused, it becomes devastating. Nothing hurts as much as the guilt, pain, and addiction of immorality. As with drugs, the worst part of the hook is never physical. What really hurts is what it does to your mind and feelings. Only Christ can heal the scars sexual addiction makes and marks on life.

9. Divorce

You know what you are looking for. You think you know where to look for what you need. *Not to be lonely anymore. Not to feel left out, unwanted, unloved. To belong to someone wonderful. To be safe. To be cared for forever.* Maybe marriage will bring you these things. But when so many marriages—even religious ones—crash and burn all around you, you need to do things right the first time.

Does sex outside of God's laws for love lead to closeness, care, and commitment? *No way.* Almost without exception, premarital sex ruins friendships and puts the lid on any chance of long-term love. Promises flow freely in the heat of the moment, but in the cold light of the morning after, caresses often turn into contempt. "If you love me, you'll prove it" puts pressure on you to perform or be rejected. The right response to such glandular fever is this: "If you really love me, you won't ask me to." A single night of compromise isn't worth a lifetime of regret. Making love doesn't make the other person love you.

The test of true love isn't sex but *trust.* "If you love someone, you will always be loyal to him no matter what the cost. You will always believe in him, always expect the best of him, and always stand your ground in defending him" (1 Corinthians 13:4–7 TLB).

The majority of marriages that fail begin with this kind of sexual involvement before marriage that scars each one's ability to love his or her partner as God intended—deeply, totally, and purely. Sex outside of marriage invariably leads to some kind of hurt, and hurt over sex sets a pattern for any future partner. *Breaking up is hard to do.* Do it often in dating and you set a precedent for your future. The pattern of dating and discarding carried into marriage is finally called divorce. God hates what happens in a divorce (Malachi 2:15–16).

Listen carefully: *You can have a marriage that lasts.* You can have a family that doesn't break up. You can stay married to one person and love them for as long as you both live. Learn from those who failed. Then *don't* do what they did. Stay clean. Save yourself for the special someone God can bring along at the right time. *He or she is worth the wait. You are worth the wait.*

The Bible says: "Don't you know that you yourselves are God's temple and that God's Spirit lives in you? If anyone destroys God's temple, God will destroy him; for God's temple is sacred, *and you are that temple*" (1 Corinthians 3:16 NIV, emphasis added). A temple is a place filled with God, where you walk with deep respect, with reverence, honor, and care. Don't go casually where you clearly don't belong.

CORE Cleanse: How to Get Clean

"Flee forbidden longings, those lusts that lure you when you are young. Press instead into what is real and right in character: conviction and faithfulness, unselfish affection. Rest content in Him with those who also call on the Lord's help for a clean heart" (2 Timothy 2:22, authors' paraphrase).

You may have already blown it. You may have failed to live purely and hurt God, yourself, and only God knows how many other people. But Jesus can do what no one else can do. He can heal you on levels no one else can see or understand. He can make a woman who has given away her sexual purity clean again, inside and out. He can give a man back his honor, manhood, and dignity and give him power to keep his promises. He can restore what is eaten away and give you courage to face the world with a new set of eyes. But afterward you must do things His way and not turn back to what hurt you before.

STEPS BACK TO PURITY

If you really want to be free, deal with your heart. Take these steps to be pure again before God:

1. *Be brutally honest with yourself.* Stop excusing what you did. Strip away any excuses you have made for your actions. Don't tell yourself that you're weak, "God knows my heart," or "I'm only doing what is natural." Stop baptizing your sexual problem with soft names. Call it sin, see it as one great habit of selfishness, and be willing to turn from the sin itself, not just be sorry for the trouble it has caused. No one can live a CORE life in the grip of sexual lust or other impurity. God can free you only if you are willing to take sides with Him against it. Begin now, before conviction goes away and you start to feel cold and hard again.

2. *Make a gift of your love to God.* Ask God to forgive and cleanse you from the rotten things you have done. Let Him deal with the stain of your past through His blood. Ask Him for the courage to face up to

what you have done. Ask Him for a new heart to love Him and serve Him as you should.

Deal with your body. "Love the LORD your God ... with all your strength" (Mark 12:30). "You were bought at a price. Therefore honor God with your body" (1 Corinthians 6:20 NIV). Do this by making a present of your body to God. Let Him take ownership. From this time on, it will not be yours to use but His.

Take it part by part. Begin now. Start with your hands. "Lord, take my hands. They have been dirtied, and your Word says, 'Cleanse your hands, you sinners.' Help me to keep them from doing wrong."

Then take your eyes. "Lord, here are my eyes. I am shaken by your Word that says, 'If your eye causes you to sin, pluck it out. . . . It is better for you to enter into life with one eye, rather than having two eyes, to be cast into hell fire' (Matthew 18:9). I make a covenant with you and my eyes right now. I will not use them to lust again. I will not look at things that lead me to sin (Job 31:1).

"Take my lips. I remember that Judas betrayed you with a kiss. I, too, have been Judas to you. Take a fire from your altar of cleansing and touch my lips. Make them clean again to sing your praises from a straight heart." Do this carefully. Give God everything (Romans 12:1–2).

3. *If someone else has been involved, confess your sin to him or her and prepare to break off the relationship.* Write a letter, but don't share all the details of why you did what you did. Sins of immorality cut so deeply that everyone knows what was wrong. Do not go to see that person unless you cannot avoid it, as doing so may start your problem all over again. If you are sexually involved, you *must* break up with him or her unless you are engaged, in which case God may want each of you to really get right with each other and stay clean for His time in marriage. This will not be easy. It will be hard for you, especially if this has gone on a long time. But if you want to be free, you must do it (Matthew 5:28–30).

4. *Set up a prayer covenant with another CORE Christian.* If the other person doesn't know what you are going through, just relate that you have a great need for victory over sin in your life and that you

would like support in prayer. If you are engaged, set up this prayer time with each other (James 5:16).

5. Stay away from sources of temptation. Avoid places where you will be alone together if that is a temptation, or stay away from the places where the person who was party to your problem is. Go out with a full crowd of disciples of Jesus. Stick together in a big family where you can have friends and learn to love and live without bringing impure activities into it (1 Thessalonians 5:22).

6. Do some solid work and exercise. Throw yourself into activities for God with all your energy. You may be surprised at how much it can help to channel the powerful sex drive into more useful outlets. It will help release sexual tension and make your happenings more fun. Set yourself tough deadlines on all that you do. Don't waste time. Challenge yourself to meet everything in Christ with all your heart, mind, and strength.

"You are already clean because of the word which I have spoken to you" (John 15:3). We can trust Jesus to keep His promises. He never lies. What He says, He has power to do.

The steps you take to becoming clean in Jesus' sight are the same basic steps you take to become a real child of God. *Confession. Repentance. Trust. Forgiveness. Trust. Cleansing.*

Three extra things will help when you are being healed by Jesus from sexual and other sins.

1. Expect miracles, not magic. God's forgiveness is real and immediate; true healing may take time. You can be cured at once; recovery from the damage may take time. Don't be discouraged if it does. When David, God's beloved in Scripture, sinned sexually, he hurt more than himself. The things he did had sad consequences, and forgiveness does not always stop consequences (2 Samuel 12:9–14).

Sin *hurts.* Do wrong and you almost always affect others (even unborn generations), even though you stop it and even after you repent. You may have many battles, but with God you will win the war. Trust Him. Rest in the real and ongoing grace of Christ. Expect God to show you what you need to be fully free, no matter what it takes (Deuteronomy 30:19–20).

2. God is faithful. "If we confess our sins, He is faithful and just to forgive us our sins and to cleanse us from *all* unrighteousness" (1 John 1:9, emphasis added). Your cleansing is not by your own devotion or your own determination. Power over sin comes from a *fresh revelation of Christ* at your own point of humble, even desperate need. Victory over sin never comes by self-effort or self-discipline. You commit your life to Jesus; He commits His life to you. Hang your life and your love on His mercy. And remember: Though you may have times of struggles, doubts, and tears, Jesus never changes. His love and commitment to you is not based on your final faithfulness to Him but on His own unchanging character. *He can keep you for the long haul.*

3. Enlist a friend. In the time of His greatest test and temptation, Jesus asked His closest disciples to be with Him in the garden to pray. Yet He himself was God. His Father was God. He had God the Holy Spirit's power without measure in His life as a man. What did Jesus need friends for? Learn the lesson: Even Jesus was not ashamed to ask for friends to be near when He most needed to be strong. If you have a close friend who knows you well enough to pray for you when you face a big battle, that person is a friend indeed (Ecclesiastes 4:9–10).

Cultivating a Pure Heart for God

"Now the purpose of the commandment is love from a pure heart, from a good conscience, and from sincere faith" (1 Timothy 1:5).

A godly girl once asked God to use her. The Lord spoke to her and said, "So many want me to *use* them. So few want to be my *friend*." How do we develop any friendship to deep intensity? A look at the habits of heart of those who feel deeply in love can help us see what it means to cultivate passion for God.

1. Priority

Make your moments together a top life priority (Psalm 139:17). Everything works toward the time when you can see each other and be together again (Psalm 106:1–2). People in love think about each other all day. Whatever else they are involved in as their job or responsibility, the focus of their thoughts is on the other person. They can't get the person they love out of their minds.

2. Purity

You clean up and make yourself up to present yourself to one you love in the very best light (Hebrews 10:22). People in love would never do or say anything that might knowingly offend, shame, or put off the acceptance of the one they most want to impress. They try to be absolutely honest and open in all they say and do (1 Timothy 1:5; 1 Peter 1:22). They are always on their best behavior (2 Timothy 2:15; Hebrews 11:16).

3. Passion

The hunger those in love have to be together is like a pain (Psalm 63:1). There is an intensity, a love that alternately can feel like a storm or fire (Psalm 42:1–2; Psalm 119:10; Jeremiah 20:9). They desire to give all they have of themselves and receive all their loved one has to give (Psalm 84:2).

4. Presence

People in love just want to be together (Isaiah 26:9). They don't want to do *anything* without the one they love, and they minimize all moments that take time away from that person, counting the minutes until they can be together again and even ending any friendships that seem to threaten their mutual commitment (1 John 2:15).

5. Pursuit

People in love seek out the one they love (Song of Solomon 3:1–2). They actively pursue their relationship and cannot stand to lose contact with the object of their dreams and desires (Psalm 27:8). If others try to draw them away, they will bend all their energies and resources to regaining lost ground (Galatians 2:20). They cannot live without their love and will do anything to bring it back (Song of Solomon 5:6).

Consider Deuteronomy 30:19b–20a: "Now choose life, so that *you* and your *children* may live and that you may love the LORD your God, listen to his voice, and hold fast to him. For the LORD is your life" (NIV, emphasis added).

A core heart that is in love with the Father would never do anything to break His heart. Nor would any prospective father or mother do anything that would harm their child. Remember, the choices we make today affect not only us but future generations!

You're blessed when you can show people how to cooperate instead of compete or fight. That's when you discover who you really are, and your place in God's family. THE MESSAGE

BLESSED ARE THE PEACEMAKERS, FOR THEY WILL BE CALLED SONS OF GOD. NIV

BLESSED ARE THE PEACEMAKERS, FOR THEY SHALL BE CALLED SONS OF GOD. NKJV

GOD BLESSES THOSE WHO WORK FOR PEACE, FOR THEY WILL BE CALLED THE CHILDREN OF GOD. NLT

Blessed are the peacemakers for they shall be called sons of God. NASB

Blessed are the peacemakers, for they shall be called sons of God. ESV

9

CORE
PEACE

BRIDGING THE GAPS

Blessed are the
peacemakers, for
they shall be called
sons of God.

MATTHEW 5:9

There is a vast difference between peacekeepers and peacemakers. Peacekeepers will let anything go to avoid rocking the boat; only fragile relationships result. Peacemakers, on the other hand, are willing to confront at the risk of being misunderstood, knowing that in confronting the situation that caused the rift, peace and unity may truly be restored. As they resolve and work through problems, growth occurs and character develops, resulting in right, lasting relationships between people. Blessed are the peacemakers—and, by God's grace, what a blessing they are to others!

CORE Peacemakers

Nothing is more difficult on earth or heaven than reconciling opposed hearts and minds. Making peace is almost always difficult and sometimes terribly costly. It cost God His Son, and it cost Jesus His life.

Being a peacemaker is not the same as being a pacifist. Peacemaking is an *active process* that brings reconciliation and restoration, not a passive acceptance of what is wrong. George Fox, gentle founder of the Quakers, would never have been known in his day as a pacifist. On the contrary, he was one of the most radical and active opposers of all that was false, evil, and unjust both in and out of the church. But a peacemaker is not a nuclear bomb, and bringing spiritual peace does not involve hand-to-hand combat.

Many barriers block true friendship and harmony in our complex world and culture: walls between old and young, male and female, rich and poor, educated and ignorant—not to mention language, nations, people groups, and tastes! Some obstacles arise out of the way things are, and differences are often a gift of God. Yet many things are not the way they were originally made to be, and bringing them back to God's intention is the peacemaker's task.

- *Old* and *Young*: Why is there constant conflict between kids and parents? What causes division when there is an age difference? The generation gap is a gap of lost love and lack of understanding.

- *Male* and *Female*: Why is it so hard to understand someone of the opposite sex? Why do so many attempts to bridge this gap meet with pain, confusion, or sometimes just plain sin? How can someone so much like us be so utterly different? The gender gap is a gap of false expectations and unrequited love.

- *Tribe* and *Tongue*: How do you reach out to people from another culture? How can we communicate? What kind of bridge do we need to build to see healing come to nations or tribes in tension, division, or even war? The gap between cultures and peoples is a chasm of different backgrounds and languages.

The common needs in these differences are the biblical requirements for unity, harmony, reconciliation, and peace: common *understanding* and common *unselfishness*.

What Is Peace?

"That they all may be one, as You, Father, are in Me, and I in You; that they also may be one in Us, that the world may believe that You sent Me" (John 17:21).

What does God want when He calls us to make peace?

In the Lord's prayer in John 17, Jesus voices the goal of God for His broken, divided world: that they may be one. The task of the peacemaker is to return divided systems and structures to divine order and harmony, to restore unity wherever there is brokenness. When this real unity takes place, it creates a powerful testimony to the unique reality of the true God and clearly points others to trusting Christ.

In so many ways, our world can go wrong. Yet despite the ugliness of the fall in our lives and in our world, God has given us the following four witnesses that point unmistakably to God. Since all people everywhere have seen these witnesses, no one has a good excuse for never thanking or worshiping God.

This is the point Paul makes in Romans 1:19–20, when he gives one reason why people who have never heard of Jesus can *still* be guilty of rejecting truth to make God angry with them (Psalm 19:1; Isaiah 40:26; Jeremiah 10:12).

OUR BODIES ✦ THE REVELATION OF NATURE IN CREATION

It is hard *not* to think of God when you look at the sweep of the stars, feel the warm sun, or smell a fragrant flower. David said, "The heavens declare the glory of God; and the firmament [the earth] shows His handiwork" (Psalm 19:1). Day after day our environment speaks to us of God (Psalm 8:3–6; 24:1; 136:1–9; Jeremiah 51:15). Nature itself can be healed during times of revival; concern for the land and its people are a part of peacemaking. But the greatest witness to the wonder of creation is closer still: our own bodies. The harmony and balance of the body's incredible systems are in themselves a living example of God's desire for unity (1 Corinthians 12).

Our very lives can "shine like stars in the universe" (Philippians 2:15b NIV). "For we are God's workmanship, created in Christ Jesus to do good works, which God prepared in advance for us to do" (Ephesians 2:10 NIV).

As God-fashioned CORE believers, we can demonstrate and be witnesses to the fact God is preparing us for good deeds that will impact our world. We can have confidence in the knowledge that in the unity and harmony of our own body we are "fearfully and wonderfully made," that even our very physical makeup has been ordained by God and written in His book (Psalm 139:14–16 NIV).

Just think: God says your body is literally His work of art. What an incredible witness!

OUR SOULS ✦ THE REVELATION OF REASON IN GOD'S WORD

Our personality or temperament tells us a lot about the God who made us. It is this that makes us sure we are not accidents of time and chance. Randomly formed brains would not be trustworthy critics of creation, but our thoughts, feelings, and free will all provide ways in which we can learn things about life and our Maker. When we think, we can see in a very small way how God reasons. When we feel hurt or happy, we learn more about God's own feelings. When we are faced with a difficult choice, we can know on a tiny scale what our Great Friend has to do when He faces problems. The written Word of God moves our emotions, enlightens our minds, and challenges our wills, affecting our whole being. The truth of the Bible flows through our lives to be expressed by our personalities in whatever work God gives us. Although the Bible is not the only source of our knowledge of God, it is His main one. People who do not have the Bible will be judged according to the knowledge they have of God from other sources, but if we also know what God says in His Book we have far fewer excuses for hurting Him.

OUR SPIRITS ✦ THE REVELATION OF INTUITION BY THE HOLY SPIRIT

Intuition is a function of our human spirits that can put us in touch with God and His truth without information from any of our five senses. God has made us moral like Him. Since being moral involves knowing what is right, He has made sure that we *instinctively sense* wrong choices. God not only wrote His law in the Bible; through intuition, He writes it on every heart (John 1:9).

Intuition makes us aware of God. Just as a growing baby with physical hunger expects to be given physical food, so there comes a time in any life when we sense a spiritual hunger and know God is there waiting to meet us. We call this time of awakening "the age of accountability," and all men and women have it. Although non-Christians do not feel the indwelling presence of God, intuition gives them a very clear witness to His reality and claims.

People also have a *sense of moral law.* Everyone starts off knowing right from wrong. God's moral law—the rule of right action—is given through our intuition, and through *conscience* directly appeals to our reason (John 1:9; 3:19–20; Romans 1:18–19).

Now, as this law directly appeals to our minds for acceptance, it can be fought off and its force dimmed by reasoning it away. Unlike the instinct of animals, it directs by *influence,* not by *control.* If we do not want to obey it, we can always think up enough reasons why we shouldn't. We can fight it or forget it for a while, argue with it or try to ignore it, but it is God's witness to right regardless, and we all know it is there.

The Bible shows us that God judges everyone according to the degree or amount of moral "light" or understanding they have. The non-Christian may know far less about God than a church member. God will judge the non-Christian by what he or she really knew, and the church member by the same rule. God is perfectly fair and just, and guilt is exactly equal to the amount of light known and rejected (Matthew 11:20–24; Luke 12:47–48; John 12:35–36, 46–48; 15:22–24; 16:8–11; Romans 2:1–16; James 4:17).

OUR SOCIETY ✦ THE REVELATION OF WITNESS BY CHRIST AND CHRISTIANS

God has given us one more testimony of His love. When He first created our human family, He made us so that we could learn from and enjoy one another. Human friendship is a beautiful thing when God is a part of it. He made us "members of one another" (Ephesians 4:25), and there is no closer link on earth than that between people who *really* know and love Him (John 17:21–23; Acts 2:41–47; 1 John 1:3–4). As others find out more about God, they can *share* their discoveries about Him and their adventures with Him. This gives us another way to learn about His greatness. All the different people that live in our world give God the chance to show us just how many ways He can meet our needs.

Right education helps people know about God. The Creator gave us minds to learn, to be excited about the truths of His universe. As we do one thing God shows us, we become ready to learn again. Each discovery should add to the excitement of the previous one. What we learn in our *souls* through our *intellect,* we should also feel right about in our *spirits* through *intuition.*

Proper examples of a God-honoring life are also needed to help us form pictures of what people who love God look like. Two thousand years ago God did the most wonderful thing possible to give us an idea of how to live. He became a man. He is the best example of love our world has ever seen (Philippians 2:5–8; Hebrews 2:14–15; 4:15; 5:5–9; 1 Peter 2:22).

Every now and then, God still intervenes in hungry lives by revealing himself directly and miraculously to sincere seeking souls. But in a world of law, miracles must always be the exception, so God needs people who will do what He tells them. This is the real purpose of the Christian's work on earth. People around the world need to see what God can do in a life. The CORE must show them. There is *nothing* more convincing than people who are actually doing what they know they should. The world needs living witnesses of God's love. Our call as CORE peacemakers is to be those witnesses (Matthew 5:14–16; Acts 1:81; Acts 26:16–18; John 2:1–17).

The CORE Conditions of Peace

Two things are necessary for agreement: common *understanding* and common *unselfishness*. There will never be unity or peace between people until they can meet these two conditions. If two friends do not agree, their friendship is in danger; if a husband and wife will not agree, their marriage is headed for the rocks; if a nation cannot agree, crime and anarchy will stalk the streets; because our countries and ideologies cannot agree, people are now afraid of terrorism and weapons of mass destruction.

COMMON UNDERSTANDING

But how can finite people agree on what is true and valuable when we cannot always see what "valuable" is? God has promised to *show* us what we need to know, provided we will use this knowledge wisely. Although we are all finite, we have an *infinite* Friend. This is one reason why God has a right to all of our lives, whether we have given them to Him or not. If two people cannot agree using their limited knowledge, they can go to God or His Word and find a principle or direction for an answer. Not many people want to do this today; it is little wonder our world is in so much trouble and has so many problems.

COMMON UNSELFISHNESS

The second condition is just as important. Knowledge is not enough. Unless we are also willing to *do* what we honestly see as the best thing, our knowledge will only get us into more trouble. Our world today is generally well educated; it also is the most frightened and confused world of all time. It is not enough to *know* what is right; we must also be willing to *do* it. Begin with selfish people, and you will always wind up with selfish societies, no matter what they call themselves and no matter how much they know. That is why God has revealed the truth to us in His law. It is not a suggestion or advice; it is a *command* that none of us can afford to break. God reinforces this law because all happiness—not only His, but that of every creature in the universe—depends on it. The Bible calls this core law love. There is no more important rule in all of God's universe.

PEACE IN THE BODY: CHRIST IS THE HEAD

Even Christians can become divided. Disunity among Christians is often caused by our not understanding our relationship to each other in Christ. "Our bodies have different parts, but all together make up only one body. With Christ it is just like that" (1 Corinthians 12:12, authors' paraphrase).

Scripture teaches that when we enter God's kingdom, our connection with the Lord Jesus is like the link between a head and a body. The two belong to each other; neither can work separately. Jesus Christ is the head of the church, and Christians all over the world make up the rest of His "body." God counts everyone who loves and serves Him as *part* of Christ (Ephesians 1:22–23), who expresses himself in and through us!

Think about the following things with this in mind:

1. The head is the most important.

All body functions are directed and controlled by the head. The head is the center and source of all operations, linking into unity the various abilities of all the body parts to enable us to do our work. So with the Lord Jesus. *He* must be the Center and Source of all our fellowship, work, and devotion. As a mindless body is helpless and powerless, so "without [Him we] can do nothing" (John 15:4–5; 1 Corinthians 1:30–31).

2. No one is more important.

Eyes see; ears hear; feet walk. Each does the job it was designed for. No *one* member of the body can do everything that needs doing. We

ULTIMATE CORE

cannot compare an "eye" with an "ear" to find out which is "better." *All* are best as long as they do the job they were created to do. The eye cannot hear and the ear cannot see. We in the body of Christ must never forget this. Comparing ourselves with others is another root of division (1 Corinthians 1:26–29).

3. All are important.

God makes everyone "princes and princesses," but only the head can wear the crown! People mistake number of talents for importance. There is only one pituitary gland in the human body. It is small—no bigger than a thumbnail. Yet without it, we have only a few minutes to live! Some Christians complain because they cannot be like some other part of the body. Because they can't do *one* thing, they refuse to do anything! It isn't the lack of five-talent people but the laziness of one-talent people that ties God's hands. Be like Mary who did "what she could" and was worthy in God's eyes of a thousand messages on His grace (Mark 14:8–9). Everyone in the body has a vital part to play. *You do yours* (1 Corinthians 12:19–21).

4. The condition of one member affects the entire Body.

A *living unity* connects all believers in Christ. We tap into this invisible unity when we pray for one another. By all being connected to the head, we must also be connected through Him to one another. A thousand pianos all tuned in to the same tuning fork are also in tune with one another. Are you tuned for harmony? What you do affects the "music" of the entire church. If you want to build up the church, you need to be restored to top working order. Your devotion to God will spark a desire for unity in others you touch in spirit (1 Corinthians 12:26; Ephesians 4:11–16).

PEACE IN OUR OWN PLACE: NO PLACE LIKE HOME

The first place for learning peacemaking is the home. *Nobody knows what goes on in our home as well as God.* Every wall is transparent to Him. Whatever is hidden carefully from the prying eye of the world is not hidden from His sight. He knows all about our family, the good and the bad. Most of all, He cares how we feel. He really understands what makes us hurt and sad, afraid and alone (Deuteronomy 5:29; Psalm 11:4; Proverbs 15:3; 1 Peter 5:5–7).

If Satan can wreck a home, he can ruin much more than one life. From a thousand secret ambushes, he springs traps on families. He worries at the love ties that bind a happy home together. He works on parents when they are tired, ill, or trapped by habits, hoping to slash apart their love and split the family in two. He tries to turn brother and sister against each other over stupid, minor differences that grow into explosions of hate and bitterness. And too often he has done it!

How do you think God feels when He sees your family? *He* began the first marriage, blessed the first home. From the beginning He chose to direct us through the structure of a home that loves and obeys Him. His basic home laws:

1. Parents should love God with their lives as well as their lips. God wants parents to be a source of strength and guidance. God longs for your parents to be like this even more than you do (Deuteronomy 5:16; Matthew 15:4–6; 19:16–19; Ephesians 6:24).

2. The Lord Jesus is to be the Head of your family. Jesus is to be the ruler and center of the home. Dad and then Mom are to be next, with the rest of the family sheltered by their direction (Ephesians 5:22–23; Colossians 3:18–19; 1 Peter 3:1–2; Titus 2:4–5). If this is not true of your family, do you want it to be?

3. You are to love, honor, and obey your parents as you would honor God. Even if you no longer live at home, God may work through your parents to use them to teach you how to live rightly. "My son, hear the instruction of your father, and do not forsake the law of your mother" (Proverbs 1:8–9). The question is not, "Are my parents doing things that hurt me or make me ashamed of them?" The question is, "Have *I* done the right things they asked me to do?" (1 Samuel 15:22; Proverbs 6:20–23; 10:17; 13:1; 15:5, 31–32; Ephesians 6:1). When you fight, struggle, or rebel against your parents, you are fighting God, too! *Get on God's side.* Nobody ever fought Him and won in the end.

4. Trouble in the family is to be taken immediately to God. If someone is in the wrong, God will deal with that person. If, for example, your parents ask you to do anything that is not wrong but you may not like, you must take it to *God* and ask *Him* to change their hearts (Proverbs 21:1). Trust the Lord to straighten out problems, and He will help you (Psalm 27:10).

If Others Sin

Peacemaking is not easy. Real peace comes only from a pure heart. Perhaps the most disobeyed command in the entire Bible is in Leviticus 19:17: "You shall not hate your brother in your heart. You shall surely *rebuke* your neighbor, and not bear sin because of him." Christians have forgotten how to rebuke sin. They sit quietly and let the world rush on to hell without a word. There is such a fear of other people today that the average Christian seems to *apologize* for being holy! Yet godly rebuke is a duty of every CORE Christian.

Most people have a strange idea of love. They imagine it is a warm feeling, a pleasant state of sensation between two people. In this dream world, even gentle rebuke is the very *opposite* of Christian fellowship. Nothing could be farther from the truth. To truly experience love and fellowship we must give and share ourselves, and this means telling the truth about ourselves. We are often not willing to pay the cost of real love and unity. The cost is largely the pain of being willing to give *and* receive reproof. Without this, there will be no true spiritual unity; without unity in truth and love, we will never experience genuine peace nor a spiritual awakening on any grand scale.

The life of the Lord Jesus was the life of love in action. Yet His actions were starred with rebukes aimed in all directions. Jesus was not a comfortable person to have around if you cherished secret sin. He not only rebuked runaway nature (Matthew 8:26), demonic forces (Matthew 17:18), and sickness (Luke 4:39), but sin in every form. He rebuked religious materialism (John 2:13-25) in church and even a proudly patronizing religious leader when sitting as a guest in the man's dining room! (John 7:36-50). He cut into religious hypocrisy in terms so scathing that the men who were exposed wanted to kill Him (Matthew 23:13-33). He even rebuked the *disciples* (Mark 8:33; 10:14; Luke 22:24-30). If Jesus was the living embodiment of love, why don't we Christians rebuke sin today?

Reproof is core. God teaches us to respond to His authority through reproof. The discipline of the family, essential to divine order in the church and the nation, is based on this (Proverbs 1:23; 6:20-23; 10:17; 12:1; 13:8; 15:5, 31-32; 29:15). *The most critical test of Christians is their growth in the ability to give and receive reproof.* If we give but do not take reproof, we become dictatorial, critical, and obnoxious. If we take it but do not give it, we are doormats. Christians become one in only one way: when we deal truthfully with one another, speaking the truth in love, receiving it from others whether it hurts or not, and giving it even if it costs us to do it.

The love we have for God plainly requires that we reprove. Sin is God's greatest enemy. A holy life grows to hate the things God hates and love the things God loves. *Sin cost God His Son, and Christ His life.* If we really love God, we will hate sin enough to rebuke it. And godly rebuke is a measure of love. The more deeply we love God, the more effectively and directly we will rebuke sin. If we love our community, we will rebuke sin.

"Righteousness exalts a nation, but sin is a reproach to any people" (Proverbs 14:34). Bad examples tend to corrupt others; they, too, must be firmly rebuked. If we love our neighbors we will reprove them if they sin. It is cruel *not* to! People who sin are injuring their reputation, respect, integrity, business, family, or body. Sin is moral madness. If people stay in their burning house, they will lose their lives; if they live and die in sin, they will lose their lives *and* souls!

God requires us to do this. There is no *stronger* command in the whole Bible. It is not only stressed in the Old Testament but underlined and underscored right through the entire Scriptures (Luke 17:3; 1 Timothy 5:20; Titus 1:13; 2:15). To refuse to rebuke ignores the Word of God, and to refuse to receive reproof is rebellion against God's rule and direction. Anyone who sees God's law flagrantly broken on all sides and does nothing in his power to oppose or prevent it betrays the Christ who died to save us from sin.

THE PEACEMAKER'S SECRET TO REPROOF

It will always be hard to reprove, especially a close friend. But we must have the courage to put principles above personalities (2 Samuel 12:1–14). The secret to reproof is to do it on God's behalf, not as some personal complaint or injury against ourselves. If we rebuke only for His sake, we will find it far simpler and more effective. The idea is "That hurts *God,*" not "This hurts me." Our *personal* displeasure is not the issue.

Think this way: "Should I be faithful to God and risk being embarrassed by this person and others, or deny the Lord, let this person keep sinning, and keep my reputation? Do I care more about my *Father's* reputation than my *own*?" Once you have settled this question, it won't matter that you may be scolded by the person you rebuke; you have done what you could for that person and obeyed Jesus, and *He himself* will share your reproach, because it is really against Him. You are not at fault for making sinners feel uncomfortable; they are at fault for breaking God's laws and God's heart, and they ought to be reminded of it.

How Do You Do It?

If you are in the right place with God, you will know when God is asking you to reprove for His sake. The Holy Spirit will give a clear sense that it is necessary to say something, and if you do not obey, you will feel a sense of loss. For Christians, the proper Bible method is to first go to the sinning parties with a loving spirit, wanting to help them back to a good place with the Lord. If they listen, you have gained a brother or sister (James 5:19–20). If they do not, after concerned prayer, take one or two other people with you who are also grieved over the hurt this brings God. If they still refuse to repent, the matter must be brought up before the whole church (Matthew 18:15–17). Even then, though, you must avoid being destructive in your criticism. If they won't repent even before the church, they should from then on be treated as a non-Christian. And what kind of attitude does God have over a "lost" person? Not ruffled-temper resignation or an I-give-up attitude, but grieved, deep concern over the sin causing separation, with an obvious willingness to forgive and forget at the least sign of repentance (Jeremiah 9:1; Luke 6:21; Acts 20:31; Philippians 3:18).

The severity of your reproof should be based on the following:

- your *relation* to the one sinning. Reproof will not always be in the same strength or form; you must take into consideration the age of the person you rebuke, since older men or women must be treated with respect (1 Timothy 5:1–2, 19). Also, the authority and familiarity that exist in your relationship should be taken into account.

CORE PEACE

- the *knowledge* the offender has. If he or she is relatively ignorant of spiritual light, reproof should be more in the form of instruction or advice; if he or she has a deep spiritual understanding of what has been done, much greater severity must be used to be effective (Matthew 23:13–33).
- the *frequency* of the offense. Rebuke for those who are doing wrong out of habit, accustomed to sin, and know the truth without obeying it should be given more sharply.

DON'T REPROVE THESE

Scripture records only four cases when a word of reproof would aggravate a situation. In such cases, a grieved silence is more eloquent than words. We are not to reprove *scoffers* (Proverbs 9:8; 15:12), as it will only make them more hateful and bitter. Nor the *self-deceived heretic* (Ephesians 5:11; Titus 3:10). When people reject truth and begin to teach the same, they are to be warned twice, then left alone. The *self-proclaimed rebel* who is known to hate God or authority (Ezekiel 3:26–27; Matthew 7:6) should not be rebuked, since it may provoke violence; nor finally, the *extremely self-righteous* (Matthew 15:14; 27:12), who are so full of pride, conceit, and self-satisfaction with their own wisdom and goodness that reproof will only bring argument. In every other case, we should follow the direction of the Spirit of God to rebuke sin.

Every disciple will be faced with the temptation to "cop out," but if we love Jesus, we will love Him enough to speak out for Him. If we become slaves of what people think of us, we will never change our world (Isaiah 51:7, 12; Jeremiah 1:6–8, 17; Romans 8:15; Hebrews 13:6; 1 John 4:18).

HOW A PEACEMAKER RECEIVES REPROOF

One characteristic of a Christian is the ability to receive reproof. God teaches us to stay on the "trail" through reproofs designed for our instruction. Such reproof can come from many different sources. Learn to recognize God's hand in these corrections that could come from

1. Scripture—The Word of God will often give you a dose of solid rebuke when you are backsliding (2 Timothy 3:16).

2. *Spirit checks*—The Holy Spirit will put "the brakes" on inside if you go off the trail (Proverbs 1:23).

3. *Conscience*—The inner voice of the moral law is an ever-present reproof against sin (Hebrews 13:18).

4. *Circumstance*—The very results of sin are a powerful reproof to the sinner (Jeremiah 2:19).

5. *Chastisement*—God allows others to punish us for correction for our own good (2 Samuel 7:14; Hebrews 12:4–11).

6. *Friends*—Never think less of friends if they point out a fault you should correct. People like that are rare (Proverbs 27:5–6; 6:3).

7. *Enemies*—Enemies sometimes can be more honest in rebuke than friends. *Always* listen.

8. *People in authority*—Those God has set over us in civil affairs—police, judges, teachers, kings, and presidents—should certainly be a source of reproof (1 Timothy 2:2; Titus 3:1).

9. *Pastors and church leaders*—Those who have been entrusted with the care of God's people (Hebrews 13:17; Ephesians 4:1–16).

10. *Parents*—We learn to obey God by learning to obey our parents. We must learn to take reproof from them (Proverbs 13:24; 23:12; 6:20–23).

CORE Leadership

While every Christian is charged with the task of peacemaking, leaders have an extra measure of responsibility. When you look for leaders, keep these two things in mind: Christ's inner circle had only two things in common—they always wanted to know and do. Choose those who show the *greatest willingness to learn* and who are the most keen to *do* what they are given. It is not always the most talented, good-looking, or gifted that make the best leaders. God's kingdom works with people with servant-learner hearts. It is consistently those who are quick to learn and obey God who know how to motivate others to do the same in His work. The quicker you learn and the sooner you do what is called for, the faster you qualify to lead others.

UNITY THROUGH HONOR

What is important to God? What is His prize for faithfulness? The Bible's reward for good leadership is not status but honor and respect for a job well done (Romans 13:7; Revelation 4:11; 1 Timothy 5:17). Honor is recognition of someone's value, significance, and service. We are to honor parents (Exodus 20:12), church elders, national leaders (Numbers 27:20, 1 Peter 2:17), older people (Leviticus 19:32), and one another (Romans 12:10). We are to honor the gift of God in someone's life, because it honors the God who gives it (Malachi 1:6; Matthew 13:54–57; John 12:26).

Honor is a vital quality if you are going to lead. If division and disunity hinder a team, a task may begin well, yet somehow fall apart. Some think there is not enough of this or too much of that. Others start to see problems they never saw before and take sides. People disagree and are hurt or become critical.

What is the key to helping people with diverse strengths work together as one? First Corinthians 12:14–18 says this:

> Now the body is not made up of one part but of many. . . . If the ear should say, "Because I am not an eye, I do not belong to the body," it would not for that reason cease to be part of the body. If the whole body were an eye, where would the sense of hearing be? If the whole body were an ear, where would the sense of smell be? But in fact God has arranged the parts in the body, every one of them, just as he wanted them to be. (NIV)

DISUNITY THROUGH INDEPENDENCE

The root of all division lies in an *independent spirit* or an attitude of self-sufficiency. It is thinking and acting as if we are the whole thing. It is imagining that because we can do one thing better than someone else, then we can do *all* things better. An independent spirit projects an "I don't need you" attitude, especially to others who have no acknowledged status or prominence. Yet the Bible says, "The eye cannot say to the hand, 'I don't need you!' And the head cannot say to the feet, 'I don't need you!'" (1 Corinthians 12:21 NIV).

Some marks of an independent spirit:

- *Pride.* Pride is an arrogant, know-it-all attitude. *Knowledge puffs up but love builds up* (1 Corinthians 8:1b; James 3:13–18; 4:6; 1 Peter 5:5).
- *Ingratitude.* Proud people cannot be thankful. They owe "nobody

nothing" (Romans 1:21; 1 Thessalonians 5:18).

- *Inability to learn or be taught.* This is especially true when our teachers are familiar or younger than we are. People marked by an independent spirit aren't good listeners and are unable to listen to something they've heard. They are anxious to "bring the balance to that," ask questions like "How long have *you* been saved? I *thought* so," or correct others' statements. *Only God has the last word.*

- *Religious deception.* The heart of every cult is an independent spirit.

So what makes the difference for unity? The Bible says it is honor. "On the contrary, those parts of the body that seem to be weaker are indispensable, and the parts that we think are less honorable we treat with special honor. . . . But God has combined the members of the body and has given greater honor to the parts that lacked it, so that there should be no division in the body, but that its parts should have equal concern for each other" (1 Corinthians 12:22–25 NIV). Do not fail to honor and give special encouragement to those who need it.

George Verwer of Operation Mobilization makes this insightful observation:

> *There is no room for the person who has all the answers.* We must take the position of learners, for a disciple is a learner. A disciple is always willing to be taught. He is always willing to listen to another's point of view and to esteem it better than his own. He does not covet a position of leadership, but only desires to be a disciple of Jesus. You must not expect that you will always agree with your leader, or see in him perfection; for remember, he is as you are, just a follower of Jesus. (emphasis added)

CORE NEGOTIATION: HANDLING CONFLICTS WITH OTHERS

One of the hard things a leader has to learn to deal with is people who disagree. One of the marks of a good leader is that they have learned to solve conflicts. They never go out of their way to stir up more trouble. If you hope to influence someone who differs from you, try these principles:

1. Find out what people actually want and ask yourself and God

how you can help them do this in a way that doesn't conflict with your long-term goal. Pharaoh told the Hebrews to throw their first-born babies in the Nile, but God's command to Israel was not to murder. Moses' parents put him in the Nile River all right—but in a boat, still obeying God! Daniel and his three friends were put under King Nebuchadnezzar's program. They neither compromised nor rebelled. They instead took the third option: They found a godly way to meet the king's expectations and wound up ruling for God under three different political systems in Babylon.

What is your long-term goal? For both Moses' mother and the boys in Babylon it was to honor and obey God, and part of that means living as peaceably as possible with all—being a peacemaker. That means trusting God to act and not just reacting when people disagree with or differ from you. No anger. No bitterness. No arrogance. "A soft answer turns away wrath" (Proverbs 15:1).

2. Forget the immediate differences between you and others. Before you say or do anything, ask yourself: "Will it make it easier or harder for me to do what I came to do?" Do your homework first. Know what the facts really are before you begin. Don't slack off here. Your goal is not to show how much smarter you are but to get the job done.

3. Put yourself in others' shoes. Take their side as much as you can. Agree with everything they say that is true and compliment them when they make a fair point. Ask yourself: "If I were in their position, what would I think and feel? Do they see what I'm saying as a request or a threat? Why might they not trust my motives? How can I say what I need to say in a way that will appeal more to the other person's interests? Is my claim convincing?"

Study the way Jesus talked with the woman at the well (John 4). He never used what He knew in a way that put her down or made her feel stupid. Jesus' words are the model of loving confrontation. Try to describe things both as *they* see them and as *you* see them as fairly as you can. Think things through as if you were they.

Remember: The Bible way to promote unity is always to honor one another. If you never fail to honor other people, no matter what the outcome or the result, you will honor God and often create a healing path for future situations.

Your goal is the highest good of God and of people, not to show off some so-called superior authority or insight. *What if you win an argument but lose a soul?* Never by word or attitude give the impression to others that you don't need them.

DEALING WITH LEADERSHIP PRESSURES

Being a leader often involves stress. Leaders deal with change, and change of *any* kind—good or bad—involves stress. If you are a leader you must answer for the decisions you make and give account for their results. Criticism produces stress. You have to deal sometimes with difficult people and difficult circumstances (2 Corinthians 1:8–11). On top of that, as a leader you become a spiritual and strategic target for attack (Mark 3:27). No wonder James said, "Don't everyone try to be a leader" (James 3:1, authors' paraphrase). How do you handle pressure that comes with leadership?

1. Lean on Jesus when you reach your limit. The power of God always operates at the perimeter of our capacity. God cannot do the new thing when we camp out in our own personal safety zone. Faith has a tensile strength. It increases by being stretched to the limit. It grows by stress, relaxation, then being stretched again (1 Corinthians 2:1–5).

God will not force you from where you are now to that edge. That step is in your hands. "In a great house there are not only vessels of gold and silver, but also of wood and clay; some for honor and some for dishonor. Therefore if anyone cleanses himself from the latter, he will be a vessel for honor, sanctified and useful for the Master, prepared for every good work" (2 Timothy 2:20–21).

Revival, healing, faith, miracles, provision, and protection always involve a voluntary risk. You must move beyond doing only what is expected and asked of you to the realm of loving and doing more than required (Luke 17:6–10).

2. Hold on to your history of hope. What God did for you in the past gives you grounds to believe Him for the future. When the stress gets bad, remember His mercy and power before (Lamentations 3:21–23). Keep a journal or a diary, some written record of God's work in your life. Often God calls us to remember His greatness and goodness (Leviticus 26:45; Deuteronomy 8:18; Psalm 103:2; 106:4–5).

3. Call in the troops. Stress and trouble can open the door to ridding us of a budding independent spirit. Sometimes we live with hidden pride in our hearts, thinking we are adequate in ourselves to get the job done. A leader's ability can involve the strength to keep going when all others have given up, the confidence to stand alone. But our strength is usually our weakness. People don't identify with our strengths and our successes. They may admire them and envy them, but they cannot share in them.

What they can identify with is our weaknesses. Paul prayed for his people. He told them he was praying for them. He told them what he was praying for. Then he asked them to pray for him (1 Thessalonians 5:23–25). Peter said: "Obey your leaders and submit to their authority. They keep watch over you as men who must give an account. Obey them so that their work will be a joy, not a burden, for that would be of no advantage to you. *Pray for us.* We are sure that we have a clear conscience and desire to live honorably in every way" (Hebrews 13:17–18 NIV, emphasis added). Let stress draw you closer to others.

When you have done all of these and still there is a breakdown in unity, move on! Sometimes it comes down to people's opinion of what should be done or not done. Stay within the boundaries of common sense and God's Word and focus on what you have been called to do!

The CORE is called to bring not only redemption but reconciliation to all areas of life. Though sin is the most hurtful thing in the universe, God in Christ has given us the pattern and the power to bring healing to our divided world.

Blessed are those who are persecuted for righteousness' sake, for theirs is the kingdom of heaven. NKJV

Blessed are those who are persecuted because of righteousness, for theirs is the kingdom of heaven. NIV

GOD BLESSES THOSE WHO ARE PERSECUTED BECAUSE THEY LIVE FOR GOD, FOR THE KINGDOM OF HEAVEN IS THEIRS. NLT

Blessed are those who have been persecuted for the sake of righteousness, for theirs is the kingdom of heaven. NASB

You're blessed when your commitment to God provokes persecution. The persecution drives you even deeper into God's kingdom. THE MESSAGE

BLESSED ARE THOSE WHO ARE PERSECUTED FOR RIGHTEOUSNESS SAKE, FOR THEIRS IS THE KINGDOM OF HEAVEN. ESV

10

CORE POLARITY

DRAWING FIRE FOR BEING DIFFERENT

Blessed are those who are persecuted for righteousness' sake, for theirs is the kingdom of heaven.

MATTHEW 5:10

To follow Christ is to polarize everyone and everything around you. If you are CORE for Christ, you won't have to look for persecution. It will follow you! The number one reason you will experience persecution is that now that Christ is establishing His character in you, you have become a major threat to the devil and his authority structure. Don't worry; God is with you. Persecution is merely an endorsement that we are living a biblically normal life.

CORE Holiness

Jesus is heaven's best. He is the standard, the criterion, the plumb line for all people. To live like Jesus is the goal of every true child of God. But we are very aware that we live in a fallen world and that, compared to His life, in many ways ours are not all they ought to be. Even worse, when we really *do* start living for Him, it seems all hell can break loose around us.

God wants us to be like His Son, and He will stop at nothing less than that. We are to learn to live like Jesus did and be to others what Jesus is to us.

Two things are obvious from the Bible: God deeply loves what He made and is committed to its rescue, restoration, and redemption. He wants us in on this great mission of mercy. We are to go out into the world and preach the Gospel to every creature (Mark 16:15). We are to make disciples, preaching and teaching what He commands. In short, *God wants us to love the world like He does* (John 3:16).

The other thing that is plain from the Bible is that we are not to live like the "fallen" world or make it the ultimate object of our affection and devotion. If people love the world and the things that are in it, they don't really love the Father (1 John 2:15). *Love* the world like

Jesus, but don't *love* the world. What can this mean?

It is perfectly possible to do both. If Jesus both loved the world and pleased the Father in all He did and said, so can His CORE. For Jesus, loving the world meant reaching out to its lost, hurting people with new life, not buying into a culture or becoming attached to things. *Holiness,* or pleasing God by becoming like Him, is the subject of over nineteen hundred Bible verses. Being like God is core. So how do *we* do it today?

Think about the biblical story of Daniel and his three friends. Back in the days when the most powerful kingdom in human history had taken over the world, they, too, were put in a place where compromising holiness for the world was easy. They were just a few friends of God against an entire culture that not only did not worship the true God but actively promoted pagan devotion. Still, "Daniel purposed in his heart that he would not defile himself" (Daniel 1:8).

Faced with powerful temptations at all levels, Daniel and his three friends did much more than survive—they thrived! *At the end of it all, they ruled the nation.*

Standing Alone in Babylon

One terrible day in Babylon, Nebuchadnezzar built an idol of himself, an astonishing creation of gold that represented him and his power over all nations in history. He then pulled together the largest gathering in history. Everyone who could had to be there (Daniel 3:1–7).

Nebuchadnezzar wanted more than money, knowledge, and power. He wanted what rightfully belongs only to God, what all of Babylon's imitators have always wanted. He wanted the *undivided worship of the whole world.*

His incentive to absolute homage was a huge furnace at the base of the towering idol. At the sound of music, all of his subjects had to bow down before his statue. If you didn't bow, you burned.

Three young Hebrew men named Shadrach, Meshach, and Abednego faced the ultimate decision. Either Nebuchadnezzar or the God they loved and worshiped was to be lord of their lives. If they bowed with the crowd, they would not be touched or harmed. No one would care.

They could have taken the easy way out and just said to themselves, "We know what we *really* believe. What difference does it make if for once we just go along outwardly with everyone else? Why risk all God has given us with our power in this place for one external show? Nebuchadnezzar is our boss and our king, after all. He should be humored. We'd be fools not to play along. Let's just kneel to Babylon on the outside but stand up for God on the inside."

But the young men knew there comes a time when what you say you believe is put to the test. They had already determined they would not compromise their trust in God and that it must always show outwardly. They made the most difficult choice any person ever faces: to die rather than conform.

When the music played, everyone fell to their knees and worshiped. Everyone, that is, except Shadrach, Meshach, and Abednego. An outraged king demanded an answer, and they gave it to him.

> O Nebuchadnezzar, we do not need to defend ourselves before you in this matter. If we are thrown into the blazing furnace, the God we serve is able to save us from it, and he will rescue us.... But *even if he does not,* we want you to know, O king, that we will not serve your gods or worship the image of gold you have set up. (Daniel 3:16–18 NIV, emphasis added)

They knew what would happen to them if they stood against the crowd and the command of the king, but they stood anyway. They made the choice that changed the world. And the God who really rules showed Babylon who really was in charge. There was a fourth figure in the furnace with the young men, and His face looked like that of the Son of God (Daniel 3:25).

You can do three things when faced with a Babylonian culture:

1. Absorption: Surrender to it. This is not recommended. Babylon is headed for destruction. Line up with it and you will head where it is headed (Revelation 18:21–19:21).

2. Segregation: Separate yourself from it. Determine to cut yourself off from the whole culture around you. Don't talk to it, listen to it, or

ULTIMATE CORE

live in it. Become a religious recluse and build a wall to hide behind. Thousands of Christians do this, but this choice faces three difficulties:

- The world is everywhere around you, and it is hard to keep it out. Before World War II broke out, a futurist realized it was going to happen. He studied the world and moved to a place where his research determined he would be safe. He moved to Guadalcanal. A Canadian family in the 1970s became concerned with rumors of war and violence. They moved to a place where the father's detailed study of history showed they would be safe, arriving in the Falkland Islands just before Britain came out of retirement to declare war on Argentina.

- To segregate yourself, you'll need to give up witnessing. If you do this, no one will ever meet Jesus through you because you won't know anyone who doesn't know Him.

- You won't be able to read the whole Bible. In order to feel good about segregating yourself from the world, you'll have to avoid verses that ask you to hang out with the kind of people Jesus hung out with.

3. Invasion: The third option. Elton Trueblood, a Quaker writer, said that though the words Jesus used to describe our relationship to the world were short—like *salt, light, fire,* and *water*—they were words of penetration. *Salt* penetrates meat and helps keep it from spoiling. *Light* penetrates darkness and drives it back. *Fire* penetrates wood and makes it burn. *Water* penetrates the ground and makes it soft. God's method of dealing with the world around us is neither isolation nor submission but *penetration.* Jesus didn't come to take sides; He came to take over. And He said, "As the Father has sent Me, I also send you" (John 20:21).

Being Holy Without Living in a Hole

Jesus is at home in our world. It is His world. He made it. He created it. He owns it by right. Its current condition is not His desire or fault. People were never made to sin. Creation was never made to struggle. Culture was never supposed to be our enemy.

But with the fall of Adam and Eve and their separation from God, everything fell apart. What started with a bad choice got out of hand and became the runaway world we see today. Nature was hurt by people's sin. Marriage and family suffered. Society hurt; culture hurt. The arts, sciences, disciplines, and structures of our world are wormy apples. What originally was meant to reflect God's glory now is a support mechanism for sin.

The world is lovely, *but it is lost*. God could have abandoned this world, but He chose to love it. Jesus loved the world by identifying with it, joining it, and finally dying for it. The way *Jesus* deals with the world that is His by right is the way He calls *us* to deal with the world. We are to be insulated not isolated. We are to live *in* the world without being *of* the world. "Don't give your highest affection to your culture" is what He says to young radicals in Babylon. "It's beautiful but ultimately empty." When you keep Christ as the center of all you say, think, and do, God sends you out into His world to heal it in His name.

SURVIVING MODERN CULTURE

How does this work out in practice in our post-modern world? We must avoid what cultural analyst Os Guiness calls the twin dangers of our culture: *privatization* and *pluralization*.

1. Privatization is the temptation to keep all of our Christian principles and practices in a separate box from the rest of our lives. When we do this, we treat our love for Jesus as a private preference we practice by ourselves on our own time.

2. Pluralization is the temptation to accept so many choices and options that you cannot make any decisions. As options increase, our ability to commit ourselves decreases.

A Christian committed to truth will always face a tension between two extremes, two errors, two opposite temptations. How do you love the world as a missionary to it without being worldly? How do you "renounce" or give up the world without losing touch with it?

PRIVATIZATION: HOLINESS IN A HOLE V. GOD IS GOD OF ALL THE EARTH

- Temptation: To split our lives into the private religious and the public "real" world.
- Greatest fear: Bringing our private Christian world into the public arena.

- Greatest embarrassment: People who bring the secular world into our private spiritual retreat.

The first way the world can hurt you is to *isolate* you. Secular culture doesn't mind that you say you believe in Christ. Secular culture doesn't even mind that you say you love and worship Jesus. As far as it is concerned, you can do anything you like—in the privacy of your own "Christian reservation." The only thing the world resents is for you to say that what is best for *you* in Christ is also best for *everyone*. Non-Christian culture can tolerate anything except intolerance of wrong. You may love Jesus, but do it on your own. You can obey any command of Christ except those that involve the world God says He owns. Being a missionary is practically a crime—where it isn't already legally a crime. Yet Paul said:

> On the contrary, we put up with anything rather than hinder the gospel of Christ. . . . Yet when I preach the gospel, I cannot boast, for I am compelled to preach. Woe to me if I do not preach the gospel! If I preach voluntarily, I have a reward; if not voluntarily, I am simply discharging the trust committed to me. (1 Corinthians 9:13, 16 NIV)

CORE STAND: Openly serve Jesus and people in the public arena.

"Though I am free and belong to no man, I make myself a slave to everyone, to win as many as possible. To the Jews I became like a Jew, to win the Jews. . . . To the weak I became weak, to win the weak. I have become all things to all men so that by all possible means I might *save some*" (1 Corinthians 9:19–20, 22 NIV, emphasis added). Determine Christ will rule in *every area* of your life.

PLURALIZATION: LIVING WORLDLY IN THE WORLD V. NO OTHER GODS BEFORE GOD

- Temptation: To continuously multiply our options to avoid the clear divine choice.
- Greatest fear: Commitment and consecration that bring a firm *no*.
- Greatest embarrassment: Seeing someone who does not compromise.

The second way secular culture can hurt you is to *immerse* you. It gives you so many possibilities, options, alternatives! Os Guiness calls this plurality of choices "The Smorgasbord Factor." In a smorgasbord, you pay one price and eat all and anything you like. Faced with multiple alternatives, people in a smorgasbord do one of three things:

- Go straight to what they always get and eat only that. Fine, safe, okay—but *boring*.
- Load up a plate with everything in sight and keep going until they run out of plates. This is the *bulimic* option. Do it all. Try everything. Go for the gusto. It is also the formula for constipation: *Absorb all and eliminate nothing.*
- Endlessly circulate around the salad bar, unable to decide on anything until they starve to death. This is the *anorexic* option. Here, there are so many choices people can't actually commit to one thing and so are practically unable to order anything.

Faced with so many options in our world, what do you do? You may play it safe and stick with the known (boring). Or you might opt out of choices altogether (irresponsibility). You may decide to hang loose and do nothing. People call this *apathy,* but a rabbit trapped in the glare of headlights isn't either daring or dumb—just dazed. Far too many inputs flood into its brain for it to know what to do! Something like that happens when our multicultural, pluralistic, have-it-your-way society demands attention. The more choices, the less ability you have to choose anything.

So what should you do? *Decrease your options.* You don't need everything. Many things are worthless for a member of the CORE, and some are dangerous. Only a few things are crucial. On the large life level, it means doing what Jesus says is right and rejecting whatever is the opposite. On smaller levels, it means simplifying your alternatives in the light of the wisdom of God's Word and the gentle direction of His Spirit.

CORE STAND: Choose Christ over all that does not bow to His lordship.

Paul wrote, "I am not ashamed of the gospel of Christ for it is the power of God to salvation" (Romans 1:16). John said, "*Do not love the world or anything in the world.* If anyone loves the world, the love of the Father is not in him" (1 John 2:15 NIV, emphasis added). Determine to live like the Lord calls you to without compromise. Trust Him to reflect His core lordship of your life in all you do.

THREE KEYS TO STAYING CORE

1. We must be clean. Always turn away from all obvious sinful and harmful indulgences, confessing and being forgiven and cleansed from every sin. There is no true salvation without repentance from known sin at the point of conversion, but unless we take care, sin has a subtle way of working itself into our hearts again. God directs us to "cleanse ourselves from all filthiness of the flesh and spirit, perfecting holiness in the fear of God" (2 Corinthians 7:1). We have His promise: "If we confess our sins, He is faithful and just to forgive us our sins and to cleanse us from all unrighteousness" (1 John 1:9). Without this daily cleansing, our witness will be worthless. Isn't it highly embarrassing to plead with sinners to give up their sin when we are holding on to some as well? Salvation is salvation *from* sin, and our lives should show it.

2. We must be set to full speed. We cannot afford to waste time. Many things do not *seem* sinful, but we may find ourselves so hung up on them that time for Christ is crowded out. The *use* we make of our lives in Christ is largely up to us. Why does God seem to use some people so powerfully? There are all kinds of containers or vessels in a house—gold, silver, wood, and clay. If we are willing not to waste time on what is unworthy or unclean, our lives will be vessels for God that are set apart—highly useful for God's use (2 Timothy 2:21). We must put crash priority on the things that count most and conserve the cream of our time and energy for that special task Jesus has given us.

3. We must be Christ dependent. Jesus is our power, our strength, our wisdom. Jesus said, "Without Me you can do nothing" (John 15:5). Where can you get the wisdom necessary to lead souls out of darkness into light? Jesus holds all the treasures of wisdom and knowledge (Colossians 2:3). Hebrews 12:1–2 sums up the secret of spiritual victory: "Let us lay aside every weight and the sin which does so easily beset us and let us run the race lying before us looking to Jesus, the Author and Finisher of our faith!" This is simple to say, difficult to learn, and amazingly powerful. Jesus *himself* is the secret of power over sin. You can't fight sin in your own strength. The more you struggle with it, the *greater* its power grows over you. But Jesus can give you instant deliverance! Learn to extract power from your Savior. Look to Jesus!

BALANCE FOR DIGITAL DISCIPLES

The church often polarizes people into either/or camps. We move toward giving ourselves completely to the precious things of faith but lose our ability to speak to the world. Or we give ourselves to ministering to the world around us and lose our ability to be different from it. Pietists had a history of retreating from the world. Reformers were known for doing the exact opposite.

In Scripture two key offerings besides the sin offering reminded God's people of their debt to Him. One was the *burnt offering*. It was an offering of abandonment and devotion. Everything went up in smoke to God, and people kept nothing of it. The other was the *meat* or *meal* offering. This took care and preparation and was offered each day. When people gave the meal offering to God, they got to eat part of it, too. Like a prayer at mealtime, this offering brought the sense of God's presence in the ordinary.

- Pietistic—the burnt offering: Everything burns, everything goes up to God.
- Reform—the meal offering: Daily hospitality in sharing ordinary life with God.

Where is the balance of these two kinds of service to God? *There is no balance.* They are two poles that pull you in two different directions. You can no more find a middle ground in both than you can find a middle pole in a magnet. We *need* both. Without the burnt offering we can become so comfortable with the world that we become just like it and no longer affect it. Without the meal offering we become so unlike the world that we can no longer talk to it. God wants us *in* the world but not *of* the world, so we can *change* the world. We could put it like this: First, God takes us out of the world. Second, He takes the world out of us. Third, He sends us back into the world.

Understand that Jesus *wants* you to live in the world (John 17:15). Everything won't be made right at this instant. We are here in His mercy to do in His strength what we can. But understand also that He is coming back. What is not set right now will be set right then. And when He does come, there will be no time to choose to serve Him. There will be only the record of when and if we served Him with all of our heart, our soul, our mind, and our strength.

ULTIMATE CORE

CORE Wealth

The great idol set in contrast to devotion and service to God in the Bible is *mammon,* the god of money (Matthew 6:24). The parables of Jesus often deal with money. God begins with an individual and brings about change from the ground up. Change a *heart,* change a home; change a home, change a *city;* change a city, change a *nation.* As a CORE Christian, you must break with the world's poisonous pattern of finances.

The world's goal of financial independence is really a desire for freedom from concerns about paying for living expenses. The quickest way to your own freedom is not to earn more but to reduce or eliminate the spending you are concerned about.

Our problem is that we want certain things in our life. We call this our *lifestyle.* Many people's desire to be free from financial concern fights against a desire for a "better" lifestyle and instant gratification. Until you settle this war in your own heart, you will never know peace in money issues (James 4:1; 1 Peter 2:11).

The United States inscribed the words *In God We Trust* on its currency. For a CORE Christian, this can be our personal declaration of a scriptural agreement with God concerning money. We trust God. *He takes care of our financial needs* (Matthew 6:31–33). People who have truly learned to trust God for their income, spending, and sharing are full of power. God is our provider. *No decision in life should ever be made solely on the basis of money.* We can experience true wealth and biblical financial freedom.

THE MONEY YOU GET

Don't work only for money. In every situation, pray and look for a job or project you can love and really enjoy. You'll find that if you do work you enjoy, you will become good at it. You will be more apt to learn, more efficient, and more creatively productive—and perhaps make more income (Ecclesiastes 5:18; 1 Peter 4:10).

If you can, try to keep from being locked into a fixed salary. While a regular paycheck is nice, it makes it hard for God to bless you financially (Malachi 3:10–11; 2 Corinthians 9:6). God delights in rewarding those who work faithfully.

Acknowledge God's divine help by tithing. Scripture says it is *God* who gives us the power to get wealth. In Old Testament times, people honored Him by giving Him a tenth of their income. This went to help the priests, who kept the temple for both the Lord and the people. In the New Testament, that covenant is fulfilled in the church through Jesus, who makes us His kings and priests for His Body and His service. As God has blessed us, we should bring gifts and offerings to Him for His work and His people. Be part of a local expression of His church doing the will of God and entrust to others a portion of what He provides (Deuteronomy 8:18; Proverbs 3:9; Malachi 3:7–11).

THE MONEY YOU SPEND

Make a distinction between needs and desires. Paul told people he always tried to take care of his own needs (Acts 20:34–35). He told friends it was right to "command respect of the outside world, being dependent on nobody and having need of nothing" (1 Thessalonians 4:12 AMP).

Plan to spend less than you earn. When you spend more than your spendable income, you become a financial mission field and not a missionary. You are a *dependent* and not a provider, a *taker* and not a giver, *needy* rather than self-supporting. To stay in need of nothing but God, you should treat your spending seriously.

Consider the two main types of spending:

1. Needs (food, shelter, clothing)—things that sustain life

2. Desires (everything not essential to daily life)

Everyone has needs (Matthew 6:25; 1 Timothy 6:8). God provides for needs when He calls a person into a career. Your work should be a *calling* from God based on the talents, skills, and mind He gave you. For every career, He knows what financial needs are unique to that work. You have a right to ask God for the things you need to do that work; things useful for serving others as one of His workers (John 16:23–24; 1 John 5:14–15). These may be anything from money for school or training to an airplane for an airline. Prayerful planning should control your spending.

Put a postcard on your mirror. Write on it these words: *You can spend it only once.* There are always more things to buy than there is money to buy them. Once money comes in, it can be spent only once. Learn to listen to the "check" of the Holy Spirit. Make sure you know what God wants done with the money He sends. God wants us to live within our income. If we spend too much on one thing, we may short-change His intentions for His provision.

Think about the *cost per use* of what you think you need. Count the *real* cost. If you buy a CD for fifteen dollars and you like only one song on it, you paid full price for just one song. If you listen to it only once, your cost per use is fifteen dollars. If you listen to it a hundred times, your cost per use is fifteen cents. Since you can spend money only once, plan to fulfill your needs with low-cost-per-use items. The money He provides for you will then go a lot further.

The Money You Save

The world will always tempt you to buy things of little or no essential need. If you never discipline your money use, you will never have extra funds to share with others in need. Beyond your real needs, you should exercise financial self-control. God may have definite plans for "excess" money that flows through your hands. Don't think for a minute it was given to you to use all on yourself (James 4:3). Trust God to give you power to say no to the "I wants" of the world (2 Timothy 3:1–5; Titus 2:11–12; 1 John 2:15–17).

Saving

Don't spend all of your income. You can reasonably anticipate some future needs: car replacements, sports gear, recreation, and repairs. One day you might even live to be old and less able to work productively! You will still have needs. Open a savings account and put some portion of every year's income in it; it is part of God's provision for future needs (Proverbs 6:6–8; 13:11; 21:20).

Debt

Christians have no option but to pay what they have promised. You must keep your word (Matthew 5:37). To spend more than you earn, you have to draw either from savings or borrow. You assume when you spend more than you earn that tomorrow you will earn more than you spend. *Bad move.* You don't know what will happen tomorrow. Only God knows that (James 4:13–16). You can't spend more than you earn unless you or someone else has previously saved. If you are in debt, pay it all back, in installments if necessary.

If you borrow to buy, it always costs you more than if you pay cash. The additional cost is called interest. Borrowing also binds you. When you borrow, the lender is either your partner or your master (Proverbs 22:7). A lender generally is a silent partner in your financial life until you fall behind in your promise to pay. You may catch yourself doing the credit-card shuffle, compounding the growth of your debt with high interest. The person who is in debt *tends to go deeper into debt.*

Each time you pull out a credit card, remember you are saying, "I promise to pay!" Rethink your purchase. If you don't have cash now to buy, what makes you think you are going to have cash later to pay the bill? If you carry plastic for convenience, don't buy on impulse. You want to spend less than your income, not go deeper into debt.

Money for Others

A person who trusts God will not be concerned about his or her future financial needs. If you see a friend in financial need, do what you can to help. Always think big when it comes to creating income in excess of your own needs that you can give away to bless others (2 Corinthians 8:12–15). God never used a man or woman to change the world who was not generous or giving.

It is very easy for people with wealth to place their trust in their money instead of in God. But money can be stolen, taken by government, or seem to evaporate in the inflating prices of things. Don't trust in it.

If God blesses you with a lot of money, He will require much more of you. Be generous, ready always to share. Your commission is to disciple and evangelize; this also takes money. Part of the purpose of Christian business is to finance this activity. This doesn't mean to throw your common sense out the window. Check out the cause; if it is worthwhile, give to it (1 Timothy 6:17–19). *"He is no fool who gives what he cannot keep to gain what he cannot lose"* (Jim Elliot, martyred missionary to the Aucas).

The CORE Faces Fire

"Martyrs die because they refuse to deny the Truth, they are unwilling to force their ways upon others, and they are unwilling to fight back when fighting back would deny the Love they are trying to show those hurting them" (*Jesus Freaks,* Vol. II, dc talk).

Jesus said that in this world you will have persecution (Luke 21:11–13). In the years since He himself was taken by cruel hands and nailed to a tree to die for Who He was and what He said, nearly *seventy million* children of His kingdom have followed Him in martyrdom. Many more will follow in this third millennium. Some of those who kill God's CORE follow other religions. Christians have even died at the hands of those who profess to follow the One Who did not come to judge the world but save it. But by far the greatest persecution of all comes from governments that enshrine in their harsh rule their hatred and rejection of God in Christ (*World Christian Trends, AD 30–AD 2200,* David B. Barrett and Todd M. Johnson).

Every nation has some kind of state religion. That "religion" may be secular humanism, atheism, a major world religion like Islam, Hinduism, or Buddhism, or even some kind of supposed Christian consensus. This national religion may not be enforced by rules. It may be no more than a common pressure on all to conform, but the idea of a nation without a belief system is as big a myth as that of objective journalism. In the last analysis, every martyred Christian dies as a result of the hatred of a religion opposed to Christ. When the truth of Jesus threatens a national religion, those who stand for Him may often be targets for bigotry, fear, and hatred. Invariably, persecution backfires. It serves only to make the church stronger, deeper, purer.

Richard Wurmbrand, the founder of Voice of the Martyrs, says,

> What encourages us to preach the gospel in captive nations is that there those who become Christians are full of love and zeal. . . . Persecution has always produced a better Christian—a witnessing Christian, a soul-winning Christian. . . . In a letter smuggled out secretly, the underground church said, "We don't pray to be better Christians, but that we may be the only kind of Christians God means us to be."

Only a national spiritual awakening and subsequent reformation can affect the laws and morals that guide a nation back to the true God. As nations come under His dealings and judgments, CORE Christians in them are often isolated, rejected, and persecuted.

Whenever possible you must use the existing laws of the land to guide your witness. You may have specific rights under the law that those who oppose your stand either do not know or ignore. Don't be afraid to use good laws to support your stand for Christ (Acts 16:37–40; 19:24–41; Romans 13:3–8). But remember that such rights are fragile and depend only on the level of true, biblical wisdom (law) and love (obedience) that exists in the country at the time. People change. Nations revive or decay. In all circumstances, Christian witness will go on till Jesus comes (Matthew 24:14; 28:18–20; Mark 16:15–20).

WHEN THE LAW IS AGAINST YOU

In some nations you will run into laws that seek to limit, block, or stop your speaking out or even meeting for Jesus. Christians through the centuries have faced the tough choices of what to do when human law conflicts with God's commands. Sometimes obeying what God says means having to break a bad man-made law (Acts 5:25–29). In every case, those who love God do not flinch from the consequences, even if it means capital punishment (Acts 4:13–31; 5:17–42).

Daniel faced exactly this in the den of lions. Shadrach, Meshach, and Abednego faced it in the fiery furnace. Stephen, the first Christian martyr, was stoned to death. James, the brother of Jesus, was killed by the sword. All of the disciples except John died a violent death at the hands of arrogant or angry governments—and even John was tortured in boiling oil. Early Christians were flogged, imprisoned, stoned, crucified. Christians in some parts of the world today face similar tortures or deaths for their beliefs. *Jesus never said it would be easy. Jesus never said it wouldn't cost.*

More Christians died for Jesus in the twentieth century than in all the others put together. *The blood of the martyrs is the seed of the church.*

FACING THE ULTIMATE TEST

"All men die. Not all men truly live" (William Wallace in *Braveheart*).

Daniel and his three friends, Shadrach, Meshach, and Abednego, were each put to the ultimate test: Deny God or die. Shadrach, Meshach, and Abednego faced the fiery furnace. Daniel had the den of lions. The Son of God came into the place of terror with each of them.

How will you face the ultimate test? God has not promised us that we will not die. All of us die, some of us sooner than others. The difference in death for a Christian and someone who is not is that a Christian is ready to meet Jesus. Death for you as a child of God is to fall asleep in His arms and awake in the other world, alive forever beyond the power of pain, safe forever from all suffering (1 Thessalonians 4:13; 1 Corinthians 15:49–55).

Daniel and his friends knew the cost of loving God and staying true to Him. Faced with the horror of agonizing death, they did not flinch or turn back. In both situations, they experienced wonderful supernatural intervention. God showed up in a way that made even the king worship. God can do it again. Miracles still happen. But remember the "if not" (Daniel 3:18): Miracles are exceptions to consequence.

From Daniel you can learn three important lessons to draw on if someday you have to face your own "den of lions":

1. *Innocence:* Keep your heart pure. When Daniel came out of the den, he said God shut the lions' mouths because he was "found innocent before Him." Don't ever go into a lions' den without a clean heart. Repent of all known sin. When Daniel was lowered into that pit he knew only one thing: His heart was right with God (Daniel 6:22; see also Psalm 24:3–5; 51:6–13; Matthew 5:8).

2. *Forgiveness:* Even though the king's own foolishness and pride created this death sentence for Daniel, Daniel held no grudges. He responded without cursing the king, without bitterness or threats of divine judgment. Daniel went to the lions holding nothing against his executors. The early Christians who also faced lions said, "These lions are not our enemies. They are our friends. They will usher us into the presence of God." Go into the den fully forgiving those who have done you wrong (Daniel 6:22; Luke 23:34; Acts 7:59–60).

3. *Trust in the Lord:* The bottom line for every den of lions is "Trust God or die." For some it will be "Trust God and die." Whatever the outcome, when you face your crisis, you must go trusting in nothing or no one except the living God. "Daniel was taken up out of the den, and no injury whatever was found on him, because he believed in his God" (Daniel 6:23; see also Psalm 37:39–40; 118:5–9; 91:1–2).

Hast thou no scar?
No wound? No scar?
Yet, as the Master shall the servant be,
And pierced are the feet that follow Me;
But thine are whole. Can he have followed far
Who has no wound nor scar?
—Amy Carmichael

Get used to persecution. Face it with the strength only God can give. It will come to the CORE as it has come to every real Christian in history.

Not only that—count yourselves blessed every time people put you down or throw you out or speak lies about you to discredit me. What it means is that the truth is too close for comfort and they are uncomfortable. THE MESSAGE

BLESSED ARE YOU WHEN THEY REVILE AND PERSECUTE YOU, AND SAY ALL KINDS OF EVIL AGAINST YOU FALSELY FOR MY SAKE. NKJV

Blessed are you when people insult you, persecute you and falsely say all kinds of evil against you because of me. NIV

God blesses you when you are mocked and persecuted and lied about because you are my followers. NLT

BLESSED ARE YOU WHEN PEOPLE INSULT YOU AND PERSECUTE YOU, AND FALSELY SAY ALL KINDS OF EVIL AGAINST YOU BECAUSE OF ME. NASB

Blessed are you when others revile you and persecute you and utter all kinds of evil against you falsely on my account. ESV

11

CORE
PRESENCE

EING WHO GOD CALLS YOU TO BE

Blessed are you when

they revile and

persecute you, and say

all kinds of evil against

you falsely for My sake.

MATTHEW 5:11

Jesus never told us it would be easy to be His friends; just that His presence and friendship are always with His CORE. Knowing who God has created us to be brings a sense of great peace and joy even in the middle of persecution. The church has always found herself in times when it is tough to be a Christian, yet if we are true to who we are in and because of Jesus, we can enjoy genuine joy in any circumstance.

Still, how should we act in a world where people criticize or cut us down because we belong to Christ? The call of the Gospel is to take God's love and care to people who do exactly that.

All of us are going to face rejection. It does not have to be from someone we know dislikes us; it can also come from our family and former friends. Mark it down: If you live a godly life, some people will hate and curse you. We can't help or do anything about being hated for that reason, but we can give attention to being criticized or rejected for the wrong reason. There is nothing more easily misunderstood than the church. Jesus said we would be blessed if we are persecuted for doing right, but there is no blessing in being hated for being religiously weird, wrong, or ignorant. We need to watch out for problems like these.

True to the CORE: Being Real

But God has chosen the foolish things of the world to put to shame the wise, and God has chosen the weak things of the world to put to shame the things which are mighty ... that no flesh should glory in His presence. (1 Corinthians 1:27, 29)

Those members of the body which seem to be weaker are necessary. And those *members* of the body which we think to be less honorable, on these we bestow greater honor. (1 Corinthians 12:22–23, emphasis added)

The worst kind of weirdness is religious hypocrisy. It lies behind more excuses for hatred toward God than any kind of false idolatry. People who claim to be spiritual but who live in a way that brings dishonor to God's name provide a platform for persecution that seems fully justifiable to the world. The great antidote to being attacked for reasons God cannot excuse is to be the real person He calls you to be.

THE PROBLEM OF PRIDE

What is pride? It is thinking we can act apart from God. It is saying we don't need Him in all we do. It is acting as if no one in the universe is more important than we are. At the most basic level, it is the *refusal to acknowledge who we actually are in the eyes of God.*

Pride appears in subtle ways. There are essentially two kinds: the pride of the "big wheel" and the pride of the "worm." The first is the most obvious. It shows in the way people look, dress, or speak. God *hates* a proud look (Proverbs 6:16–17). It can raise its ugly head in business, athletic, or social life. The worst variety of this pride is the most widespread, because it goes around in Christian clothes. We can preach on the pride of race, face, and place, but the most deceitful is pride of *grace.* Unfortunately, you do not have to look far to spot it in most churches.

One form of this pride attempts to trade on God's *goodness.* It involves "reminding" Him of how much you have done for Him in the past. You suggest to your conscience that since you have accomplished some great things for God, you are entitled to a short moral holiday. Don't fool yourself. Do you honestly think our holy Lord can simply *overlook* calculated sin, especially on the basis of how much you may have done? (Ezekiel 18:24). Too often His children fall into sin right after they have done some really significant work for Him. Grace cannot be stored up so you can sin a little thanks to your reputation. The closer you get to God, the more carefully you must guard your life, because He will deal with you *more* severely for failure than someone with less spiritual understanding (James 3:1). He cannot balance our present sin against past faithfulness. Neither His faithfulness nor His love are altered by our actions if we do wrong: He will hold us accountable, no matter how good our spiritual reputation. Paul counted his tremendous accomplishments as *loss* (Philippians 3:7-9). Peter lived for today and the day (2 Peter 3:10-14) when Christ will return, forgetting the past. "No one," said Jesus, "who puts his hand to the plow and looks back is fit for the kingdom of God" (Luke 9:62 ESV).

Self-dependence is another common pride sin. As long as there is someone bigger and better, the person with "big wheel" pride can never be content; they appear to forget that God is always going to be infinitely greater than any person can ever be. People who want to be king of their own universe never want to meet God because it would mean they have to answer for their false estimates of their own importance.

On the other hand, overdone *self-condemnation* can be pride, too. This is pride pretending to be humility. Words like, "Oh, I would never consider myself to be a saint!" or "I am too unworthy to work for God" can be symptoms of spiritual *disease*.

This pride of the "worm" devalues what God says we are worth in *His* eyes. He cares for us regardless of our lack of greatness because He made us and knows what we can be in His hands. Yes, if we compare ourselves to His greatness, we will feel very small and insignificant, like a worm in contrast to His infinite power and glory (Job 25:4-6; Isaiah 41:14). But remember that God made us in His own image and then himself became human. And the Lord Jesus has called us not just servants but *friends* (Luke 12:4; John 15:13-15). We are in His royal family (John 1:12; 2 Corinthians 6:18; Galatians 4:6; Hebrews 2:10-11) and inherit all the riches of His family privileges (Ephesians 2:4-7).

Many people are unaware there *is* a "pride of the worm." But it is this lack of holy boldness and failure to grasp the hand of God that holds back God's kingdom. If He saves, calls, and equips us for a task, we *can* do it! We cannot stand on the sidelines murmuring sanctimonious things about being unworthy when Christ has given His army standing orders to fight for righteousness. Too much self-pity disguises itself as humility. God values each one of us. What you as *one* can do in faithfulness is just as important to Him as the work of any saint. We must stop thinking of our limits and start thinking about His resources. The Lord Jesus was as dependent on His Father's power when He walked the earth as you and I are now (John 5:17–47). He simply did His work, giving glory to His Father (John 12:26, 28). *True humility forgets self, not debases it.* People focused on Christ stop being self-conscious and start being God-conscious. *This* is true humility: being willing to be known and accepted for what you really are in the sight of the Lord.

Satan uses both extremes of pride in his attacks on Christians. If he cannot puff you up, he will try to push you down. He will alternate thrusts of great elation or great depression following spiritual victories or failures. Watch out for these two kinds of pride, *recognize* them for what they are, and *resist* them. Avoid both extremes by thinking of yourself as a forgiven child of God. And remember, too, the secret to dealing with self is not to wrestle with it but to become so caught up in the Lord Jesus and His work that you forget it.

THE PROBLEM OF MASKS

Almost everyone wears a mask to cover the real us—our true inner souls. Behind many smiles lie defeat, discouragement, and despair. We live in a pretend world. Daily, people practice their smiles in the mirror and go out to live with other masked people. It often seems like no one understands us and our problems, since most everyone we meet seems to live a relaxed life. Not seeing anyone with problems like ours, we cover the lines of guilt and worry, fix our smile up carefully again, and go back to pretending. From childhood we are taught to be unreal, to look as if we are happy when we aren't, to laugh when we feel like crying, to act as if nothing has happened when we are hurt, to carefully cover the tears and go on with the business of living again. But it is this kind of automatic deceit that makes it hard for God to get through to us.

When Jesus came, He wore no mask. He was *exactly* what He

seemed to be. People came to Him, pretending, and found they couldn't fool Him! He looked into their souls and showed them without saying that He understood why they wore their masks. Gently, He helped them take them off, and the people behind them saw light as they faced the world honestly for the first time. When Paul saw himself as God saw him, he said, "I am chief of sinners" (1 Timothy 1:15, authors' paraphrase).

God wants to show you who you are. It may take Him a long time, but He will stop at nothing short of perfection once you let Him have your life. But He can't start until you know the *truth* about yourself— "Nothing good lives in me!" (Psalm 53:3; Romans 7:18 NIV). All our righteousness rests in our relationship to Him. Cut off from Jesus, we would all go down the tubes. We are like ugly ducklings wanting to be something other than what we are. Until we despair of ever changing ourselves, God cannot make us into beautiful swans.

Taking off the mask can be frightening and often more than a little painful. But when we learn to do this together before God, we take a giant step to family unity as His children. Many personal problems grow out of people failing to believe they are what they actually are. Check your life for these:

1. SELF-CONSCIOUSNESS

"Nobody wants me; nobody likes me; nobody accepts me."

Afraid of meeting others? The self-consciousness we sometimes call shyness is really only another form of *pride*. Isn't it true that our real fear of meeting people is primarily worry about what they may think of us or that we will not measure up to their standards? Signals like this show you have not yet accepted yourself as God made you. The less you think about what others think of you, the more power and freedom you can have in your life as you walk before your Father's eyes.

2. CONCERN FOR LOOKS

"I hate the way I look—my hair, clothes, face, etc."

Think about how many more great needs would be met if God's people spent as much time on their hearts as they do their looks! If you could change the way you look, would you? You can! Your looks reflect the state of your heart. When it is honest and free from guilt, your face will be lit with the clear radiance of God. A person who is truly beautiful *inside* will be attractive *outside*. Take care of the inside and the outward appearance will take care of itself (Romans 12:1–2; 2 Corinthians 3:18; 1 Timothy 2:9–10).

3. CRAZY FOR SPIRITUALITY

"Nobody really understands me and God."

Do you know people who seem to try *too* hard to be Christians? They appear intent on being super-holy, want only to do spiritual things, or act as God's judge of the sins of the world. Yet those who know them smell a rat. Their passion doesn't ring true, and the fruit of the Spirit is strangely absent from their lives. Wrapped up in themselves, their hyper-spirituality is often a religious shell covering a desperate need to be accepted.

4. CRITICAL SPIRIT

"Nothing I do turns out right!"

Continual self-criticism can be a sign you have not taken your proper place in God's family as one who belongs to Him. Such criticism can lash out against others in envy, jealousy, or backbiting, or in the frustrating civil war of your own life. Perhaps you want to be like someone else you admire but can't, or you wish someone would think you are something you know you're not. When you think like this, you actually *blame* God. If you hate yourself for what God intended you to be, you will always feel like a failure.

Why do you think Jesus asks people to confess their sin? It is certainly not because He doesn't see or notice it. It is because *we* need to see it. It is because unless we take responsibility for what we are and what we have done, we can never be right before Him and others.

You are what you are. There is no use pretending differently. Once you truly accept yourself for who you are, frustration will vanish and you'll be ready to be molded into all God intends you to be (Psalm 73:26). Your life can be clean, honest, and glowing with His power.

THE PROBLEM OF LONELINESS

Being alone doesn't necessarily need to be a time of depression. If we think of being alone as an opportunity to leave old things in the past and prepare to make new friends, it can seem easier. Any sense of loneliness that we may have can ultimately be overcome in prayer, as we grow closer in our relationship to God. You can use times of feeling alone to pour out your heart to Jesus. As a boy, King David felt lonely and rejected. Often alone with no one but his sheep, David learned friendship with God. He said, "When my father and my mother forsake me, then the LORD will take care of me" (Psalm 27:10). God chose David out of all Israel to make him its greatest king. God even called him "a man after My own heart" (Acts 13:22).

Yet extended times of aloneness are rarely from God, who is himself a community of Persons. He sets the solitary in families (Psalm 68:6), and His will is that we have friends. We cannot love our neighbor if we have no neighbors.

The Bible says that when we show ourselves friendly, we will usually be befriended (Proverbs 18:24). While not always the case, it at least opens the door for others to find out about us. Maybe you are thinking that you don't *want* friends right now. Well, the desire for friendship must exist in order for you to conquer loneliness. God must heal your heart of hurt from bad friendships and broken relationships before you can be free to start again.

Sometimes someone may treat you as if you are annoying, obnoxious, threatening, timid, or just plain boring. You may not be any of those things at all, but it hurts when no one seems to want you around. If you are snubbed or rejected by those you try to know better, take it bravely. Not even Jesus was loved by everybody. He said, "If they persecuted Me, they also will persecute you" (John 15:19–20).

Sometimes people don't like us because we try too hard, or we just don't fit their circle of interests and goals. Take such rejections with a grain of salt. Not all of your loneliness has a spiritual root. Learn from a snub. Maybe there is something you can change. A rejection that you learn from now may open a door later to touch many more people for the Lord. Ask Him to show you your low points or things that you should change in order to relate to others better. You can even ask people you would like to get to know what they don't like about you. Say something like this: "Look, I like you. I know there's a lot in my life that I need to know to be a better person, and I'm sure you can see things I can change. Is there something I could do differently?" There is nothing wrong with being to the point. Just keep in mind others' feelings and the fact they have problems, too.

CORE SOLITUDE

The ability to stand alone is core to Christian life. God seeks out those who dare walk alone. If the willingness to stand alone is a mark of our own true conviction, the willingness to walk alone is a test of our own true sense of worth. But the willingness to live alone is an even greater gift. Few can live like that and sacrifice the provision of God for friendships and family. Yet there comes a time in any CORE life when you may feel His call to do just that for a time. Some of the greatest spiritual times of your life will come when you are all alone with God. No great man or woman of God ever lived without learning to seek God in silence. Don't despise the discipline of aloneness.

MAKING FRIENDS WITH CHRIST'S FRIENDS

Often we are so afraid of rejection from the people we desire friendship with that we build up a defensive wall. We then end up cutting ourselves off from the very people we desire friendship from.

Don't be afraid of trying and failing. We all make mistakes in this life, but learning is what it's all about. Give both yourself and the people you want to get to know better a chance.

Perhaps you have had trouble making friends before. You may be shy or feel that people won't like you. It is true that some people in the world will *never* like you. If you live for Jesus, there will be runaways from God's love who will not want to know you too well. You will meet bitter people who have been hurt and do not trust anyone. No, Christians can't expect to be popular with everyone, but Jesus had many friends. He was a supremely friendly, understanding person. Anyone could come to Him and always be sure of a welcome.

The world has a strange idea of Christians. The very word is often a cold shoulder. They think of us in terms of being too weird, intolerant of other views or faiths, unable to enjoy a little "fun" in life. Non-Christians often create a miserable picture of Christianity. But remember, those reasons are not why the Pharisees criticized Jesus. They said He was the "friend of tax collectors and sinners" (Luke 7:34). In other words, *sinners liked Him too much.* No one ever came to Him with a need and was not made to feel welcome. Jesus had a knack of mixing with people and building them up even when He was brushing away their wrong.

Every disciple of Jesus must be a friend to all. If we really love God, we love the One who loved the world—and the world means *everyone.*

Of course, your closest friends will be Christ's friends. That small, core group of people we enjoy sharing our deepest feelings and hopes with are those with whom we can really have fellowship. We can help one another grow spiritually by joining our efforts with theirs on some common task for God. We can expect them to lovingly show us if we are doing something wrong, and they expect us to do the same. This inner circle will be close to our hearts, and we must make sure they are Christ's friends.

The Lord Jesus gave us an interesting principle. He said, "If two of you agree on earth concerning anything that they ask, it will be done for them by My Father in heaven" (Matthew 18:19). The phrase "two or three" that follows in Matthew 18:20 is important. Unity in prayer comes only through a close, common bond of understanding, affection, and friendship. Jesus put His team of disciples together on that basis. Your closest friends should be people of similar likings and interests, people who think like you do in most situations. They should also have a similar level of spiritual growth in Jesus. They should be ones with whom you can share new discoveries of the work and Word of God in your life.

When we walk together with God, under His control, doing a common task He has given to us, we will really begin to know the joys of divine friendship. With friends that are Christ's friends, we can know God's love among us every day.

THE PROBLEM OF OPPRESSION

"Heathen kings lord it over them, and those in authority over them are called benefactors. But it *shall not be so with you;* rather the greatest among you must become like the youngest and the leader like one who serves" (Luke 22:24–27; see also 12:37).

Oppression is when someone assumes the unjustified right to lord it over others by means of power, wealth, or education. Oppression can be legally enforced to carry out domination over others and public devaluing and diminishing of their lives. Dictatorial governments do it to citizens, cynical teachers do it to students, pastors do it to their congregations, parents or older brothers or sisters do it in our own homes, and churches have done it to control people they should have served. Even Christians do it when we try to wrongly use the Word of God as if it is *our* sword and not the sword of the Spirit.

Powers, principalities, and dominions are structures given originally by God to bring honor to Him and blessing to His world (Romans 13:1; Colossians 1:16). But the Bible teaches us that, in our fallen world, many have become instruments of hurt instead (Romans 8:38–39; Ephesians 6:12). Even the things we look to most often to tell us what is success—wealth, education, and power—can become avenues of arrogance.

"Let not the wise man glory in his wisdom, let not the mighty man glory in his might, nor let the rich man glory in his riches; but let him who glories glory in this, that he understands and knows Me, that I am the LORD, exercising lovingkindness, judgment, and righteousness in the earth. For in these I delight" (Jeremiah 9:23–24). From this passage, we learn a few things:

- Knowledge without God leads to arrogance (1 Samuel 2:3; Romans 1:21; 1 Corinthians 1:20).
- Wealth without God leads to unrighteousness (Luke 16:11; 1 Timothy 6:9–10).
- Power without God leads to injustice (Luke 16:10; Proverbs 28:8).

God, the most wonderfully wise being in the universe, is full of lovingkindness (Psalm 63:3). God, the richest being in the universe, is utterly true and righteous (Psalm 50:10; Revelation 16:7). And God, the most powerful being in the universe, is completely just in all of His dealings (Isaiah 61:7-8).

Oppression can function in every life system to create human or demonic dominion. These structures of domination create an atmosphere of arrogance, accusation, legality, and mockery to create strongholds of anger, slavery, and hopelessness. The weapons of hell are accusation, bondage, and despair, but evil cannot break evil. "The weapons of our warfare are not carnal but mighty in God for pulling down strongholds" (2 Corinthians 10:4).

God's heart is utterly unlike the heart of a fallen creature. He never uses His powers unjustly. God loves His enemies. He is kind to those who do not deserve it. He is gracious to pests, kindly listens to what He already knows, and serves and ministers to those who ought to be ministering to and serving Him. God loved Adam and Eve just as much after they sinned as He did before. God does not reference His responses to our behavior but to His own unchanging character. He does not want anyone to die but wants all to repent. He may change His actions or mind, but He will never change His purpose or His love. He is faithful and true.

If we want to be like God, we should strive to seek not titles but blessings, not status but honor. The kingdom belongs to the poor in spirit, the merciful obtain mercy, and the meek inherit the earth.

HOW JESUS DEALT WITH OPPRESSION

How did Jesus engage the oppressive powers of our world?

Truth

The root of oppression always rests in a lie. It draws power from false presuppositions and has to hide its real history. Jesus dealt with oppression by exposing it with the truth of who He was and what He said. He reminded those who attacked Him of what the same lies they tried to live by had done to people before them. Christ's enemies watched Him and listened and came back empty-handed. "No man ever spoke like this Man!" (John 7:46). When dealing with oppression, stick with Bible truth and the record of history.

Humor

Oppressive powers are almost always humorless, arrogant, and proud. True humor flows from truth and humility and sees the ridiculousness of posturing and imposition. Jesus sometimes exposed haughty lies with gentle, redemptive ridicule (Luke 6:43; Matthew 5:38–45; 16:1–4). Keep your God-given ability to see and smile.

Nonviolence

The most pervasive and reinforced lie in all human history is that the answer to violent wrong is a *more* violent right, the myth of "redemptive violence." It is *never right* to answer evil in the same way. Jesus, who could call on ten thousand angels to help Him, did not call them at the cross. He who could still the wind continually resisted evil in a nonviolent, righteous way (Matthew 26:52; 1 Peter 2:23).

Love

Jesus never shamed, belittled, or despised people. He loved His enemies and did good even to those who used Him. Perfect love casts out all fear (1 John 4:18).

Purity

Entrenched evil in people or systems uses immorality to guard its boundaries on all levels. Nothing challenges an oppressive power more foundationally than the light cast in the darkness by a holy life. The best way to convict of evil is to live a contrasting life that is pure and unselfish. Jesus had no ulterior motives in loving people.

Acceptance

Evil loves rules, mysterious and complex structures, and keeping others at a distance. Oppressive powers promote hierarchy, flourish in bureaucracy, and thrive in impersonality. Jesus penetrated those powers at every level of contact. He lived better than by the rules and sent His followers to live and minister like innocent, trusting, caring, welcoming children. Stay childlike and simple.

Fearlessness

Fear maintains oppression. Evil keeps order through legal enforcement; it uses hope and fear, threat and bribe, to make people obey. Jesus called people to die to a self-centered way of life. You cannot threaten or bribe those who are dead to themselves and live only for Christ. Conscious of His origin and destiny and moved by love, Jesus lived unafraid. The CORE who follow Him can draw on His grace to do the same.

Substitution

When faced with the ultimate threat, Jesus took it on himself. Like a bodyguard, He took the bullet meant for us. "Greater love has no one than this, than to lay down one's life for his friends" (John 15:13). "For a good man someone would even dare to die. But God demonstrates His own love toward us, in that while we were still sinners, Christ died for us" (Romans 5:7–8).

When the Son of God came to His own creation, "He came to His own, and His own did not receive Him" (John 1:11). This is one of the saddest records in history. Not even Jesus' parents understood Him. Though He did more for people in His short life than any other person in human history, many still treated Him with criticism and even curses. In the end, He was betrayed by a friend and abandoned by almost all of His followers. Jesus could have cried from the cross, "That's it! I can't take this any longer. Angel legions three, four, and five, this is it. End the world!"

He could have said it, but He didn't. Instead He said, "Father, forgive them, for they do not know what they do" (Luke 23:34).

When the world hurts you, stand with Jesus and do and say what He did. Be strong in your hour of need and He will not fail you. When the world hurts you, it is core to forgive. That is the only way to be free from its power.

A CORE TASK: BREAKING THE POWER OF OPPRESSION

True followers of Jesus are called to break the power of oppression in His name, by the power of His Spirit, according to His Word, and because of His blood (Revelation 12:11). We are authorized ambassadors of the rightful King of Kings, called to declare the truth of His righteous law. We are called to fight, but not with the same weapons as the oppressive powers of this world. "We do not wrestle against flesh and blood, but against principalities, against powers" (Ephesians 6:12). We must *minister in the opposite spirit* to defeat oppressive powers (Matthew 10:7–42). If we try to fight evil in the same spirit, we will become oppressors ourselves.

There are many unredeemed, unrighteous, and unreconciled structures in areas of tradition or acceptance all over the world. We see human and demonic oppression in relationships between men and women, parent and child, employer and employee, old and young, rich and poor, tradition and innovation. It can even be reinforced by God-unauthorized traditions found even in His house: "clergy/laity" (Matthew 23:8: "you are all brothers"), "pulpit/pew" (1 Corinthians 3:5), and "church/parachurch" (1 Corinthians 3:5–10).

It was not this way in the beginning. The task of His church has

ULTIMATE CORE

always been to engage the powers of oppression.

Starting in our own hearts and homes, the Gospel brings true life, freedom, and redemption to the fallen, sinful structures of the world (Ephesians 4:1–16). It is part of the task of the CORE to share this freedom and redemption with a hurting, fearful world.

We will never find a verse in Scripture that calls the CORE to be popular with the general populace, nor to look for favor in a fallen world that rarely honors its Maker. Misused, mistreated, and misunderstood we may be, but our Leader still commands us to seek our world's greatest good. To befriend the Lord is to be a friend to all and to seek their highest happiness for His sake. As poet John Masefield said, "I knew that Christ had given me birth / to brother all the souls of earth." That, to the CORE, is true joy.

Be happy about it! Be very glad! For a great reward awaits you in heaven. And remember, the ancient prophets were persecuted, too. NLT

You can be glad when that happens— give a cheer, even!—for though they don't like it, I do! And all heaven applauds. And know that you are in good company. My prophets and witnesses have always gotten into this kind of trouble. THE MESSAGE

Rejoice and be glad, for your reward in heaven is great; for in the same way they persecuted the prophets who were before you. NASB

REJOICE AND BE GLAD, FOR YOUR REWARD IS GREAT IN HEAVEN, FOR SO THEY PERSECUTED THE PROPHETS WHO WERE BEFORE YOU. ESV

Rejoice and be exceedingly glad, for great your reward in heaven, for so they persecuted the prophets who were before you. NKJV

Rejoice and be glad, because great is your reward in heaven, for in the same way they persecuted the prophets who were before you. NIV

CORE
WORSHIP

THE SECRET TO JOY

Rejoice and be
exceedingly glad, for
great is your reward in
heaven, for so they
persecuted the prophets
who were before you.

MATTHEW 5:12

How strange it seems to us today for Jesus to link trouble and opposition with joy and great gladness! He is not speaking about a grim-lipped tolerance for trial here, but something utterly out of the ordinary: a happiness that totally transcends natural explanation. Joy comes not from excess but abandonment. True joy comes only from God as we learn to give our whole lives to Him and celebrate His faithfulness to us in every circumstance. It is this ongoing celebration of God and who He is that is core worship.

CORE Focus

Worship is not a word that rolls with ease off the lips of most people. It's an odd old-fashioned word that doesn't seem to have a place in the vocabulary of our post-modern world. In spite of this, we were created with a longing to worship, and worship continues to play a huge role in our self-absorbed, self-indulgent society.

Worship is focus: the focus of one's affections and desire to please. Worship is adoration, ardent devotion, and admiration for one we love. To worship is to idolize, honor, adore, glorify, and esteem the one at the center of our devotion. We were created with an incredible capacity to worship, and the focus of this worship was to be our Creator, the one true God. When we chose to live independently, in rebellion to God, this innate desire to worship was not destroyed. It was simply redirected to focus on someone or something other than God.

It's not hard to determine who or what is at the focus of our worship. The truth is, "Where your treasure is, there your heart will be also" (Matthew 6:21). Jesus knew and understood the human heart so well! The simplest way to reveal the central object of your devotion is to determine where you spend your time, what you treasure, what consumes your thoughts and desires in the course of daily life. The questions with which we must search our hearts are these:

- "Whom do we give our allegiance to?"
- "Whom or what do we direct the major part of our time to?"
- "Where and on what do we spend most of our money?"
- "Whom or what do we hold up as an idol?"
- "Whom do we honor and love?"
- "Whom or what are we most devoted to?"
- "Whom do we most desire to be like?"

As you honestly answer these questions, you will discover the object of your worship.

Some people worship man-made idols: idols of "success" in sports, music, entertainment, religion, or business. Many others are consumed with an inordinate affection for themselves that doesn't just border on worship but is entirely submerged in it. Hours are spent at the gym or in front of the mirror working on the perfect look. Millions are spent on "labels" and cosmetics to beautify our outward appearance. We wouldn't be seen dead in the wrong car, with the wrong friends, or at the wrong party. We strive simultaneously to "stand out in a crowd," all the while "fitting in" with the computer-enhanced, blemish-removed, breast- or muscle-boosted, teeth-whitened images of the marketing predators. Such obsession is self-worship.

The heart of God is looking and longing for a people who will denounce the worship of every idol and return in their hearts to the purity of devotion to Jesus alone. Jesus knew the cry of His Father's heart: "Yet a time is coming and has now come when the true worshipers will worship the Father in spirit and truth, for they are the kind of worshipers the Father seeks. God is spirit, and his worshipers must worship in spirit and in truth" (John 4:23–24 NIV).

God requires us to worship Him in spirit and in truth. Is this just thirty minutes or an hour on a Sunday morning at church when we try to forget those around us, put the week's activities aside, and press in to see if we can feel God? Surely not! "Worship" on Sunday is a valid but minuscule segment of an authentic worshipful life.

Worshiping God "in spirit" implies a depth, intimacy, and friendship that goes far beyond the offering of a small segment of our lives encapsulated in an ordered, predictable, and queued time slot each week. Worship is life. It is a life given over to God 24–7. A life that lives its worship through vital, minute-by-minute, authentic contact with the object of our adoration. It is a mutually satisfying, spiritually normal interaction with the Creator of the universe. Worship was never intended to be reserved for those few short fragmented minutes when we "feel spiritual."

True worship is based on the reality of God, not on our circumstances. God knows the heart that will worship Him in the wilderness of affliction will continue to worship Him in the promised land of plenty. This is what He desires—people who will worship Him in spirit and in truth. People who don't deny their circumstances but, in spite of how things look to the natural eye or how "unspiritual" they may feel, choose to praise, adore, and worship their God. Not just during a church meeting, but with their lives.

> It's who you are and the way you live that count before God. Your worship must engage your spirit in the pursuit of truth. That's the kind of people the Father is looking for: those who are simply and honestly themselves before him in their worship. God is sheer being itself—Spirit. Those who worship him must do it out of their very being, their spirits, their true selves, in adoration. (John 4:24 THE MESSAGE)

CORE Thankfulness

Happiness comes from heaven. It is a gift of God, a by-product of His holiness, a relaxed trust in His wisdom, truth, and Person (Psalm 146:5; Proverbs 3:13, 18; 29:18; John 13:17). We can't fake true happiness.

What cultivates a happy heart? The answer may surprise you. *Develop the habit of being thankful.* Does Jesus love you? Do you have the ability and calling to serve God? These alone are reasons enough to be thankful.

Learn to be content with what you have been given and to be thankful for what you have been kept from. Thankfulness keeps a heart humble. Many take for granted all the opportunities and blessings God gives them. *Proud people are never grateful.* Why should they be thankful when they take credit for all they have and have done? It is a mark of the last days that people will be ungrateful (2 Timothy 3:1–2).

God remembers the leper who returns to thank Him. The least we can do is appreciate Him for who He is and what He has done. To give thanks for your food like Jesus did is not just a formality but a day-to-day privilege, a reminder that all we have comes from Him. What do we have that we have not been given? (1 Corinthians 4:7).

Ingratitude leads to lack of contentment, one of the great sins of our world. If we had no one to compare ourselves with other than God, our values would be much different. We would be content with what He knows we need. In our "age of envy," wanting what others have is cool. We get caught up in the lust of *better* and *more*. But envy is a deadly serious sin according to Scripture (Exodus 20:17; Deuteronomy 5:21). It is a corrosive poison that rots and kills (Proverbs 14:30; Job 5:2).

Make a habit of thanking God daily. We remain close to God by remembering what He has done for us and by staying in an atmosphere of worship and prayer. Doing so guards the heart against darkness, depression, and dangerous fantasy (Romans 1:21–22) and keeps us content and grateful. Giving thanks recognizes the power and mercy of God in our life and gives us power over the idol of wanting more.

Over thirty times in the Bible we are told to "give thanks" to the Lord (Psalm 118:1, 29; 136:1–3). "In everything give thanks; for this is the will of God in Christ Jesus for you" (1 Thessalonians 5:18). A thankful heart is a condition of fearless witness and worship.

Worship and Work

The separation between the sacred and the secular has for centuries kept Christians from fulfilling God's highest purposes. The early Christians understood their lives were to be lived for God, and this in essence was an expression of their worship. "Therefore, I urge you, brothers, in view of God's mercy, to offer your bodies as living sacrifices, holy and pleasing to God—this is your spiritual act of worship" (Romans 12:1 NIV).

Most adults spend almost forty percent of their waking time at work. In contrast, the average Christian spends less than *two percent* of their time in church meetings during their working years. Core to the life of a disciple of Christ is the understanding of work as a spiritual activity that has the potential to be part of our worship. Yet for most, we feel strangely unspiritual at work because we have not made the connection that "whether we eat, drink, or whatever we do, we do it all to the glory of God" (1 Corinthians 10:31, authors' paraphrase). Giving God glory through a good, hard, honest day's work is a legitimate means of worship that adds dignity to our God-given vocation. It is a door-opener to advancing our destiny and career for the kingdom of God. Promotion for the Christian is not about power, prestige, or money. On the contrary, it is simply another way to bring honor and credibility to the Christian faith and glory to our Father and Friend in heaven.

We have been taught that work was part of the curse that came on humankind when Adam and Eve sinned in the Garden of Eden. This is simply not the case. Before the fall, Adam and Eve were instructed to tend the Garden and to have dominion over all creation. In other words, they were to "work it" as God's representatives. They were actually created to enjoy laboring on behalf of God in His creation; it was only after the fall that their work became harder. God himself is a God who works. When He considered the results of His work of creation, God declared it was good! Work was never intended to be a curse but rather part of the divine nature that was instilled in our lives as God fashioned us in His image.

When done with the right attitude, work produces within us

- purpose
- dignity
- value
- a sense of accomplishment
- joy
- life

These are the blessings God will impart to our lives as we learn to worship Him through our work.

THE CORE AT WORK

Work was not originally intended to simply be the means by which we earn money. The blessings of work are for the rich and the poor alike. The outcome of our work is not to earn sufficient money that we never have to work again or about earning enough to retire early. A wise man of God was once asked at the age of eighty-three, "When are you going to retire?" His response was immediate: "When I find it in the Bible!" We have heard of those who retire, only to become sick and pass away. It would seem as though they lost their purpose. As Christians, we have a higher purpose, an eternal purpose. It is the purpose and plan of God, and as we continue to actively participate in its fulfillment, old age brings many new beginnings instead of redundancy.

For the Christian, no work is secular. We are spiritual people, and that spirituality directs our lives regardless of the activity we are involved in. All our work, every activity, takes place in a sacred space where God is at work. No matter what we do as our daily occupation, if done for the purpose of God, it will bring glory and honor to Him. This is worship. Every occupation contains an element of the nature and image of our Creator. This makes it possible for us to glorify Him through our work. Through their work, for example, the builder, engineer, and architect all reflect the nature of the God who designed, engineered, and fashioned the world and everything in it. The artist reflects the creative flair of the One who paints the sky with sunsets and clothes the fields with flowers. The musician brings honor to the Creator of sound and nature's songs. The medical worker reflects the healing nature of the greatest Physician of all time. The administrator brings glory to the One who sustains all things, keeping order of time and seasons. We simply need a revelation about those things we consider secular. We need God's perspective on our work. We need a new mind-set that recognizes every ability as a gift from God and an opportunity to give glory to His name. We must discover a faith that we can wear more naturally and comfortably in the marketplace of life.

The Bible contains many illustrations of what can happen when the people of God learn to couple faith with work in a positive way. Consider Joseph, who, finding himself a slave in a foreign, pagan nation, determined in his heart to give one hundred percent to everything that was assigned to him. His willingness to humbly serve people, knowing in his heart he was serving and worshiping the living God, paved the way for his promotion to second-in-command in the greatest nation in the world. Through his seemingly "secular" work, Joseph was used in the plan of God to save His people during a time of famine.

Consider Nehemiah, a servant in the king's palace, who heard the call of God to rebuild the wall of the city of Jerusalem. He literally put his life on the line to motivate and oversee the citizens of Jerusalem as the wall was rebuilt. It was the plain, simple, hard work of laying brick upon brick. Doesn't sound very spiritual at all! Yet Scripture describes the people's enthusiasm, stating, "They set their hands to this good work" (Nehemiah 2:18), and "So [the people] rebuilt the wall till all of it reached half its height, for the people worked with all their heart" (Nehemiah 4:6 NIV). These people were not clock watchers! Their heart and motivation was for the work they had to do to complete the wall. In spite of the opposition that came their way, they persevered in their work until the wall was complete and the city of Jerusalem was secure once more from its enemies. Through their work these men and women of faith worshiped God, bringing glory and honor to His name as they partnered in His purposes in the world.

Likewise, you also have the privilege and responsibility to live your life as worship to God, every day, during every moment, and involving every activity. Think about your own life. Is God glorified by your attitude and actions at work? Does your work reflect the nature of Christ? Are you diligent, trustworthy, and thorough, completing what is assigned you with integrity and excellence? Are you honoring God through your work?

> And whatever you do, whether in word or deed, do it all in the name of the Lord Jesus, giving thanks to God the Father through him. . . . Whatever you do, work at it with all your heart, as working for the Lord, not for men, since you know that you will receive an inheritance from the Lord as a reward. It is the Lord Christ you are serving. (Colossians 3:17, 23–24 NIV)

Count It All Joy!

Every now and then we may encounter a trial that doesn't seem to go away even when we ask God to deal with it. Thinking that perhaps it is the work of the Enemy, we resist him in the name of Jesus, but nothing seems to happen. What is the biblical answer to trials like this? Scripture says to "Count it all joy!" (James 1:2).

> Rejoice in the Lord always. Again I will say, rejoice! Let your gentleness be known to all men. The Lord is at hand. Be anxious for nothing, but in everything by prayer and supplication, with thanksgiving, let your requests be made known to God; and the peace of God, which surpasses all understanding, will guide your hearts and minds through Christ Jesus. (Philippians 4:4–7)

No matter what we may face in this world, we have two firm assurances: (1) We are in the will of God, and (2) He loves us. Everything that happens to us has been filtered through His hands. The only thing the devil can do to us is to tempt us—and he has to get permission from God to do that!

Rejoicing and praising are habits formed by practice. We *become* what we dwell on. Christians need to practice "confessing" Christ as much as our sins. Daily confession of His glory and grace will bring daily deliverance from the more subtle sins of depression and doubt. Praise is the positive confession of the faithfulness of God, the outward expression of "counting it all joy" (Psalm 22:23; 42:5, 11; Philippians 4:8).

The early disciples were filled with hope and enthusiasm and completely possessed by a desire to save their world. Their preaching and teaching was an exciting series of surprises. Christianity without enthusiasm is like a body without life. Discipleship is not dreary resignation. The early disciples were beaten but rejoiced that they were "counted worthy to suffer shame for His Name" (Acts 5:41). In prison Paul and Silas prayed, sang praises, and started a *church* right where they were! Even Jesus went to the cross *for the joy that was set before Him.* In discipleship the pearl, not the price, is important (Matthew 13:44–45; Acts 16:25–32; Hebrews 12:2).

Praising God allows you to focus on Him. When you rejoice, you demonstrate true discipleship to a darkened, hopeless world, convincing them more than words could of the priceless gain of life you've received from Jesus. Joy draws like a magnet. When you praise, you

1. PROVE YOUR FAITH

Nothing shakes non-Christians more than to see the joy a Christian can have, even in the most difficult of circumstances. When you are supposed to moan and don't, they know you have something very real. Praise is a living expression of faith. Never speak *negatively.* Death and life are in the power of the tongue (Proverbs 18:21). Words have great power to affect attitudes, and we are ruled by our words more than we realize. Don't express a feeling of defeat! Say you can't do it, and you are beaten before you begin. Speak your fear of trouble, and you call hell into action. Don't be snared by the words of your mouth (Proverbs 6:2). Demonstrate your faith in God through praise.

2. EXPRESS GRATITUDE

Praise keeps requests in perspective. We tend to think more of our troubles and less of our Father, who is closer than our hands or breathing. The devil cannot get you if he cannot discourage you! Praise is a song of deliverance, a hymn of victory sung before joining the battle. Nothing is more disturbing to hell than a core band of disciples singing about conquest *before* the encounter, with perfect confidence in their Captain. Remember that God will make you capable to do the job He calls you to do—but strength is supplied in service, not before. Praise keeps Christ King in your life.

Filling our hearts and minds with *music* is a wonderful way to praise. If you don't like current praise music, write your own in a spirit of love and worship.

You may face giants you cannot conquer, needs you cannot meet. But God is on your side. Your battles are His battles! Fear and depression disintegrate under the power of praise. It brings Christ-consciousness into every problem. You need difficulties and trials to learn to depend on Him.

You *must* worship . . . even when you feel least like doing so. All of us have our gray days when God's light goes behind a cloud. Do you trust in feeling or in God's love? Take joy in God and you affirm your faith in His unchanging promises regardless of changing feelings and seemingly impossible circumstances. When trouble comes, look back on your blessings. Maybe even write a list of what God has done for you. Praise is core, and it lifts our hearts into the very presence of Christ.

The life of the disciple is a life that emanates gratitude, praise, and worship, regardless of circumstances or situations. God is looking for worshipers. He is looking for people who, when they experience the difficulties of life, the routines of daily living, the trials and the periods of waiting, look to their God with love and devotion. Will you be such a person?

You are the salt of the earth; but if the salt loses its flavor, how shall it be seasoned? It is then good for nothing but to be thrown out and trampled underfoot by men. NKJV

Let me tell you why you are here. You're here to be salt-seasoning that brings out the God-flavors of this earth. If you lose your saltiness, how will people taste godliness? You've lost your usefulness and will end up in the garbage. THE MESSAGE

You are the salt of the earth. But if the salt loses its saltiness, how can it be made salty again? It is no longer good for anything, except to be thrown out and trampled by men. NIV

You are the salt of the earth; but if the salt has become tasteless, how can it be made salty again? It is no longer good for anything, except to be thrown out and trampled under foot by men. NASB

YOU ARE THE SALT OF THE EARTH. BUT WHAT GOOD IS SALT IF IT HAS LOST ITS FLAVOR? CAN YOU MAKE IT USEFUL AGAIN? IT WILL BE THROWN OUT AND TRAMPLED UNDERFOOT AS WORTHLESS. NLT

YOU ARE THE SALT OF THE EARTH, BUT IF SALT HAS LOST ITS TASTE, HOW SHALL ITS SALTINESS BE RESTORED? IT IS NO LONGER GOOD FOR ANYTHING EXCEPT TO BE THROWN OUT AND TRAMPLED UNDER PEOPLE'S FEET. RSV

CORE CULTURE

IN THE WORLD, NOT OF IT

You are the salt of the earth; but if the salt loses its flavor, how shall it be seasoned? It is then good for nothing but to be thrown out and trampled underfoot by men.

MATTHEW 5:13

Jesus has commanded His CORE to be the salt of the earth, but what exactly does that mean? Salt is one of the chemical wonders of the world. Made from two highly reactive and even dangerous elements, it is essential to life. In ancient times salt was so precious it was actually used for money! People used it to not only help preserve food but to help bring out the flavor in everything it was added to. Salt not only stops things from spoiling and going bad, but it helps make people thirsty and brings the flavor of heaven back into the world.

In order to retain our God-given flavor, we must guard against losing our "saltiness" by becoming too similar to the larger culture around us. Of course, when transformed by a CORE perspective for God's glory, culture—from media and the arts to the way people speak and behave on a daily basis—can be a powerful Christian force. The reality, though, is that most of the culture we are exposed to today is anything but God-honoring. At times, we may even be tempted to worship it instead of Christ. How is the CORE to deal with multiple forms of temptation from an often anti-Christian culture? How do we stop that culture from hurting our hearts? Even more, how can we affect that culture so that it brings joy to God's heart?

CORE You

The world tells you that to win you must be invincible. It tells you to be independent, stand on your own two feet, and listen to no one. *God says the exact opposite.* He says that to win we have to know our weaknesses and how quickly we can fall. He says that to triumph we must learn to trust Him, to expect His help, to be a continual learner. God delights in taking those the world writes off as losers and making them thoroughly awe-inspiring. He loves to use the least, the littlest, the last. Your unchangeable limitations—the things you can't change about yourself—are great blessings in disguise. They are opportunities for others to see that you serve an invisible Someone who can make anyone who hangs with Him the greatest mover and shaker ever (1 Corinthians 1:26–31).

You can take the first step by doing the *exact opposite* of what your culture tells you. Jesus never said, "Find yourself." He said, "He who finds his life will lose it" (Matthew 10:39). Focus on yourself and you will wind up with nothing more than yourself.

Understand this: When an infinite God expresses himself finitely, it always comes out differently. The secret to standing out in a culture is simple: *Forget yourself.* Give yourself away to Jesus. *Deny yourself.* Give up your life to the infinite God and His eternal purposes. Lose your life in Him. Seek only to serve Him and others for Him. Let Him express His personality and power through you. When you do this you will become wonderfully unlike anyone else in history. You will find that in losing your life, you find it forever (Mark 8:34–36; 1 John 2:15–17).

Living in the World Without Being Worldly

"I do not pray that You should take them out of the world, but that You should keep them from the evil one" (John 17:15).

When people become Christians, why don't we just go straight to heaven? It would allow us to avoid so many pressures and trials. The simple answer is we still have something to do. Far from having us leave the world, Jesus is praying instead that *we will stay in it* (John 17:15).

If we have to live as men and women of God in a culture largely against Him, how do we do it? What does God expect of us? How do we learn to share with the world without it seducing us?

You are a missionary. The difference between being a missionary to a culture like ours and a culture of the past is that this one changes all the time. You need to keep in touch with this mission field yet still take steps to limit your exposure to only what you need to know in order to be salt and effectively communicate God's truth. You can do this in part by increasing your sensitivity to what you are *already* exposed to. There are many things you see and hear each day. What you need is to learn to *really see, really hear* what is being said and shown in the light of God's work in your world.

"BRAILLING" YOUR CULTURE

If you were blind and you wanted to find out what something was like, how would you do it? You would use what senses you still had—smell, sound, and especially touch. So, too, you can keep up with what is going on all around you. The best way to learn what something feels like is to lightly touch it in as many ways as you can. "Braille" what goes on wherever you go. No one expects you to be an expert in every-thing; don't try. What people do hope is that you are *interested in everything* important to them. There are three levels of brailling a cul-ture:

1. Spend time with the natives. Spend time with those you would like to reach. Take whatever time they will give you. Just listen. If you are going to go fishing for souls, go where the fish are.

2. Soak yourself in their world. You pick up more than a language when you live with people; you also pick up their accent. If you speak about someone's culture without ever taking the time to live any part of your life in it, you speak with an accent that gives you away. Such sensitivity to nuances can't be taught. You catch it, not learn it. You can be forgiven for not knowing something, but if you don't *care* enough to learn more, you will lose your audience.

3. Study the movers and the shakers. Who are the *leaders* of the culture you are trying to reach? Learn something about your mission field's heroes. Whom do they admire and listen to? Whom do they look up to and model their lives after? Make it your business to find out all you can about those key people. Appreciate what you can of what you find. Ask God to show you the hunger behind this admiration so Jesus can fill it with His grace.

CORE APPEARANCE: THE WAY YOU LOOK

Clothes are centrally important to a culture. They can take up a tremendous amount of our money, attention, and time, and they do say something about the focus of our lives. Clothes are an outward sign of our *inward* choices and lifestyles.

When Jesus spoke about John the Baptist, He asked people what they expected to see in him: "But what did you go out to see? A man clothed in soft garments? Indeed those who are gorgeously appareled and live in luxury are in kings' courts" (Luke 7:25). John didn't wear the clothes of his popular culture; he wore a camel-hair coat. His clothes said something to the watching world. *What he wore was part of his message.*

What you wear is part of *your* message. You say something to people by the way you dress. Now, what are you saying to people with your clothes? Do they say something positive about what a friend of Jesus is like?

The people who "overcome by the blood of the Lamb" in the book of Revelation are known by their clothes (Revelation 3:4–5). Their dress is part of their testimony. The distinguishing marks of Babylon, the "mother of harlots," were her clothes and jewelry; what she looked like outside was an integral part of what she was inside (Revelation 17:4–5). How you dress is important to God. It is not just a hang-up of religious formalism.

We must dress as Christians in a way that speaks as loudly as our words of what is clean and valuable and real (Matthew 6:28–29; 1 Timothy 2:9). Learn to dress in a way that honors Christ.

The Bible does not tell us *what* to wear, but it does give us some guidelines.

1. Be *simple.* Don't follow the latest fad or buy into the lie that the more expensive something is the better it makes you look. Dress appro-

priately for what you need to do without calling too much attention to yourself.

> And I want women to be modest in their appearance. They should wear decent and appropriate clothing and not draw attention to themselves by the way they fix their hair or by wearing gold or pearls or expensive clothes. For women who claim to be devoted to God should make themselves attractive by the good things they do. (1 Timothy 2:9–10 NLT)

> Don't be concerned about the outward beauty that depends on fancy hairstyles, expensive jewelry, or beautiful clothes. Be known for the beauty that comes from within, the unfading beauty of a gentle and quiet spirit, which is so precious to God. (1 Peter 3:3–4 NLT)

2. Be *modest*. The way you dress should not draw unnecessary attention to your body. Clothes should be a backdrop, not a showroom. Never look cheap or sexually suggestive. Remember that, as a CORE Christian, you represent Christ to the world. You should dress to please Jesus and no one else.

COUNTERING THE DRUG CULTURE

People who have not given in to the real God have tried to find the key to life in another god: chemical consciousness. We are surrounded by a culture that looks to illegal and legal drugs not only for its pain and problems but for its parties.

The Bible mentions powerful drugs like wormwood, hemlock, gall, and myrrh and specifically forbids their use. Revelation 18:23 uses a special word to describe drugs: *sorceries*. The word is *pharmakeia* in Greek. The source of the English word *pharmacy*, it refers to seeking "spiritual" experiences through drug use. God says this dangerous practice will fool many people in the last days and warns that no one who uses drugs or sells them to others for this purpose will be in heaven (Revelation 21:8).

More common than the use of illegal drugs, though, is the use of legal drugs like alcohol and tobacco. One single drink of alcohol permanently kills irreplaceable brain cells, and tobacco, whether smoked or chewed, leads to often-fatal cancers of the mouth, throat, and

ULTIMATE CORE

lungs, among other terrible diseases. While both are addictive, tobacco in particular is one of the most lethally addictive drugs in the world today, often leading users to even more powerful and destructive drug use. You may know or have heard of church people, even leaders, who smoke and drink and yet seem to serve God, but too many people who have flaunted their freedom in these areas have lived to regret its consequences on themselves and eventually their families.

In the Bible, smoke is negatively associated with shortness of life, wasting destruction, and judgment (Psalm 68:2; 102:3; Proverbs 10:26; Revelation 9:2–3, 17–18). The Bible also has negative things to say of alcohol: "Wine is a mocker, strong drink is a brawler, and whoever is led astray by it is not wise" (Proverbs 20:1; see also Isaiah 5:11, 22; 28:7). No King's child is to touch alcohol (Proverbs 31:4). Wine is for no one in ministry (Leviticus 10:9); you are to get your bravery, happiness, and loudness from the Holy Spirit! (Ephesians 5:18; Acts 2:13). The only legitimate use of strong drink in the Bible is to medically dull the pain of someone who is dying (Proverbs 31:6). It is wise for the CORE not to smoke or drink at all.

CORE PRINCIPLES ON CULTURAL CHOICES

1. "To the pure all things are pure, but to those who are defiled and unbelieving nothing is pure; but even their mind and conscience are defiled" (Titus 1:15). God made *everything beautiful* in His time (Ecclesiastes 3:11). If you have a clean heart and really love God more than everything else in the world, you will see God's hand in everything. If you don't, almost anything can cripple you and make you more dirty (Revelation 22:11).

2. "Therefore do not let your good be spoken of as evil. . . . Therefore let us pursue the things which make for peace and the things by which one may edify another. . . . All things indeed are pure, but it is evil for the man who eats with offense" (Romans 14:16, 19–20). What is fine and allowable for you may cause someone else to criticize you or Christ. If you are strong enough to deliberately not celebrate God's goodness in a way that you enjoy but that may offend someone who is watching you, make that choice.

3. "Do you have faith? Have it to yourself before God. Happy is he

who does not condemn himself in what he approves. . . . Whatever is not from faith is sin" (Romans 14:22–23). How do you know if something is personally wrong for you even if others may think it is okay? If you doubt the legitimacy of something, *don't do it*. Even if it turns out later to be right, for you *at that time* it will be wrong. Don't hurt your conscience, especially if your spirit is weak. If you can't honestly and freely do something as if for God, don't do it at all. Anything done in doubt is always wrong (Romans 14:1–3).

4. "We then who are strong ought to bear with the scruples of the weak, and not to please ourselves. Let each of us please his neighbor for his good, leading to edification" (Romans 15:1–2). You may not be moved by public opinion. You may believe what you are doing is acceptable to God and know you have a *right* to do it. Yet a loving Christian does not disregard another's life. You can still surrender that right for the Lord's sake even though He won't ask it of you, because it is not a simple matter of right or wrong. If you can and will, you can put aside your own preferences and choose to encourage someone else who cannot think and act with the same spiritual understanding you have. Your pleasure is secondary to caring for people you can affect for Christ.

CORE Art and Media

Whether intended for entertainment, information, or to promote a worldview, media plays a central role in any culture. While we have already looked in chapter 8 at some dangers posed by the dominant, secular media, we should also look at how the CORE can use media to penetrate the non-Christian world around us. In God's hands, the media offerings created by Christians can be an exciting and effective way to glorify Him, communicate His truth, and bring real flavor to the world. How can we recognize such an offering?

WHAT MAKES IT "CHRISTIAN"?

Apart from the motive or worldview of a writer, singer, actor, painter, or other artist, can we establish any criteria for Christian art and media? We can talk about the choice of certain words, the effects of different kinds of sounds and lyrics, the power of a presentation, or the subject matter. Yet none of these *makes* art Christian.

Today we label things *Christian* to describe something that conforms to a certain religious or sometimes cultural standard. There is a difference between songs, books, art, and other creations with Christian *themes,* and songs, books, drama, dance, etc., written or performed *by* committed Christians. But although God gave specific instructions to people on how to build and shape things, there is no "Christian" art in the Bible. Artists who write songs out of their lives, thoughts, struggles, and defeats tell what they see or feel from their own point of view. For Christians, that point of view will be Christ-centered and reflect the truth of His world, bringing glory to Him. Whatever we create, do, or practice will reflect our own inner vision and commitment, whether we intend our work to be specifically religious or not.

It is important to note that a creation in any of the arts need not be religious to be Christian. Some of the best-loved stories of Jesus are *not religious at all*. The parables of the soils, the prodigal son, the lost sheep, and the unjust judge don't even have the word *God* in them, but no one would deny they are divinely given and full of truth! (The same is true for the Song of Solomon and the book of Ruth.) Songs, art, poetry, or writing born of God's Spirit need not always be obviously or particularly religious, though it will be true to the way God sees and shows life. Someone spiritually altered by God has a wholly different perspective on the world, life, and faith. CORE art always holds up what is good and real and stands against what is evil and false. *Whatever we do, we are to do all for the glory of God* (1 Corinthians 10:31). He sees our hearts and knows why we do the work we do. There is no "secular" or "sacred" to God if your heart is set to please Him in your creation; He doesn't care if it is "Christian" or not!

History is full of Christians who created great art. How poor our world would be if there had been no music from Bach, Handel, Watts, or Charles Wesley, no timeless tales from Dante or Bunyan, no children's stories from a Hans Christian Anderson or a George MacDonald, no science or fantasy fiction from a C. S. Lewis, Charles Williams, or J. R. R. Tolkien, no novels or dramas from a Dorothy Sayers or John Grisham, no poetry from a G. K. Chesterton or T. S. Eliot! Among the myriad forms of music, dance, film, animation, writing, theater, graphics, or other arts, there are some that can be your chosen avenue to share your devotion for and to the Lord. Not all will like or prefer what you do. You should not expect even Christians to always agree with your choices. While you may have true freedom in Christ not to feel locked into any one kind of expression of worship or artistic declaration, you can and ought to be considerate of others. They may struggle in areas you do not, or they may be hurt by things that do not bother you at all. "All things are lawful for me, but all things are not helpful. All things are lawful for me, but I will not be brought under the power of any" (1 Corinthians 6:12). Stick with what God is after in your life. And know this: You are free in any realm to *do anything at all* to make God's heart glad. "Now the purpose of the commandment is love from a pure heart, from a good conscience, and from sincere faith" (1 Timothy 1:5).

CORE Rules

Even two millennia ago, the clash of culture between the world and the church was a big deal. When the early church met in Acts 15 to decide on the core rules for the next generations of new, non-Jewish converts, the way they met and their final conclusions and even the way they came to them were radical. So what did they decide? We can sum up the core elements of the Christian life in dealing with the dangers of a culture in two key commandments.

1. Put no other gods before the real God.

2. Sanctify the ordinary—"Whether you eat or drink, or whatever you do, do all to the glory of God" (1 Corinthians 10:31). Don't divide life into the secular and sacred.

If God would say one more thing to those who would claim to be His CORE, it would probably be this: "Don't embarrass Me." God is looking for people He can be proud of, a people of whom He is not ashamed to be called their God. "Give no offense, either to the Jews or to the Greeks or to the church of God" (1 Corinthians 10:32).

Listen to God and do what He wants for your life. As His salt, we are blessed to be able to creatively give back to Him and His world in any of those multitudes of ways that display His wisdom, grace, and love, leaving people thirsty for the Source. Your life is a gift from Him for your world; what you can become by His power is your gift to God.

You're here to be light, bringing out the God-colors in the world. God is not a secret to be kept. We're going public with this, as public as a city on a hill.
THE MESSAGE

You are the light of the world. A city set on a hill cannot be hidden. NASB

YOU ARE THE LIGHT OF THE WORLD. A CITY THAT IS SET ON A HILL CANNOT BE HIDDEN.
NKJV

You are the light of the world—like a city on a mountain, glowing in the night for all see. NLT

You are the light of the world. A city set on a hill cannot be hidden. ESV

You are the light of the world. A city on a hill cannot be hidden. NIV

14

CORE
COMMUNICATION

S P E A K I N G   T O   S O C I E T Y

You are the light of

the world. A city that

is set on a hill

cannotbe hidden.

MATTHEW 5:14

You do not have to learn to be a witness. You already are one! You are telling the world right now who or what you **really** belong to by what you talk about and center your life around. Your words and your life are tied inseparably together. You will always convey to others around you what you really love and live for, and your words will either back this up or show you up. Anyone who watches you closely can tell if you truly mean what you claim with your lips.

If we call ourselves Christians, we are already witnessing for or against Jesus. If we say we belong to Him but our lives do not back up our words, people may reject Christ and the Gospel because of us. That is why Jesus said, "He who is not with Me is against Me, and he who does not gather with Me scatters abroad" (Matthew 12:30).

You cannot present Christ to others without your own life being Christlike. CORE Christianity **is** Christ! You cannot present Christ to another until you properly **represent** Him and His love. If you want to be a witness, you must really **know** Him to **show** Him.

CORE Motive

The world is filled with movements for evangelism and methods of witness today. Some work inside structured churches, some work outside; some are planned and highly organized, while others arise loosely and spontaneously to try to minister to needs. But none of these has a right to exist—*unless* staffed by people who have the right motives! God is looking for people who want to see Him glorified above everything else and who want to stop people from hurting Him, others, and themselves by their selfishness and stupidity. Our evangelism *will* fail if we do not serve God for the right reasons.

The Lord Jesus saw saving *one soul* as worth more than the whole world. He spent much of His time talking with one person at a time about that person's relationship to God. Bringing people to Christ is impossible without concerned, *personal contact.* Jesus put the life and the love of His Father on exhibition to the world. When the world is lost and running from God, He must look for people to convince them of His love and concern despite their sin. He wants to do this by living His life through and in CORE Christians who will yield to His direction as they bring others the message of reconciliation and forgiveness.

To be Christlike in attitude means to be absolutely real. God hates phoniness. If you have any other reason for wanting to witness to others apart from a genuine concern and love for them and for God, forget about trying to "witness." You will only do more harm than good. Love is the only acceptable core motive for witness—an honest, unselfish concern for the highest good of God and His wayward creation. It involves a level of concern that made even Christ cry (Matthew 9:36). Love is not something you feel; it is something you *do,* directly measured in unselfish sacrifice.

Witnessing like Jesus means being Christlike in conduct. The world is full of selfish people who think only of themselves, care only for themselves, and live only for themselves. God's CORE people are to be totally different—they are to live like *Jesus.* It does no good to say, "I'm full of sin—look only to Jesus!" to non-Christians. They have every right to respond with, "But I can't *see* Jesus. I can only see *you.* And if He hasn't helped you, what makes you think He can change me?"

Jesus said, "As long as I am *in* the world, I am the light of the world" (John 9:5). But Jesus is no longer in the world, and He has left us as His witnesses. "As the Father has sent Me, I also send you" (John 20:21). "You will be my witnesses . . . to the ends of the earth" (Acts 1:8 NIV). To be effective witnesses for Jesus we must live above the world's standards and values so unbelievers take notice and ask what our secret is. We should live so that we can say with Paul, "The things which you learned and received and heard and saw in me, these do, and the God of peace will be with you" (Philippians 4:9). People must be able to be "followers of us and of the Lord" at the same time (1 Thessalonians 1:6).

God's blueprint for Christian witness is outlined in 1 Timothy 4:12. There is no real reason why a young adult cannot be as effective for God as an older adult, provided there is a basic understanding of what is involved and a consistent life to back it up. We are to be examples by *word* (what we say), *conversation* (what we do), *charity* (why we do it), *spirit* (where we do it), *faith* (when we do it), and *purity* (how we do it). God is globally mobilizing today's younger generations for the mightiest awakening history has ever seen.

Witnessing like Jesus means having consistency—the ability to be the same all the time. To be like Jesus, we must be changed daily by His Holy Spirit. Following Jesus doesn't mean adhering to a set of rules, but having a friendship with a living, loving Person. It is "Christ in you, the hope of glory" (Colossians 1:27). In this life of grace and faith, we are to be marked by the sign that "sin shall not have dominion over you" (Romans 6:14). Christianity *is* Christ—resurrected, real, and bringing peace and power (2 Corinthians 3:18).

CORE Witness

FOUR ELEMENTS IN WITNESS

When the Lord Jesus was on earth, He did not use a "plan" for witnessing. Because He really understood how salvation takes place, He was able to adapt his approach to everyone who came to Him, meeting that person where he or she was. A thorough understanding of the basic facts of sin, responsibility, grace, love, repentance, and faith in Christ are essential to proper witness. To know the Word of God is to understand that no one is *ever* saved without God investing a good deal of supernatural persuasion in his or her life. Keep in mind these four interacting elements that make up a part of any conversion experience:

GOD IS SPIRIT

The work Jesus did when He witnessed is done today by the *Holy Spirit*. His work is to convict us of sin by guiding our thoughts back over our sad past to reveal our true lost state before God (John 16:7–13). The Bible shows us that He can speak directly to the conscience of unsaved people. Expect His help when witnessing. He knows everything about the people you are talking to, and by direct intuition can give you the right words to say that will hit them at the core of their selfishness.

The Holy Spirit gives truth vividness, authority, and clarity. Under His power, the Word of God burns and cuts like a blade of fire (John 4:23–24; 16:7–11; 2 Corinthians 3:5–6; Ephesians 3:5–6; Revelation 3:20).

People do not naturally want to obey God because their selfishness has too strong a hold on their lives. According to the Bible, sinners are deceitful, self-satisfied, proud, and stubborn. They resist God, reject truth, and although guided by Satan, are unconscious of bondage (John 8:33; Acts 7:51; Romans 7:7; 1 Timothy 6:4; 2 Timothy 4:4; Titus 3:3; Revelation 3:17). Before the message of salvation makes any sense to non-Christians, they must *see* that they are in big trouble and that nothing they can do or say for themselves can excuse their guilt. They must see that their rebellion has made them rebels against God. But you must learn how to *work with the Holy Spirit* in speaking about this to people you are trying to win. Truth without His compassion will only further harden people's hearts, making them less receptive to God's truth.

GOD IS HOLY

Sinners live in a pretend world. They convince themselves that what they do is right, knowing all the time they are wrong. They *want* to be self-deceived. Pride keeps them dishonest whenever by circumstance or conviction they realize they need to surrender to God. Instead, they appease their consciences by comparing themselves with the rest of the selfish world around them. By avoiding any standard of truth and holiness, they may manage for a while, until God brings someone across their paths to demonstrate the truth. Faced with a living demonstration of God's love, their own guilt becomes painfully real.

Non-Christians become aware of God's holiness in direct proportion to how much *you* are filled with God's Spirit. This is why it is so vitally important to know the Spirit's gift of power and to spend time in God's presence in prayer. Non-Christians must sense God's reality in *you*.

GOD IS LOVE

Truth first shows the ugliness of sin in contrast to God's goodness. Today we must spend far more time showing pre-Christians their true guilt before God than was needed a century ago. People no longer think their guilt feelings are a symptom of any *real* wrong; they try to live instead without absolutes. They must know the bad news about themselves and their broken relationship with God before the Good News makes any sense. Witnesses need divine wisdom here "to open their eyes, in order to turn them from darkness to light" (Acts 26:18). As Catherine Booth wrote in *Godliness,* "The eyes of the soul must be opened to such a realization of sin and such an apprehension of the consequences of sin, as shall lead to an earnest desire to be saved from sin."

The Holy Spirit uses the law to show up excuses and drive people into the mercy and love of Jesus. Yet the law has no power *in itself* to change sinners or to make them love God. Only the truth of God's concern and love contrasted with their own selfishness can subdue their proud wills and break their hearts. Non-Christians must realize that *Jesus is their Friend* and will welcome them the moment they are willing to turn their backs on sin and give themselves up to God. Unless they sense this divine concern, they will only go on into deeper rebellion and despair.

It is your job to demonstrate God's concern. How can people see that God cares? By *your* care. How can they know that God loves them? By *your* love! For this reason, you must *never* argue or give any impression you are looking down on others. This does not mean you should excuse sin or talk about it as if others were helpless and had nothing to do with it. Don't treat sin as an unavoidable weakness. You certainly cannot show love by making it seem as if it's easier to be saved than it actually is—God expects total honesty, complete repent-

ULTIMATE CORE

ance, and an entire consecration of the heart to Him. Show your love by earnest concern, presenting the truth and praying for others to be "saved and to come to the knowledge of the truth" (1 Timothy 2:4). Expose sin and show the insanity of living in it.

GOD IS LIGHT

Non-Christians don't want to face reality. They *always know* right. Never forget this. The sole reason for their sin is an *intentional choice* to please themselves against the advice of their own initial reason and conscience. You have a powerful ally in the consciences of those you talk to. The conscience says "Amen" to every truth the Holy Spirit makes real from your lips. People are forced, inwardly at least, to admit the truth.

What would you say to people who said that they "could" not believe or repent or forsake some particular sin? What is the first step toward getting real with God? Honesty! When people are willing to lay out before Him all their excuses, problems, doubts, or difficulties, then conviction of sin, faith, and salvation will follow in short order. Your task is by the power of the Word and Spirit of God to get people to be honest *before* and *toward* God. When that happens, the light of the Gospel will shine into their hearts. It is then up to them to repent and respond to your message from the Lord. In short, sinners have a part to play in their own salvation—by giving their free response out of a Spirit-awakened love for God (Isaiah 55:7; Ezekiel 14:6; 18:30–32; Acts 2:38; 3:19; 17:30–31; 20:21).

CORE FACTS FOR NON-CHRISTIANS

God, in loving wisdom and infinite kindness, has communicated to us in two amazing ways:

1. By *indirectly* speaking to us in real history through people who love Him, passing on His offer of pardon and the conditions under which it can be given. The basics of this message are in the Bible, which describes why God made us, what He had intended for us, and what has happened through sin. Despite our rebellion and persistence in selfishness, God still loves us and longs to restore us.

2. By *directly* meeting His creation in person. The most amazing of

all these contacts occurred some two thousand years ago when God *himself* miraculously became one of us as Jesus Christ. He was born uniquely, lived incomparably, died prophetically, and rose again from the dead triumphantly. Jesus' earthly mission was threefold:

- to show us what our *Maker* is really like;
- to show us how *we* are supposed to live;
- to *die* an agonizing death out of love for us, as a *substitute* for the penalty of our sins.

Because of Jesus' sacrifice, God can offer forgiveness, full pardon, and restoration to us on two conditions:

1. Our repentance: We need to be willing to forsake our selfish way of life, whatever the cost to our plans, our pride, or public image.

2. Our faith: We need to be willing to trust Jesus Christ as our own personal Substitute for the penalty of our sins and love and obey Him forever as our true and rightful Lord.

When we surrender to God and make Him our core choice, we must willingly give our whole selves to Him and obey Him in everything. When this happens, a divine transformation from a state of selfishness to love takes place that the Bible calls being "born again."

The Holy Spirit searches out the excuses and hiding places of the heart to draw us to submit to God. Objections and difficulties are as different as people are. As you witness, God will direct you to find the places where the Holy Spirit is pressing on people's consciences. Press those same places, and you may lead them to God.

OVERPLANNING

There are many "soul-winning plans" and "salvation outlines" for Christians today. Be careful of the following:

1. A "pat" approach. If a memorized outline involves psychological "traps" to cut out people's excuses, they may resist or resent these even while being forced by the preplanned words to continue the conversation. Although some of these pat approaches have been effective in teaching people how to witness, they have two dangerous weaknesses:

- They can make our witness mechanical by inviting complete reliance on the plan and leaving no option for the Holy Spirit's own *specialized* witness.

- They may not allow enough *scope* to search to the roots of people's selfishness. In this case, a "decision" may be made to relieve the psychological pressure of the "traps" without a *true* change of heart. The depth quality of a convert depends on how clearly he or she understands and commits to the truth of God. Any plan that minimizes either the guilt of sin, our responsibility and need for total surrender to God, or our own dependence on the Holy Spirit is inadequate and can produce converts that are at best weak in faith.

Not everyone should be given the same directions. A general pill cannot cure all ills. It is the Holy Spirit's task to "customize" our witness to the person at hand. This means that for *every person* there will be a *different message,* although each will follow a general pattern of instruction, with the Holy Spirit underscoring the points that will most cut home to the sinner's heart.

2. False presentation of what it is to be saved. Unscriptural ideas of sin and guilt and our required response in conversion will result in "converts" who rapidly return to their old ways. Which is better: for a person not to hear, or for a person to hear what is untrue, get a false hope, and still go to hell? What you say to non-Christians may vary, but whatever is said, you should not give any directions that are incomplete and leave them without a clear picture of what God requires them to do. Challenge them to give their hearts to the One who made them and loves them. They should be fully ready to die and meet God the moment after they follow your instructions. When apparent converts turn away from their new faith, we can't always blame them or circumstances. We must always also ask ourselves: "Did I do my job and give them the full and honest truth?"

DO IT DAILY

Most of the time, daily loving contact with others will create natural opportunities to witness. As you live the life of Jesus Christ in you, His Spirit will draw those who need help across your path. Ask God for this;

your task is to be alert to *see* those people when they come and be ready to help them.

Don't try to scheme how you will lead conversations around to spiritual things. *Honestly, sincerely be concerned about others and listen!* Find out their real problems and needs. If you try to launch some canned plan or presentation, they will sense you have something on your mind not related to what they are saying and may think you don't really care about them at all. If you listen carefully, God will show you their greatest point of need and what false "god" needs to be surrendered for salvation.

The best way to bring people's attention to Jesus when a divine opportunity occurs is by *raising a question at a point of interest.* This was Christ's way of witness. He either created a situation that made the other person ask a question or directly asked one himself. These questions were always loving, geared to the other's basic need, and never offensive. They also could not be answered with a yes or a no, creating opportunities for further questions. Jesus answered these replies in the same way, encouraging people to face their sin and give Him their trust. Here are some such questions:

- Are you interested in spiritual things?
- If someone asked you, "What is a follower of Jesus?" what would you answer?
- Have you ever had God deal personally with you?
- How did you give your life to the Lord?
- Someday when you stand before God, what reason are you going to give Him as to why He should let you into His kingdom?

OVERCOMING FEAR

Fear in witness is created by three basic factors: (1) inadequate training or preparation; (2) self-consciousness from insufficient prayer or concern for the other person; and (3) not knowing what might happen when the truth is presented. You will lift a load off your mind if you realize there are only five basic attitudes non-Christians can adopt when witness occurs:

INDIFFERENCE

The Bible shows this is the ordinary state of truly lost people. They don't know or care that they are sinners, and only God can open their eyes to their sad situation. Prayer, care, and a loving but firm warning from the Word of God, coupled with your invitation to further consideration, are your only tools here.

CURIOSITY

This is a sign of an awakened hunger for reality or further consideration. Present as simply as possible God's claims on their lives. Love them, smile at yourself now and then, but be firm and concerned. Ask questions to make sure others understand what you say.

HESITANCY

This is often a sign of sin being exposed. If people ask questions, use them to try to point them back to their personal responsibility to God. Answer as briefly as possible. If you feel the questions are only some kind of excuse, show them you understand they are excuses and that they are not sincere about giving themselves to God.

For example: "How do you know God isn't just your imagination?"

"That's the same sort of thing I said when I lived for myself. I knew God was real all the time, but I didn't want to live for Him. It was easier to deny His reality than to answer His claims on my life."

"Yes, but He might be real only to you; He's not real to me!"

"Of course He's not real to you. He never *will* be as long as you keep serving and living for yourself. You will only find Him when you quit living in sin and honestly face Him. . . ." etc.

ACCEPTANCE

If this is real, acceptance is usually a sign God has already been working to lead these people to Him. Check very carefully to be sure they fully understand what they are doing and grasp the cost of total surrender to Jesus. Suspect quick decisions made without question and without signs of struggle, surrender, or change after prayer. That can mean they made a fake decision in order to escape conviction.

REJECTION

Don't be too quick to give up when people reject your witness. God doesn't give up on us, and patient love has won out many times. But if the truth is fully faced and finally rejected, you should give people the chance to *completely understand* what they are doing to God's offer of love and mercy and what they are choosing forever as their destiny. Show your grief and concern. Sometimes a final clarification has brought home what it means to reject Christ and His Gospel, and people have at last turned to God. Never close the book on people. Only God has that sad right. Tell them you will keep praying.

CORE FACTS FOR NON-CHRISTIANS WHO COULDN'T CARE LESS

When witnessing to unconcerned non-Christians, you need to give them a sense of their true guilt before God. Keep in mind these facts as you witness to people who couldn't appear to care less:

1. All happiness depends on each moral creature living unselfishly, including people.

2. People were made to be governed *by motives* and not by mere force. We need a Ruler who can direct us into the wisest choices and so bring all the highest happiness. We need Someone smart enough and good enough to show anyone anywhere what is true and best.

3. God has the supreme right to be the core focus of our lives. He is not only our Leader and Director but our original loving Father and Friend.

God's right does not come from the fact that He made us, loves us, or even that He died for us. His right rests in the truth that we need guidance, direction, and ultimate authority. Why is He the only one who is qualified to give us these things? Because

- He is everywhere present and can see all that is happening in the universe.
- He knows every fact fully and perfectly and has perfect wisdom.
- He has endless power and energy to help and direct or enforce right.
- He is our only example of perfect justice and completely unselfish conduct.

These qualifications both mandate Him to rule us and oblige us to obey Him. To refuse to do so is unintelligent, dangerous to the universe, destructive to the happiness of others, and ultimately deserving of punishment. Selfishness is the essence of sin. It denies God's right to be God and ignores the happiness of others except when it contributes to a sinner's own happiness. Left unchecked, selfishness would ultimately destroy the universe, and a terribly great penalty comes by committing it. This penalty is endless death on an eternal scale. If people insist on breaking the known guidelines for happiness, God must curb the cancer of their rebellion by sentencing them to preserve the highest good of the universe. When this happens, unrepentant sinners bring on themselves an agony equal to the guilt they have incurred. This terrible sentence of judgment and death grieves God, but without harming the universe He cannot wisely suspend it unless a substitute is found for the penalty that satisfies justice.

TALKING WITH THOSE WHO COULDN'T CARE LESS: TIMING

Most people don't care about Christ. When you do witness, don't go when they are:

1. Busy. People won't think your message is as urgent as their work at hand. Wait until they are more relaxed and ready to listen before you begin to witness.

2. Under chemical influence. If you can smell alcoholic breath or sense drug use in people you want to witness to, they may be too under the influence to be fully responsible. People affected by alcohol or drugs often talk readily about God, but their talk is seldom sincere and decisions for Christ made under these conditions rarely last. If you want to talk, wait until they sober up first or wait for another chance.

3. Excited. It takes a far greater passion on your part to turn people's thoughts to God when they are excited or angry. If you spark people's natural animosity toward God while they are angry, it may turn into open violence. Don't provoke wrath—speak gently when you witness. If the person you are talking to gets louder, speak more softly (Proverbs 15:1).

Do go:

1. In God's timing. He often changes situations through prayer, creating a need for sensitivity to His Spirit. You may be strongly directed to speak to someone at a certain time, and this might be God's time to talk. Go immediately, as soon as God opens the way to witness. He knows the times when we are most strongly influenced for truth.

2. Early. Don't put off witnessing, hoping for a better time. It's *always* a bad time to witness! Look for a chance to talk, and if none comes, make one. Make an appointment so people will know it is important. Follow it up until they give their lives to God or you are sure you can do nothing more for them but pray.

3. Alone. People hide their true feelings about God when they are in a group. Pride can stop them from being honest, and they resist what they normally would yield to if alone. Get them away from the group, and you will see their true state.

TALKING WITH THOSE WHO COULDN'T CARE LESS: ATTITUDE

DO

1. Be short. Don't "spin out" what you have to say. Get to the point as soon as you can. If you sense people are close to making a decision, if possible call them to make a choice. Try not to give the impression they can repent later. God expects and will empower them to repent now, although they *may* need more time to allow the Spirit to work in their lives.

2. Be kind. If you lose your temper, you lose your witness. If you are snubbed or laughed at, guard your spirit from anger. Don't embarrass God.

3. Be serious. Don't have a light attitude. You are talking about eternal issues, and you won't seem really convinced that these people's destiny is for eternity. You don't want anyone to try laughing off what God has to say through you. Earnestness will convince more than words that what He says is true.

4. Be patient. Stick with people if they have real difficulty in understanding. Repeat what you say and illustrate it. If you know a question is an excuse, make them see it is an excuse and that they aren't sincere in making it. Let God enlist people's own consciences.

5. Be direct. Don't ignore anything He shows you about others' character or relationship to God that may prick their pride. Be open and up-front about what you know, not to wound or to offend but because they need to see where their problem is. Only a careless surgeon leaves rotting tissue in patients. Don't hide the truth. It may hurt, but be up-front or you won't help.

6. Be particular. Don't talk about sin abstractly. Make people feel you mean them. Don't be afraid of underlining particular sins you may know they are guilty of in an effort to avoid hurting their feelings. Hell is far worse than momentary embarrassment! Plainly but kindly face them with these to show how they are fighting God.

7. Stick to the point. Don't wander around the main issues, get side-tracked, or yield to smoke screens. This does more harm than good. If people bring something up that leads you off course, simply tell them you will be happy to look at that with them later, but right now you want to know what they are going to do with Jesus.

8. Aim at the conscience. Again, your greatest internal ally in dealing with non-Christians is their conscience. Impress on them the sad effects of past failures in their lives and those of others, and the Holy Spirit will ram truth home with a pile-driving impact. The Word of God and the response of conscience go hand-in-hand.

DON'T

1. Be hard. Show that you love people and want them to have the best for time and eternity. If you are pushy and bossy, you will needlessly offend.

2. Be harsh. There is no need to be abrupt or rude. Give the right impression about the Christ you love and represent (1 Peter 3:8–9).

3. Apologize. If people blame Christians or churches for past wrongs, *don't* agree or they will think you are siding with them against God. Tell them we don't have to answer for others but for ourselves and our sins. (Never apologize for your own life! If you have to always do this, you shouldn't be witnessing!)

TALKING WITH THOSE WHO COULDN'T CARE LESS: BARRIERS

When God's truth comes in power to the hearts of non-Christians, prepare for possible barriers of defense. They usually take one or a combination of these four forms:

1. MENTAL—*Argument.* Don't argue back! Answer only by raising a further question or by further defining what you have just said. Answer with facts. Don't raise your voice, get angry or sarcastic, or ridicule people. If you know they are making excuses, point that out.

2. PHYSICAL—*Attack.* You may be physically assaulted in your wit-

ness for Christ. This is rare in countries with Christian backgrounds if your witness is not offensive or belligerent, but it can happen. In this case, you are under direct command "not to resist an evil person" (Matthew 5:38–48; see also Titus 3:2; Colossians 3:13; Ephesians 4:2). You may not be able to control your feelings of hurt or anger if this happens, but you can cry out inside to Christ to help you make the right choice and not hit back. This is showing true love. Remember, the word *martyr* means witness.

3. SOCIAL—*Avoiding you.* This is one of the most common barriers. If your witness hits home, non-Christians may try to steer clear of you. Don't trail them around if this is happening; just be there at key times. It is not really *you* they are trying to hide from but God. They may avoid your words and eyes, but you might be able to communicate your love and prayers to them in a way that they cannot avoid.

4. SPIRITUAL—"Assuring" you that they are already saved, belong to a church, have their own religion, etc. You can clarify religious non-Christians' stands before Christ by asking them about the events leading up to the time of their conversion and what took place. Point out the essential difference between true Christians and religiously selfish people—a true devotion to Jesus Christ and the Christian love that marks the unselfish life. This is the hardest kind of barrier to crack because it seems strikingly similar to true faith.

Non-Christians take any road to escape truth when presented with the Good News. Provided they are not objecting to your timing or attitude, many excuses come from the sinners' commitment to remaining selfish. If they can make you think they are not *able* to do what God asks, you will never witness with power and confidence.

TALKING WITH OTHER KINDS OF NON-CHRISTIANS

THOSE WHO ARE SHAKEN UP

Sometimes events happen that make non-Christians think about God. Sickness, disaster, death in the family, some disappointment or near tragedy can waken us to God's claims and prepare us to listen with attention and seriousness. This openness is not the same as being convicted of sin! Don't lose the opportunity if you meet people like this. Pour light and love in on their hearts and minds. Let God use truth to reveal their sins and need of a Savior.

Once people are awakened, the work of years can be done in minutes. Bring them *at once* to the point of decision. If you miss your chance, you may miss it forever. Don't shrug off your responsibility or be silent if God places people like this in your path.

THOSE WHO ARE CONVICTED BUT NOT CONVERTED

There is always some reason for a convicted sinner not yielding to God. Our task is to find it, bring it out, and deal with it. Many times they know what is wrong but try to hide it from you. Other times they are self-deceived and may not see the reason. Ask these questions:

- Have you done something wrong you are not willing to make right?
- Is there something you are not willing to give to God?
- Is there an idol in your life you are not willing to give up for Christ?
- Has someone hurt you whom you are not willing to forgive?
- Did you do something in the past you don't want to confess?
- Are you prejudiced against someone? (Maybe a Christian with a poor witness?)
- Are you waiting for God to do something before you give yourself to Him?
- Do you think you have committed the unpardonable sin?
- Have you been playing with spiritual powers outside of Jesus Christ?

If you meet hesitation, confusion, or silence in response to any of these, you should probe deeper. Usually it is just *one point* God is waiting for us to yield. The moment we give in simply because God asks us to, true conversion begins. People often ask, "Will I have to give up _____?" Whatever it is, tell them plainly, "Yes." It is probably the very thing they do have to give up because it is their god. If God is dealing with them on one point, don't compromise or pass it by, or they will get a false hope and a sham experience. Jesus didn't give in to the rich young ruler even though He loved him (Luke 18:18–25). If the young man had been allowed to keep the god of his possessions, he would have felt relieved, called himself a true disciple, joined the church, and still gone to hell. Don't try to make salvation easier than *God* has.

COVERING THE FACTS

Here is a simple outline of steps in salvation that can be used as a starting point in talking to the convicted. With each person, emphasize the particular sections that he or she needs to clearly understand. Work with the Holy Spirit to find these, and ask after each: "Are you ready to do this?"

1. Rethink

Stop running away from the voice of God and look at your life. We do not naturally *want* to obey God; only if we let the Holy Spirit show us our sin as God sees it will we realize just how bad we have been. To do this, you must be totally honest!

Don't pretend.

Don't play down your sin.

Don't make excuses!

Admit it from your heart: "God, I am all wrong!"

If necessary, get a paper and pencil and write down the things that have come between you and God and stopped you from serving Him as you should.

2. Repent

Turn your back on your old way of life. Be willing to lose any habit, any plan, any friend that you have been living your life for instead of God. This is not easy, but Jesus said if we wanted to follow Him, we must first *count the cost* (Luke 14:25–33). Salvation is like a marriage. Two people promise themselves to each other and pledge their love to each other before a watching world. In doing this, they give up all their old dates. This is what God wants you to do to know His love.

3. Renounce

Give up all *rights* to your own life. If you are going to be a part of God's world-changing family, you cannot be your own boss any longer. You must die to your own plans, dreams, and ambitions and be willing to do whatever God wants you to do. It may hurt to surrender everything at first, but God knows best and will *never* ask you to do anything that you will regret in the end. He knows exactly what will make you most happy. True Christians have nothing of their own. Time, talents, money, possessions, friends, career, and future—all must be surrendered for God's service wherever and whenever He wants them.

4. Replan

Be prepared to make many *changes* in your life! The very moment you make this heart choice for God, the old "you" will die and a new person will begin to live inside you. If the Holy Spirit is speaking to you about getting something right with someone, you must be *willing* to do it. Wherever you need to confess wrong or restore or repay something to someone, Jesus will give you the courage and the words to say. Becoming a Christian implies the willingness, as far as humanly possible, to right all known wrong (Proverbs 28:13). If you have written out a list of things that have come between you and God, ask His forgiveness for those against Him. Plan to make things right with people you know you have wronged. The circle of confession should fit the circle of the sin committed. Those sins only against God, confess only to Him; those only against one person, to that person alone; those against a group, to the whole group.

5. Receive

Ask Jesus Christ by faith to rule in your heart as King. He must be your absolute Boss from now on! This act of faith is neither an idea nor a feeling but an act, a choice of your will made intelligently and carefully. Give Him your doubts, your weakness, and your loneliness. Your heart will never have peace, your doubts will never clear up, and you will never die to the world until you trust, surrender, and believe from your heart! *Be totally honest with Him.* Receive Christ into your life as your Lord and Master to live for Him from this moment on (Romans 10:9–10).

WHAT TO TELL NEW CHRISTIANS

What instructions should you give people whom you lead to God? Help them begin the process of surrendering to Christ by suggesting they tell Him something like, "Lord Jesus, please forgive me for my sin. I admit to you honestly today that all my life I've lived for myself. I want to give up all rights to my life right now and ask you to forgive my sin and make me one of your children. Be my Boss from this moment forward in everything I say and do. Thank you, Lord. Amen." Then leave them a few suggestions for beginning a life with the Lord Jesus.

Whatever you do, don't say

1. *"Now you are saved!"*

It is better not to say this because

- *You* don't keep the Book of Life, *God* does. He knows if a prayer was a heart cry or not and whether new life has begun. You don't. You have no right to tell others what God alone can assure them of.

- Better they find out their salvation is real for themselves. Faith is strengthened by testing, not propping. If it is real, it will stand life's hard honesty.

- If you tell people this, it is *your* word they rely on. You might find they are *your* convert, not God's, and *you* will have to keep them instead of God! Letting only God grant assurance soon proves if their stand was an experiment or an experience.

2. *"How do you feel?"*

The Christian life is an outflow of faith by trust of the will. Choose God's way, and feeling will follow. But don't give the impression that feelings are a guide to whether people are saved, or they will lose assurance with a headache! Teach their *duty,* feelings or not.

3. *Too much!*

Keep some instruction for another time. If you give people too much at once, they won't remember it, will get confused, or will feel like a failure. Babies don't start learning the more complex truths of life the moment they are born; it is the same with spiritual babies.

Whatever you do, do say

1. *"Did you really mean what you just asked God?"*

This will help you discover doubt. If people still doubt, there is often still something to be done. Perhaps they are holding something back and haven't completely given themselves up to God. Don't be afraid to dig deeply here. Unless a conversion is deep and thorough, the resulting Christian life will be less fruitful, useful, and blessed. Give clear, strong, and firm directions. Tell people it is sin to have reason to doubt and sin to doubt without reason (Romans 14:23). If you leave them uncertain, they will at best be sickly, shaky Christians.

2. *"Would you like to thank God for what you just did?"*

This is an acid test of reality: If they can honestly thank God for their salvation, you can be reasonably sure it is genuine.

Do teach them to

1. Expect to enjoy God's love and favor.

This won't mean they will always be excited or always be directly thinking of God, but their hearts should be at peace and enjoying the blessing of Christ. If you give the impression it doesn't matter if they lose the sense of God's love and favor, you shouldn't be surprised when they backslide from God. Sin *should* cause doubt and worry in Christians so that they will tearfully go back to God to confess their wrong. The only real evidence of salvation is lovingly obeying God from the heart (Luke 6:43–49).

2. Spend time with other Christians who love Christ wholeheartedly.

Don't leave people with backsliders or hypocrites or they may try to take their standards from them. If, however, they don't *want* to be with God's people, there is probably something wrong with their salvation (1 John 1:7).

3. Renounce ownership of all they have—time, talents, money, and possessions.

Unless they have truly done this to the best of their present knowledge, they are not Christians. They should not be left to think *anything* still belongs to them. Nothing is their own anymore—property, influence, body, or soul. All belongs to God. They have chosen to be not their own but God's servants, to be ruled and directed at His pleasure. They have chosen to be CORE.

CORE Signs of Salvation

True Christians will show *definite signs* of a real experience with God that has resulted in a genuine conversion to Christ. The following are evidences—*not* proof!—that a person has become a Christian. The first evidences are *external*—ones that you, the witness, can recognize. The second are *internal,* things new Christians should look for in their own lives.

OUTWARD SIGNS

1. Desire for Scripture. True Christians want to read the Bible to find out what God expects of them. Scripture is spiritual "food." "Man shall not live by bread alone, but by every word that proceeds from the mouth of God" (Matthew 4:4; see also Deuteronomy 6:5–7; Job 23:12; Jeremiah 15:16; Romans 10:17; 15:4; 1 Peter 2:2).

2. Difference in standards. New Christians begin to show a radical change in habit, action, and purpose. They want to be different in word, thought, and action. It may take time for the inward change to show outwardly in some things, but never condemn new converts for what they *are* until you find out first what they want to *be*! "Therefore, if anyone is in Christ, he is a new creation; old things have passed away; behold, all things have become new" (2 Corinthians 5:17; see also Galatians 6:15–16; Ephesians 4:20–24; 1 John 3:1–3).

3. Difference of self. A child of God begins to tighten the rein on old habits of self-indulgence even in the ordinary areas of life, like eating and drinking. Harmful stimulants, too many late nights or late mornings, extravagant clothes, empty entertainment, coarse language, and spending patterns all come up for inspection and change. "And everyone who has this hope in Him purifies himself, just as He is pure" (1 John 3:3; see also Matthew 16:24; 1 Corinthians 10:13).

4. Despised by the surrounding culture. New Christians may experience trouble from those who know them well but who don't understand their new life, or from those who have backslidden into old ways and priorities and whose lukewarm faith a new convert may show up. "All who desire to live godly in Christ Jesus will suffer persecution" (2 Timothy 3:12; see also Acts 5:40–41; Romans 8:18; 2 Timothy 2:12; Philippians 1:28–29; 1 Peter 2:20–21).

5. Seek other Christians. Wanting to be with other Christians and a real love for true children of God is a sure sign of new birth. "By this all will know that you are My disciples, if you have love for one another" (John 13:35; see also Acts 2:42; Romans 15:5–6; Ephesians 3:17–19; Hebrews 10:25; 1 Peter 1:22; 1 John 1:2, 7; 3:14).

6. Serve God. New Christians look for ways and means to please Jesus. They begin to witness for Him and want to bring other people into a right relationship with Him. "For to me, to live is Christ, and to die is gain" (Philippians 1:21; see also Matthew 10:32; 1 Peter 3:15).

7. Stick to the task. New Christians keep pushing forward for God despite failure or setbacks. They are determined to stay true to God no matter what. "One thing I do, forgetting those things which are behind and reaching forward to those things which are ahead, I press toward the goal" (Psalm 37:23–24; Romans 6:1–14; Philippians 3:13–14; 2 Peter 1:10).

INWARD SIGNS

1. Assurance of God's love. This clears away doubt for Christians and makes them active for God, decided in faith, and holy. "All that the Father gives Me will come to Me, and the one who comes to Me I will by no means cast out" (John 6:37; see also 5:24; 16:27–33; Acts 13:39; Romans 15:13; 8:38–39; 1 John 1:2; 4:18; 5:12–13).

2. All-sustaining peace. The peace Christians experience upholds them through trials and hard times. Christians have a freedom from fear no matter how dangerous, difficult, or deadly a situation may be. "The peace of God, which passes all understanding, will guard your hearts and minds through Jesus Christ" (Philippians 4:7; see also Luke 12:32; John 14:1–2, 27; 2 Timothy 1:7; 2 Corinthians 5:1, 8).

3. Awakened conscience. Christians have a greater awareness of thoughts, words, or actions that are not pleasing to God. Christians respect the power of sin and keep God's commandments. "We know that we are of God, and the whole world lies under the sway of the wicked one" (John 14:15, 21; Romans 12:2; 1 Corinthians 2:14; James 1:12; 1 Peter 1:13–16; 1 John 5:19).

4. Search for truth. Christians show genuine desire for reality and a solid foundation on which to build the new life. They turn to both the Word of God and to other spiritual Christians. "For everyone practicing evil hates the light. . . . But he who does the truth comes to the light, that his deeds may be clearly seen, that they have been done in God" (John 3:20–21; see also 5:39; 8:12, 31; Acts 17:11; 1 Corinthians 2:9–16).

5. Spirit witness. The Holy Spirit gives Christians a consciousness of *acceptance* with God on the merit of Jesus. "For as many as are led by the Spirit of God, these are sons of God" (Romans 8:14; see also 8:9; John 14:17; 1 John 4:13; 5:10).

6. Sonship awareness. When God is truly Father, Christians have a warm sense of *parental affection* and care from Him. "And because you are sons, God has sent forth the Spirit of His Son into your hearts, crying out, 'Abba, Father!'" (Galatians 4:6; see also Romans 8:15-17, 28-29; John 1:12; 2 Corinthians 6:16-18; Ephesians 2:18; 1 John 3:1-2).

7. *Social concern.* Christians are interested in the needs of others, desire to promote righteousness and study, and they think of ways to convert, sanctify, and reform others. "But whoever has this world's goods, and sees his brother in need, and shuts up his heart from him, how does the love of God abide in him?" (1 John 3:17; see also Proverbs 11:25; 3:16-24; 2 Corinthians 9:6-8).

Signs People Have Rejected God

Those who have deliberately hurt and turned away God's Spirit by continually rebelling against truth are in great danger of being forever lost to God. There are some evidences—again, not proof—that show people have gone down this path and further attempts at witness may be pointless:

1. *Rich in sin over a long period.* People who profit, especially a lot, from sin and its consequences are in danger of sacrificing eternal rights and riches for material wealth. "I was envious . . . when I saw the prosperity of the wicked. . . . Until I went into the sanctuary of God; then I understood their end" (Psalm 73:3-17; see also Psalm 49; Jeremiah 5:27-29; Luke 12:15-21).

2. *Run from truth.* Those who have rejected God make a habit of avoiding places and people connected with salvation. They don't go to church, don't read the Bible, and avoid CORE Christians. If a fatal disease is spreading, the ones *sure* to die are those who ignore the cure. "'As I live,' says the Lord GOD, 'I have no pleasure in the death of the wicked. . . . Turn, turn from your evil ways! For why should you die, O house of Israel?' " (Ezekiel 33:11; see also John 5:39-40; 8:24; 9:41).

3. *Rebel instead of repent* when corrected or punished. When troubles intended to make people turn in desperation to God come along, those who have rejected God become more and more bitter against Him. "My son, do not despise the chastening of the LORD, nor detest His correction; for whom the LORD loves He corrects, just as a father

the son in whom he delights" (Proverbs 3:11–12). "Why should you be stricken again? You will revolt more and more" (Isaiah 1:5; see also Psalm 94:12; Revelation 3:19).

4. *Age in sin.* Most people are saved under the age of twenty-five. The older people are, the less likely it is they will repent. Those who set their hearts on making their mark in the world while coldly calculating to give their lives to God later are trying to take advantage of God's patience. They hope to give the jaded remnant of a devil-serving life to God before it is too late. This will not work. "My Spirit shall not strive with man forever, for he is indeed flesh" (Genesis 6:3; see also Ecclesiastes 12:1; Romans 2:4–10).

5. *Absence of correction or punishment.* When people have *no* trouble in their lives they are *in* trouble! Satan never seems to bother much with people who have no interest in the things of God. "Do not despise the chastening of the LORD . . . for whom the LORD loves He chastens" (Hebrews 12:5–8; see also Psalm 94:12; Proverbs 3:11; Revelation 3:19).

6. *Accepts a damning heresy.* God sends strong delusions so that those who reject Him believe a lie, because "they did not believe the truth but had pleasure in unrighteousness" (2 Thessalonians 2:12). The more certain their damnation is, the more certainly they believe the lie. Charles Finney wrote, "Beware how you trifle with God's truth. How often have individuals begun to argue in favor of heresy for the sake of argument . . . until they have finally come to believe their own lie, and are lost forever." (See also Romans 1:28–32; 2 Peter 2:1–3.)

Creating a Holy Epidemic

The core temperature of a body is the minimum heat needed to sustain life. If the body temperature drops below this mark for too long, we die. God's way of reversing core death in His world is by revivals in the church and evangelism in the world. Just as sin that brings death spreads like an epidemic, Gods answer is a witness like a divine countervirus.

True revivals and evangelism spread like a healing epidemic. The force and power of an epidemic depend on these things:

- The seriousness of the sickness. How deeply does it affect people, how long does it last, and will it threaten their very lives?
- How rapidly and effectively an infection is transmitted. How quickly does it jump from person to person, and how easily or simply can it be caught?
- Community. How many people will it affect? Where might it touch large groups of people?

Epidemics stop spreading for the same reason revivals, evangelism, and missions come to an end: If our life as a witness is no longer infectious enough to be taken seriously, if what we profess to have cannot seriously threaten a diseased culture, or if some system succeeds in keeping us isolated from people, our witness will die.

For this reason, we must take care to radiate a God-authorized and God-centered message with power to genuinely and practically transform lives. We must maintain a life before God as challenging and infectious as His to everyone we meet. And we must resist the powers and structures that would hinder His work and go where the people are, most especially to those areas where rapid and powerful change in one person cannot fail to affect and transmit to others.

Nor do they light a lamp and put it under a basket, but on a lampstand, and it gives light to all who are in the house. NKJV

Neither do people light a lamp and put it under a bowl. Instead they put it on its stand, and it gives light to everyone in the house. NIV

Don't hide your light under a basket! Instead, put it on a stand and let it shine for all. NLT

NOR DO PEOPLE LIGHT A LAMP AND PUT IT UNDER A BASKET, BUT ON A STAND, AND IT GIVES LIGHT TO ALL IN THE HOUSE. ESV

If I make you light-bearers, you don't think I'm going to hide you under a bucket, do you? I'm putting you on a light stand.
THE MESSAGE

Nor does anyone light a lamp and put it under a basket, but on the lampstand, and it gives light to all who are in the house. NASB

15

CORE
COMMUNITY

COMING TOGETHER IN CHRIST

Nor do they light a lamp and put it under a basket, but on a lampstand, and it gives light to all who are in the house.

MATTHEW 5:15

What does God most want for His creation? God, who is in himself a Trinity of loving, caring Persons, most wants us to form a real and lasting friendship with Him and with one another. No matter what our backgrounds, nationalities, or circumstances, this hunger is written deep in all our hearts. We all long for a real home, family, friendship, and love. We long to care and be cared for, to share joy. Salvation is restoration to God's family, and His kingdom is built on CORE community.

CORE Church

The idea of community and a desire for it are very strong in a generation that often feels alienated from family and other social groups. A longing for community, especially one that can make a difference in this world, is one of the reasons many young adults first come to church.

The Bible definition of church is a "company of believers" or "called-out ones"—a witness to God's power and glory (Romans 1:7; 1 Corinthians 1:2). It is not a building but a group of Christian *people,* wherever and however they are able to meet. The way they are organized, where they meet, or the methods they use are unimportant. The *Person* around whom they meet is their supreme common ground (1 Corinthians 1:2; 2 Corinthians 1:1; 1 Thessalonians 1:1; Ephesians 2:19–22).

Though the church is not a building, it is still God's house—one built not of bricks and wood but of people. There is no place we can build adequate to honor who He is, and there is no sense in putting fortunes into doing so when the world's spiritual needs are unmet. But God's church *is* called to provide all a physical house can offer: shelter, care, community, comfort, protection, provision, rest. The church is to radiate Christ like a light on a stand.

The Church at Home

The early church thrived in actual house churches, informal meetings of CORE Christians that took place in people's homes. In this environment, they practiced personal evangelism daily and easily cared for new converts. The house church is simple in principle but far-reaching in practice. It costs nothing extra yet meets every need. It can never become too big. It is the perfect place of Christian fellowship.

Throughout the Bible the home is central. God frequently uses the illustration of the church as a family. He is our Father; we are His children. The home is the basic unit of society, the real strength of a nation, and God planned Christian life to begin in the home.

There is a beautiful simplicity in the home gathering. In Bible times the door of a home was always open to people's needs. No one had to put on special clothes to go and hear a special man in a special place. It is a perfect place to invite even unbelievers. Informal, natural, and without stigma, people can meet there simply and without stuffiness.

Community built around common interests and callings is effective because it isn't artificial. No mass meeting can ever take the place of the honesty and hunger for truth that reveals itself in a home or other small-group setting. Early disciples never used the temple or a public place of worship for fellowship with the CORE community but as a public witness and as a place of prayer.

Meeting in small groups can temper the temptation a leader can have to be too self-important in ministering. Pride can be a very real danger to those God puts into places of authority. In a home or small-group meeting, leaders have to be real, instead of putting on a "show" to impress a crowd. Teaching can be more specific and practical, and people's needs can receive personal attention.

For early Christians, when a group grew too large, it very naturally split. Another home was opened and another group began. Dividing to multiply, the early church evangelized by leaps and bounds. In just two years *all Asia* was reached with the Gospel (Acts 5:42; 19:20; 20:20).

Multitudes around the world hungry for genuine Christian community are meeting in homes for prayer and Bible study. God is preparing His worldwide CORE for the greatest evangelism thrust of all time, and you can be a part of it.

Wherever you meet, give yourself to a community of Christians who really love God and love people. Ideally their goal will be to help and reach the community God has called them to care for. Go to a place where they love you enough to tell you the truth, to comfort you when you are down, and to correct you when you are not doing well. Choose to be a part of a community where the focus is Jesus as Lord, wisdom is grounded in God's Word, and the desire to see people meet Him is pursued with passion and priority.

How to Multiply the Message

If the "seed" God scatters is His CORE, how do new "plants" take root? There must be *growth* before there is reproduction. Crowd work is effective in mass evangelism but not in training and teaching. How can new disciples be taught truth, built up in faith, and trained for world conquest? There are challenges involved in starting a core of Christian life. Unless discipled honestly and realistically, new Christians may never mature in their faith in Christ, and some may spiritually die.

1. Groups must be small.

- Members should know one another. When groups become too large, it is impossible to form meaningful relationships and keep one another accountable to living a pure life before God.

- Everyone *learns* better in a small group. When there are questions, it is easier to ask them, and answers are given rather than missed or ignored.

- Larger groups have a greater tendency to fall into formality or a set pattern. Small groups are more flexible and adaptable.

- *Everyone* has to take part. Each member of the body of Christ has something to contribute. Everyone, even the shyest and youngest, needs a chance to add to the CORE's effectiveness.

2. People must be available . . .

- *for instruction.* New Christians tend to have crises and concerns at unpredictable hours. Some problems are too urgent to be put off for another time. The group must be able to meet often but always be available to help one another when difficulties come.

- *for fellowship.* A fire burns best when all the wood shares the flame equally. God doesn't want anyone in His body to be independent because a body can't function that way. We all need the Lord Jesus and we all need one another. We need to find a place where we can meet to worship God and share our love for Him.

- *for refuge.* Never forget—true Christianity always brings *persecution.* Jesus' disciples lived in constant danger. Enemies of the Gospel, faced with living truth and rejecting it, must either run from or destroy it to live unconvicted. The meeting place must also be a *place of safety* emotionally, spiritually, and physically.

Revival in the Church

Revival is what happens when Christians return to obeying God. Two conditions mark every revival in history, and no one will experience a true spiritual awakening unless both are present: *prayer* and *unity* (Matthew 18:19; John 17:20-23; Acts 1:14; 2:1). Unity can come through love expressed in forgiveness, discipline, and the willingness to receive correction and criticism. It also comes through the forces that shape a genuine spiritual awakening.

1. VISION—Proverbs 29:18.

People need to see, experience, and feel that God is at work in an active, vital way. Whenever God wants to give a vision, He looks for a person who will trust Him and do His will. Vision is born out of true prayer, obedience, and genuine, unselfish love. It comes when people are cleansed from all sin and begin to pray that God will supercharge them by His Holy Spirit (Joel 2:28; Habakkuk 2:2).

2. KNOWLEDGE—Hosea 4:6.

The experiences of vision must be married to facts of knowledge. We must know from God what is important to Him and His purposes and commit ourselves to His truth. People unite around common facts. To create true unity, these facts must be true, or there will be no unity under the Spirit of truth. These facts also must be valuable—important to the time in which they are preached. God wants to speak to us about what is important to shape our time. Unless Christians can discern and obey the truth, no revival is possible (Proverbs 22:17–21; Romans 10:2). We must return to what He has said in His Word.

When these essentials of vision and knowledge are split apart from each other, people can easily become experience- or knowledge-centered, and these divisions can mar any part of the Christian church. If your Christian community does not display evidence of an awakening, you are called to pray for and bring change in both areas. We must learn together what it means to love the Lord with all our heart and soul and mind.

Why Different Churches?

Why are there so many denominations? Why can't Christians agree on a common set of ideas and unite? We all know we cannot do God's work alone; working together is the only way we will reach an entire world.

It is true that division often comes from sin (1 Corinthians 3:3) and is marked by fighting, envy, and bitterness (James 3:14–18). Sometimes, though, division is simply a consequence of place or size or other neutral factors, such as:

1. We are limited in knowing one another.

Only God has *all* knowledge. From His infinite perspective, He knows what is right in every case, and we can turn to His revealed wisdom. Agreement comes from common understanding, but that is not always possible for finite people. We have not all grown up together, experiencing the same kind of life situations, and we don't all respond the same way to different things. If we do not share a common understanding, we will not agree.

Yet time is too short for us to grasp God's whole reality. We need *eternity* to learn and share all God wants to show us as a Christian family. Since we can't see the whole picture, we all need to do what God asks of us. If each of us obeys that small part God reveals to us, He will shape our lives together to change our world (Isaiah 55:8–9; Romans 11:33; 1 Corinthians 13:9).

2. We have different personalities.

Some of us are naturally quiet, others active. Part of this depends on the way we were brought up and natural hereditary factors. God does not change our personalities when He saves us but only redirects them for His glory. To some God has given the gifts of speaking in public; to others ministering in loneliness. We cannot all act alike because we were not all born alike (1 Corinthians 3:3–11). God gave us this diversity for His purposes.

3. God calls people to work together on the basis of their being able to agree together.

Remember, the goal is always the same: God himself! All CORE Christians agree on the goal (1 Corinthians 8:5-7 KJV). But if we differ basically in our understanding of how to plan the work God gives us to do, we will not work well as a team (Matthew 18:19; Luke 10:1). The subchoices we make to reach the goal are *human* decisions made on our limited, available knowledge of situations, and we may not agree on these.

If we feel before God that we can serve Him best one way, we should team with those who agree with this calling. There is no need or sense in fighting over the *means* to accomplish the goal (Mark 9:38–40). If Christians cannot agree on a plan, it is not *sin* to part but common sense. Separation in this case lets us carry out God's intended work for each of us in the best way possible (Acts 13:1–3; 15:36–40).

4. The world has different needs.

Christ has set different offices in the church to take care of the various spiritual needs of the world (Romans 12:3–9; 1 Corinthians 12:28). Often a particular form of witness is needed to reach certain kinds of people. You cannot reach everyone effectively; others, through background and training, are better qualified to present truth to some than you, and no one is sufficient by him or herself. All of us need one another just as we need God. God points out a task and fits people into it, and He has equipped each of us to do a task uniquely so as to show His great diversity and creativity.

MULTIPLICATION BY DIVISION

Too often Christians unwittingly fight God by trying to herd together an ever-enlarging group. God wants Christians to spread out thin so that the message of the Gospel can touch many lives. If seeds aren't spread, growing plants will choke each other. Here are some reasons why a Christian community should divide:

1. Small group unity

While large gatherings have power to impress the public and will always have a key place in showing the world God's glory, the smaller a group, the more chance of its members building *unity* in understanding. Jesus first focused on a few, which made it easier to teach, correct, or discipline. We pray best in "twos and threes" because we can agree for one thing together more easily than in a crowd. God divides to multiply His kingdom. The CORE must consist of trained and dedicated Christians who spread out to light the world for God.

2. Fixed group comfort

Armchair Christianity is not God's idea. When we have completed a task God has given us, we tend to rest on our laurels, but a comfortable religion is not discipleship. If we dig in our heels, God will dig us out again. When the disciples began to hole up in Jerusalem, God allowed persecution, scattering them to the four corners of the world (Acts 11:19–21). When useful believers get too settled in one place, God may stir up trouble or persecution to break them up and move them out to where the need is (James 1:1; 1 Peter 1:1).

3. Large group formality.

The larger the group becomes, the greater its tendency to drift into a rut of *formalism.* Organization in the New Testament was always simple and only used when absolutely necessary. Life precedes the letter, and form follows function. The need determines the structure. With God, the simpler the better (2 Corinthians 1:12; 11:3).

If a Christian community becomes too large, there is also a greater chance its members will ignore the *spiritual* and push the *material.* Group method becomes more important than God's message. If the community becomes *too* complex, God must break it up so it again becomes teachable and functional. God has done this often in history, and we would be wise not to grieve over this kind of dissolving when it comes from Him. What God blesses, He breaks. If we object to our *own* community structure being shattered, God may leave it alone—

and us, too. All that will then remain is a monument to our failure to move.

When Jesus talked about the cost of following Him, He used two illustrations: fighting a war and forming a tower—building and battle (Luke 14:28–33). The CORE community kneels before God and stands to face the world as soldiers that build and workers that battle. *Visibility. Stability. Locality.* These are the bricks of the building. *Mobility. Flexibility. Specialty.* These are the marks of the military. One births the other and each needs the other. Local or global, until Jesus comes, the CORE should be found both building His House and fighting His battles.

Let your light shine before men in such a way that they may see your good works, and glorify your Father who is in heaven.NASB

Let your good deeds shine out for all to see, so that everyone will praise your heavenly Father.NLT

LET YOUR LIGHT SO SHINE BEFORE MEN, THAT THEY MAY SEE YOUR GOOD WORKS AND GLORIFY YOUR FATHER IN HEAVEN.

NKJV

Now that I've put you there on a hilltop, on a light stand—shine! Keep open house; be generous with your lives. By opening up to others, you'll prompt people to open up with God, this generous Father in heaven.

THE MESSAGE

Let your light shine before others, so that they may see your good works and give glory to your Father who is in heaven. ESV

Let your light shine before men, that they may see your good deeds and praise your Father in heaven.NIV

16

CORE
RADIATION

WITNESS TO ALL THE WORLD

Let your light so shine
before men, that they
may see your good
works and glorify your
Father in heaven.

MATTHEW 5:16

Every true follower of the Lord Jesus is a missionary; every lost

man or woman is a mission field. The fire begins with one person

and shines on out until the whole world is alight. As a part of God's

CORE, you stand at the end of a long line of men and women who

have carried the flame before you. Now it is your turn to

radiate His light.

Radiate Christ

Long ago God spoke to Abraham, the man recognized as the "father of the faithful" by the three great monotheistic religions of the world (Genesis 13:16; 15:5; Romans 4:18). This man listened to heaven and went out not knowing where he was going; it was to him God gave the first missionary call. Thousands of years later, that seemingly impossible call is heading toward completion. God's light radiates again in heaven and earth, and CORE Christians have inherited the honor of completing the Great Commission.

Every Christian in the world is to be in some way or another involved in worldwide missions. There are no exemptions from this responsibility. You, too, have a call to world missions. Whatever else your calling and vocation, your greatest task is to somehow be involved in God's Great Unfinished Task.

"As long as I am in the world, I am the light of the world," Jesus said (John 9:5). He is no longer in this world, but we are! His plan for us is both simple and daunting. He intends to incarnate himself again in those who trust and follow Him, to radiate through His CORE the light of His love and wisdom to the people we meet. It is an innate characteristic of a true core to radiate, to permanently affect everything and everyone around it.

Scripture gives us divine strategy for affecting entire nations. God, who gave himself to us to take away our sins, wants to purify for himself "His own special people" who are completely enthusiastic about and dedicated to doing His good works (Titus 2:14).

This tells us three things:

1. The purpose of Christ's coming to earth to die and rise again was to make possible a *genuinely pure and unselfish people* who are like Him. Prophets can make promises and gurus may pose as guides, but only Jesus can purify.

2. These people are to be completely distinct from the selfish world around them. *You can't change the world if you are just like it.*

3. What will impress non-Christians is not words but *actions*. The world will never be moved by what you say you believe but by how you live. God wants to show off His children, to show up the contrast between life in Him and without, and to show others practically how to live.

"Go into all the world and witness. If need be, use words," said Saint Francis. The power of the Gospel of the kingdom to give us a pure, peculiar, and practical life is unmatched.

KEEPING UP WITH CHANGES

How do we shine our light in a place where everything is utterly dark? Daniel and his band of brothers were subjected to changes of exponential proportions. Uprooted from their homes, their families, and everything they knew, they were marched off into captivity in a totally alien culture. In hardly more than a generation, they had to learn to adjust to a new ruling power and culture all over again when yet *another* military power conquered their world. Yet Daniel and his brothers learned so quickly that they were able to triumph for God. Like them, your culture has been conquered by Babylon. Like them, you inherit great change. Like them, you must learn to adapt your approach to reaching others for God without compromising your convictions.

You are a missionary to your world. That world changes every day. Its interests, fears, loves, hates, and heroes keep shifting. Every missionary needs to know the people, culture, customs, and language of his or her chosen field. If you just recently became a child of God, you know the culture that surrounds you and so have a great advantage. You do not have far to go to bridge the gap. Besides knowing the culture, though, you must know what to say and when to say it.

HOW TO SPEAK SO PEOPLE LISTEN

"If you talk to people in a language they don't understand, how will they know what you mean? You might as well be talking to an empty room" (1 Corinthians 14:9 NLT). A famous preacher of another century at first had great difficulty getting through to his congregation. He was a good scholar and devoted to God, but his inability to communicate deeply concerned him. When he asked God what to do, the Holy Spirit directed him to study the public and private witness of the early church in the book of Acts. There he found three common principles that he diligently applied to his next morning message. Scores of people responded. He said, "Now I know how to preach the Gospel." What did he find? The three basic elements he discovered are vital principles in talking with anyone about Christ, no matter where your mission field.

1. Establish common ground. When Paul spoke to Jewish people, he spoke as a Jewish rabbi. When his audience was Roman, he identified with them as a Roman citizen. To the Greek philosophers on Mars Hill in Athens, he quoted Greek poets, calling on what the Greeks already knew and were interested in before he spoke of Jesus and the Resurrection. Find something you and your audience, however small or large, have in common. Ask God for ideas.

All true communication is a gift of His grace. Pray for

- *Communication—the ability to make a spiritual connection with people you talk to.*
- *Conviction—that through you the Holy Spirit will make people aware of sins that need to be dealt with and forgiven, or will give them needed challenges and encouragement.*
- *Compassion—people need to sense from God that He loved them enough to die for them. When Jesus wanted to talk to us, He came to us. Actively find people to talk to and go to them in Christ.*

2. Tell people what they know to be true. To repeat, tell them what *they* know to be true. There are many things *you* know to be true, and of course you want to tell others about the truth they need to know but don't. But that is not where you start. First, tell people what they *already* know is true. Tell them the same thing in as many ways as you can.

Paul said to Agrippa, "You are expert in all customs and questions. . . . The king, before whom I also speak freely, knows these things" (Acts 26:3, 26). Use this expertise in "custom" to tell people what they already know to be true. Use every relevant popular illustration you know—songs, movies, games, stories, news, magazines. Think of what happens when you do this ten, twenty times. People hear you say something they know is true and they think, *"Well, that's true."* Then they hear you say the next thing, and the next. *"That's true, too."* If they know what you say is true each time they hear it, they will really be listening when you tell them the truth about God and His Good News, truth they may never have heard before. Remember: *All truth is God's truth, even if it isn't religious truth.* God speaks in many ways to people even when they have not heard His Word.

3. Tie what you have to say back to the Gospel. When you have established common ground and have told people many times over what they already know is true, bring everything back to Christ and His kingdom. Relate what you say to Jesus. Paul said, "To this day I stand . . . saying no other things than those which the prophets and Moses said would come— 'that the Christ would suffer . . . rise from the dead. . . . *Do you believe the prophets?* I know that you do believe" (Acts 26:22–23, 27, emphasis added).

Approach every message, every witness in this way and in this order. ("Have you ever been lonely?" "I remember when my best friend died. . . ." "This book said . . . this movie shows . . . that reporter on channel 4 said yesterday . . . this woman was so lonely she . . . I read this morning that . . .") Then put the truth back into the context of Christ. ("There is a way out of loneliness. There is a Friend who sticks closer than a brother. His name is Jesus. He said, 'Come to Me and I will give you rest.' He said, 'I will never leave you nor forsake you.'") Common ground. Culturally known truth. Context returns to Christ.

ACTIONS THAT SHINE

"For we are His workmanship, created in Christ Jesus *for good works,* which God prepared beforehand that we should walk in them" (Ephesians 2:10, emphasis added).

How do you witness to a world where people think any lifestyle is valid and all teaching—especially religious—is at heart the same? The Bible makes it plain: The best way to witness is through a loving life of good works. What we do and how we live provide irrefutable evidence of a good life. Jesus said to those who accused Him, "Many good works I have shown you from My Father. For which of those works do you stone Me?" (John 10:32). Not even government leaders can easily threaten people whose lives are full of good works (Romans 13:3).

What are "good works"? They are things that make a Christlike life valuable to others. Good works are the mark of people who freely and generously give what they can to those in need without expecting any return. This may be food, clothes, money, shelter, skills, or even opportunity. People who do good works for God are willing to communicate; they go out of their way to make friends and are ready to speak encouraging words. No matter how much such Christians' lives may challenge sin, everyone still looks forward to seeing them (1 Timothy 5:25; 6:18; 2 Timothy 3:17).

Good works aren't just *actions;* they can also be our approach to message and ministry. Those who work hard to represent Jesus both by being uncorrupted in who they are and serious and sincere about what they say show the pattern of good works (Titus 2:7). Billy Graham is known and respected around the world. His life has been a "good work." Many godly people are commended for the way they help others, from taking care of orphaned children, giving shelter to strangers, relieving the sick, to blessing other believers (Acts 9:36; 1 Timothy 2:10; 5:10). Mother Teresa's life was an example of this.

One missionary ministry tried this by searching out people and places needing help when they came to town. They went door to door saying, "We have come to town to help the neighborhood. Our team is donating to each street a gift of time and work for one week. Is there anything that we might be able to help you with for a few hours? No strings attached." Lawns, baby-sitting, housecleaning for invalids or the sick, yard cleaning, free car washes: All become silent testimonies to the power of a life transformed by unselfish love. Another church in a small city with one of the worst crime and family situations in the

ULTIMATE CORE

292

nation has become a beacon in a community eaten by robbery, addiction, and prostitution. They feed the hungry, provide safe places for children to play, and once even raised money to help their bankrupt city council pay their firemen and neighborhood security.

You might wonder whether people will be suspicious. After all, in this fallen world no one does anything for free. Real, unselfish love, the kind that comes only from God, is so rare the early church had to use an obscure word, *agape,* to describe it. But if we do good works for the right reason, simply because God asks us to and with no expectation of return, people will begin to understand just what *agape* love is. The power of good works not only blesses people, it also brings glory to God (1 Peter 2:12). The world around us will see Jesus in His people, loving them.

Preparing for the Work God Has for You

While you wait for God to make His will for you plain, there are things you can do right away, in the time you are seeking to know His purpose for your life. Don't be worried if you don't immediately know the night after you give your life to Jesus what God wants you to do! Often He puts us through training to see if we will trust Him before He makes clear what He has on His heart for us. Use these years to learn patience, divine discipline, and obedience from Him and expect that He will open the pathway to your new future. In the meantime, do these things:

1. *Follow your interests and abilities.* Sometimes our backgrounds are part of God's purpose for us; the lessons we have learned from life, the responses and the choices we have made in the past, are all used by God and woven into His ultimate purposes. Find out what you can do well and what you can't. God wants to use us as we are. What makes you different from anyone else in the world? Sometimes God may use your talents; sometimes it is your very lack of talents that makes you special to Him. Hudson Taylor, a missionary to China, said, "When God wanted to evangelize China, He looked for a man weak enough to use." Learn what you like to do well, what abilities God has given you, and try to develop them.

2. Have many interests. Learn to do many things and be interested in more than just the few things you have already done. Try your hand at different sports; they may help develop your body in ways that will make it stronger and more serviceable for Jesus in the years ahead. Experiment with different hobbies; some of the things you learn in recreational times will become valuable tools in the future, especially hobbies like radio or electronics, photography, art, or crafts. The more things you know a little about, the more people you may be able to reach for Jesus.

3. Read about the things you'd like to do. If you think God might be calling you to some form of missionary work, read biographies of famous missionaries. If you think God has called you to be a Christian artist or a mechanic or a scientist, read books about art, mechanics, and science. Read often and wisely. If you learn to like books, you'll have a wider picture of the world God wants to reach.

4. Get some practical experience early. Take a part- or full-time job or internship in the area of your interest. Sign up for a short-term mission. Try to meet people who are doing what you may be led to do. During holidays or vacation times, ask if you can do an odd temp job around the place you would like to work in, and talk to others already in that job. On spare time, ask a lot of questions. Do others find the work interesting? What does it require in terms of time, study, and commitment? Can you grow in it? Could God use it to take care of your financial needs? Might it be useful on the mission field or in ministry? Of course, whatever work you do must honor God.

5. Study God's Word. No matter what work you choose to do, you will benefit from a year or more in a good part-time Bible school, Christian college, or correspondence course in Scripture. And *pray;* talk over new developments and disappointments with Jesus.

The Radiation Principle

The Lord Jesus commanded us to go into the world and preach the Gospel (Mark 16:15). Christians today need guidance before deciding to *stay home* rather than wait to be told to go! As martyred missionary Jim Elliot said, "Most Christians don't need a call—they need a kick in the pants!" You don't become a missionary by crossing the sea but by seeing the cross. Every Christian is called to reach out to the lost people Jesus died to save. When God gets ready to change history, He radiates His CORE to every corner of the globe.

It might seem hard to believe, but strangers to a country have always had the greatest impact on it for the Gospel. A Jew brought the Good News to Rome; a Roman took it to France; a Frenchman to Scandinavia; a Scandinavian to Scotland. A Scotsman took it to Ireland, and an Irishman made mission conquest of Scotland. The Englishmen John Wesley and George Whitfield took revival to America.

Jesus Christ ordained His twelve disciples that they might "be with Him" and so that He could send them out to preach (Mark 3:14). *Evangelism* is telling a world the Good News of the Cross. Christ still calls us. If you *go out* in His name, your presentation of the Gospel will be more effective for reasons like these:

1. A spirit of adventure.

The challenge of new mission fields demands we give our all to the task. Everywhere, there are new conditions, new people, and new perils to face—situations that, because of their newness, draw out the best in the CORE (Luke 9:1–6; Acts 1:8). Routine tends to produce rusty or dusty Christians.

2. A sense of abandonment.

When we leave all that is naturally close and dear, we have a chance to *prove* the reality of our consecration to God. All of us have only so much time, talent, and devotion. By moving out from our settled home conditions, we can give God and unreached others the shares of what we would have used on those who may have already heard the Good News. When there is no God-given home responsibility, there may be no good reason for you to stay. To tell the Lord we have "given Him all" while clinging selfishly to our safe, comfortable lives is hypocrisy (Matthew 10:37; Mark 10:45; Luke 9:23–25; John 20:21).

3. A stranger is accepted.

People tend to ignore the authority of someone they already know. Almost every one of God's prophets was rejected by his own nation. In Jesus' day people refused to accept His message because they knew His lowly background (Matthew 13:53–58). He said, "A prophet is not without honor except in his own country, among his own relatives, and in his own house" (Mark 6:4). God wants us to be strangers in the earth, the attractive unknown (Hebrews 11:13). When newcomers bring a message they claim is important, they draw the curious. God can use this natural tendency to attract sinners to the truth by sending His disciples to "regions beyond" (Acts 17:18–20).

Understanding a Mission Field

With so many bewildering networks of groups and relationships within a society or local community, how can we identify possible areas of opportunity? Christ's commission to His CORE in Matthew 28:18–20 and Mark 16:15 gives us a model of society to use when doing this. Each forms a three-dimensional target area.

1. "Into all the world": We need to look at geographic location—where we and the people we hope to reach actually live.

2. "Discipling all nations": We need to look at societal strata—who we and the people we want to reach associate with.

3. "Teaching all things": Last, we need to look at life structures—what we and the people we hope to reach do and are involved with.

There are two approaches to penetrating any sector of a community:

- Top Down: Reformation—"We have God's message. Where are the openings?"
- Bottom Up: Renaissance—"We have an opening here. What is God's message?"

For example, we may have God's blueprint for what restored family life should look like but need to be looking for ways to bring this into different socioeconomic groups or ethnic communities. On the other hand, we may be able to get entry into local schools, businesses, or government but not yet be clear on the message we ought to bring. Both approaches are legitimate and have their place. Talking one on one, our approach will often be top down, but when we aim to impact societal structures for the kingdom it is more likely to be bottom up. In other words, we may come at witness two ways:

1. What is the biblical ground plan for this area of life? How did

God's pattern for a life structure get lost, corrupted, or distorted, and how can we restore it?

OR

2. We see obvious problems or needs. How can we solve these problems or alleviate the distress they cause to people, communities, and to God?

IDENTIFYING OPPORTUNITIES FOR PENETRATION

Think of the possibilities of witness as you analyze the society around you. What are some indicators that may give you keys to finding openings for ministry?

1. Areas of obvious or growing evidence that society is failing to provide an answer—help for the poor, the oppressed, or the addicted; gangs, aid for the sick or the hungry, etc.

2. Growing discontent with the world's versions of education, employment, finance, etc.

3. Areas where an underlying worldview is being challenged or even bypassed by disciplines such as the human sciences, biology, psychology, medicine, sociology, etc.

4. Areas where we already have a nearby and reasonably strong base from which we can work—counselors can do career planning, those with a strong family and marriage can mentor couples and families, etc.

5. Areas never addressed or challenged may show us overlooked opportunities.

6. Areas where the church was once strong but has lost or abandoned its original position, such as working with children; creating art, film, animation and drama; science; communications; learning; etc.

7. Areas with strategic influence—like media and leadership training, for instance.

8. Areas where we could possibly achieve local leadership or significant impact—small towns, rural areas, school student councils, athletic teams.

9. Areas where successful penetration can lead to other advances or where success would provide resources for further advance. Business, for example, can offer financial support and creative skills; youth min-

istry can create manpower for missions and evangelism, etc.

Jesus said, "Lift up your eyes and look at the fields, for *they are already white for harvest*" (John 4:35, emphasis added). All around you there are places and people that by right belong to the great King.

Do not ask God for a call to go but for clear sight. You do not need a call to these mission fields; you need *only to see which ones are yours.* There can never be too many workers for God. Join His mission to help take back His world!

The road to a radiant life begins with one small step in the right direction. Take it. Do the first core thing, and God will show you the next. By His grace and in His Spirit, you can be a part of His Church on the Radical Edge . . . and so help to transform the world.

Train With the CORE
Lifeway College

Being CORE means taking on the very nature of Christ. This can be done only by dying to oneself, putting on the mind of Christ, and hungering after a relationship with Him so that we feel His very heartbeat. Then we will truly be touched by the divine and begin to walk toward the goal He has for our lives—being world changers.

Then Jesus came to them and said, "All authority in heaven and on earth has been given to me. Therefore go and make disciples of all nations, baptizing them in the name of the Father and of the Son and of the Holy Spirit, and teaching them to obey everything I have commanded you. And surely I am with you always, to the very end of the age." (Matthew 28:18–20 NIV)

John Wesley said:

Give me one hundred preachers who fear nothing but sin, and desire nothing but God, and I care not a straw whether they be clergymen or laymen; such alone will shake the gates of hell and set up the kingdom of heaven on earth. God does nothing but in answer to prayer.

This quote sums up a vision that has been on our heart for over fifteen years. We believe that God has said "the time is right" to train people to shake the gates of hell and extend the kingdom of heaven on earth. God has spoken clearly to our hearts and said, "This is the day—the time is now."

In response to the challenge that God has laid before us, Lifeway Ministries Trust has developed a number of intensive training programs that will enable the CORE to be trained and equipped to fulfill their role in the task to disciple the nations and set up His kingdom here on earth.

Ministry Courses
- Certificate in Evangelism
- First Wave Army
- R18 Youth Leadership Training
- Certificate in Christian Ministry
- Diploma in Christian Ministry
- Ministry Internship Programme

Media Course
- Certificate in Television and Video Production
- Diploma in 3D Character Animation

Business Courses
- Certificate in Business Administration
- Diploma in Business Administration
- BA in Business Administration
- Diploma in Business Information Systems
- BSC in Business Information Systems
- English as a Second Language

Contact us for more information and a free prospectus at

The Registrar
P.O. Box 303
Warkworth, New Zealand
Phone: +64-9-425-4054

Fax: +64-9-425-4053
E-mail: *registrar@lifeway.ac.nz*
Web site: *www.slic.ac.nz*

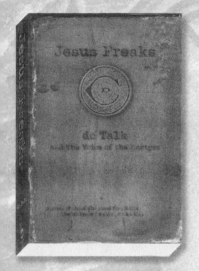

Learn about some of the biggest Jesus Freaks of all time: those who stood out from the crowd enough to be called martyrs. If Jesus was willing to give His life for me, and if these people, these martyrs, were willing to give up their lives for Him, how much does it take for me to truly dedicate my days on earth to Him?

Jesus Freaks by dc Talk and The Voice of the Martyrs

NSPIRATION

REVOLUTION

Learn about those who stood against the culture of their day and made a difference in the name of Jesus. Our mission may not involve hanging on a cross, being jailed, or being burned at the stake, but we have other, more invisible obstacles. Ours is a society built by pride, materialism, and dedication to the status quo. While we may not be called to martyr our lives, we must martyr our way of life. We must put our selfish ways to death and march to a different beat. Then the world will see Jesus. *Jesus Freaks: Vol II* by dc Talk

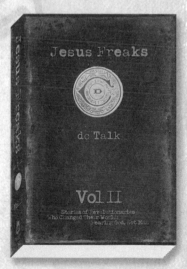

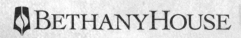